Zoho® FOR DUMMIES®

by Steve Holzner

WILEY

John Wiley & Sons, Inc.

Zoho® For Dummies®

Published by
John Wiley & Sons, Inc.
111 River Street
Hoboken, NJ 07030-5774
www.wiley.com

WILEY

About the Author

Steve Holzner is the award-winning author of many books, and he special-izes in online topics and applications like Zoho. He's been working with Zoho since it first appeared. He's been on the faculty of both MIT and Cornell University.

Dedication

To Nancy, of course!

Author's Acknowledgments

The book you hold in your hands is the product of many people's work. I'd particularly like to thank Kim Darosett, project editor; Katie Mohr, acquisitions editor; and Teresa Artman, senior copy editor.

Publisher's Acknowledgments

We're proud of this book; please send us your comments through our online registration form located at `http://dummies.custhelp.com`. For other comments, please contact our Customer Care Department within the U.S. at 877-762-2974, outside the U.S. at 317-572-3993, or fax 317-572-4002.

Some of the people who helped bring this book to market include the following:

Acquisitions and Editorial

Project Editor: Kim Darosett

Acquisitions Editor: Katie Mohr

Senior Copy Editor: Teresa Artman

Technical Editor: Raju Vesgesna

Editorial Manager: Leah Cameron

Editorial Assistant: Amanda Foxworth

Sr. Editorial Assistant: Cherie Case

Cartoons: Rich Tennant
(`www.the5thwave.com`)

Composition Services

Project Coordinator: Patrick Redmond

Layout and Graphics: Reuben W. Davis, Timothy Detrick, Christine Williams

Proofreader: Laura L. Bowman

Indexer: Broccoli Information Management

Publishing and Editorial for Technology Dummies

    Richard Swadley, Vice President and Executive Group Publisher

    Andy Cummings, Vice President and Publisher

    Mary Bednarek, Executive Acquisitions Director

    Mary C. Corder, Editorial Director

Publishing for Consumer Dummies

    Kathleen Nebenhaus, Vice President and Executive Publisher

Composition Services

    Debbie Stailey, Director of Composition Services

Contents at a Glance

Introduction *1*

Part I: Working with Documents *5*
Chapter 1: Getting Started with Zoho 7
Chapter 2: Zoho Writer: Getting It Down in Print 21
Chapter 3: Zoho Writer: Publishing, Sharing, and Working Offline........45
Chapter 4: Zoho Show: Lights, Camera, Action!.....................................63
Chapter 5: Zoho Notebook: Organizing and Storing Content..................87

Part II: Scheduling and Communicating *113*
Chapter 6: Zoho Planner: Organizing Your Life 115
Chapter 7: Zoho Mail: Your Communication Center 139

Part III: Managing Data *167*
Chapter 8: Zoho Sheet: All Your Data Cell by Cell.................................169
Chapter 9: Zoho Reports: Creating Online Databases 197

Part IV: Using Zoho for Your Business *223*
Chapter 10: Zoho Projects: Managing Your Team's Timeline...................225
Chapter 11: Zoho Invoice: Billing Your Customers 251
Chapter 12: Zoho CRM: ManagingYour Customers 275

Part V: The Part of Tens *297*
Chapter 13: Top Ten Zoho Help Resources...299
Chapter 14: Top Ten Online Zoho Tutorials 303

Index *307*

Table of Contents

Introduction 1

About This Book 1
Foolish Assumptions 1
How This Book Is Organized 2
    Part I: Working with Documents 2
    Part II: Scheduling and Communicating 2
    Part III: Managing Data 2
    Part IV: Using Zoho for Your Business 3
    Part V: The Part of Tens 3
Icons Used in This Book 3
Where to Go from Here 4

Part 1: Working with Documents 5

Chapter 1: Getting Started with Zoho 7

Signing Up for Zoho 8
    Setting up your account 8
    Signing in for the first time 10
Taking a Look at the Zoho Apps Covered in This Book 12
    Writer: Your word processor 12
    Show: Your presentation manager 13
    Notebook: Your online scrapbook 14
    Planner: Your online organizer 15
    Mail: Your communication center 15
    Sheet: Your spreadsheet 16
    Reports: Your database 16
    Projects: Your team scheduler 18
    Invoice: Your billing application 18
    CRM: Your customer relationship management system 19

Chapter 2: Zoho Writer: Getting It Down in Print 21

Signing In and Starting Zoho Writer 21
Taking a Quick Tour of Zoho Writer 22
    Document management 22
    General functions 23
    Toolbars 23
    Left pane 24
    The Writer links 25
    Document tabs 26

Creating, Saving, and Naming Documents..................................26
Formatting Tips and Tricks in Writer 29
    Saving time with keyboard shortcuts 29
    Aligning page elements 30
    Making your text look pretty...32
Inserting Elements in a Writer Document 34
    Inserting images in Writer 34
    Inserting a hyperlink...35
Creating and Refining Tables in Writer....................................36
All the Full Facts: Getting Your Document's History 38
Organizing Your Documents with Tags 39
Like a Cookie Cutter: Templates..40
    Finding and downloading a template 41
    Using a template 42
    Creating your own template 43
    Exporting a template to the Template Library 44

Chapter 3: Zoho Writer: Publishing, Sharing, and Working Offline....45

Having Your Say with Comments 45
Getting the Word Out: Printing and Publishing to the Web.................47
What's Mine Is Yours: Sharing Documents 49
    Inviting collaborators..49
    When collaborators edit a shared document 52
    Communicating with a document's collaborators 53
    Collaborating with groups of collaborators 54
    Inviting a group of collaborators to share a document.................56
    Managing groups...56
Importing and Exporting Documents.......................................58
Taking It off the Internet: Working Offline...............................60
    Installing Gears from Google 60
    Using Writer with Gears...61
    Synching your offline documents with Writer online 62

Chapter 4: Zoho Show: Lights, Camera, Action!...................63

Creating a Presentation 63
    Creating a new presentation 64
    Importing an existing presentation 65
Welcome to Zoho Show 66
    Getting to know the interface.......................................66
    Understanding presentation views...............................67
Customizing Your Presentation..68
    Adding slides 68
    Adding text 70
    Working with bullets 71
    Adding shapes 72
    Changing themes on the fly 79
    Adding images 80
Sharing Presentations with Other Show Users.........................82

Showtime! Presenting Your Presentation......................................83
   Showing your presentation in person................................83
   Controlling your presentation remotely.............................84

Chapter 5: Zoho Notebook: Organizing and Storing Content 87

Getting Started with Notebook 88
   Renaming and saving your notebook..............................88
   Growing your notebook: Adding pages............................89
Adding Stuff to Notebook 91
   Adding text to a page...91
   Adding images 93
   Adding video..94
   Adding audio files 96
   Adding HTML..97
   Adding a URL 97
   Adding RSS feeds 98
Embedding Documents...99
   Embedding a non-Zoho document..................................99
   Adding a Zoho Sheet or Writer document.......................100
   Adding a Show document...100
Adding Shapes 101
   Drawing shapes 102
   Copying, pasting, and deleting shapes.........................103
   Inserting shapes 104
   Editing shapes 105
Finessing Content: Arranging, Fixing, Freeing, and Stacking 106
   Arranging content on the page 106
   Fixing and unfixing content 106
   Stacking content...107
   Deleting content...108
Clipping on the Web (For Firefox Users Only)...............................108
   Snapping a whole Web page.......................................109
   Snapping part of a Web page......................................109
Getting Others Involved: Sharing a Notebook 110

Part II: Scheduling and Communicating 113

Chapter 6: Zoho Planner: Organizing Your Life...................115

Starting Planner 116
Creating a To-Do List..116
Amending a To-Do List..119
   Checking items off a list 120
   Reordering a to-do list...121
   Adding a new list item 121
   Editing and deleting a list item.................................122
Setting Due Dates for List Items...122
Setting Reminders 123

Scheduling Appointments 125
        Setting your time zone 125
        Creating your first appointment 126
        Setting a recurring appointment.. 127
        Adding more appointments.. 128
        Editing and deleting appointments 129
Recording More Details with Planner Notes 129
Adding Attachments.. 131
        Uploading an attachment... 131
        Opening an attachment... 132
        Adding more attachments 132
        Deleting an attachment.. 133
Creating a New Page... 133
Even More Organization: Adding Tags to Planner Items....................... 134
        Adding a tag to a page.. 135
        Searching for a page with tags 136
Sharing Planner Pages... 136
        Inviting someone to share a page 136
        When someone shares your page.. 137
        Chatting with someone sharing your page.............................. 138

Chapter 7: Zoho Mail: Your Communication Center. 139
Getting Started with Zoho Mail.. 139
Composing Your Zoho E-Mails.. 141
        Getting return receipts for your e-mails 142
        Setting a priority level 143
        Personalizing your e-mail: Adding a signature...................... 143
        Taking a look at your sent mail 144
Receiving and Reading Your E-Mails... 146
Replying To and Forwarding Your E-Mail... 147
        Replying to an e-mail 147
        Forwarding an e-mail 148
        Setting a vacation reply.. 149
Managing Your Inbox 151
        It's outta here: Deleting e-mail 151
        Organizing your e-mail with folders 152
        A word about spam 153
        Marking e-mail with flags and bolding..................................... 153
Handling Attachments in Zoho E-Mail 154
        Adding attachments to your e-mail 154
        Opening e-mail attachments.. 156
Searching Your E-Mail.. 157
        Searching all messages 157
        Restricting searches 158
        Searching specific folders 159
Saving E-Mail on Your Computer and Printing E-Mail........................ 159
Working with Your Address Book Contacts 160

Organizing Your E-Mail with Labels and Folders 161

Creating and using labels...161

Creating new folders...163

Reading Your E-Mail Offline..164

Part III: Managing Data *167*

Chapter 8: Zoho Sheet: All Your Data Cell by Cell **169**

Getting Started with Zoho Sheet...170

Entering Data..171

Adding and Deleting Rows and Columns....................................174

Adding a new column...174

Adding a new row 175

Adding Comments and Data Formats 176

Adding a comment...176

Using date, currency, and percentage formats...........................177

Organizing Your Data by Sorting..178

Performing a standard sort 178

Performing a custom sort 179

A Picture Is Worth a Thousand Words: Creating Charts............180

Serious Data Crunching: Using Formulas and Functions 182

Using the Sum button 183

Creating a formula 183

Using functions in Sheet...185

Sharing Spreadsheets..186

Inviting others to share a spreadsheet 187

When others share your spreadsheet....................................189

Handling changes made by others 190

Publishing on the Web 191

The Cool Stuff: Creating Pivot Tables 192

Chapter 9: Zoho Reports: Creating Online Databases **197**

Getting Started: Creating a Database 197

Importing a database...198

Creating a database from a template 202

Creating a database right away..204

Creating a blank database 205

Giving Your Data a Home: Creating Database Tables............206

Entering Data into a Database Table..209

Creating a standard table 209

Creating related tables 210

Making Changes to a Table 212

Making changes to the columns 212

Making changes to the rows...213

Sorting and Filtering the Datain a Database Table.......................214

From A to Z: Sorting data..214

Getting selective: Filtering your data....................................214

Querying the Data in a Database Table with SQL.................................217
A Window into Your Tables: Viewing Your Data...............................219
    The standard: Tabular view 219
    Graphics at work: Chart view 219
    Reorganize data with Pivot view......................................220
    Summarizing with Summary view 221
Sharing a Database 222

Part IV: Using Zoho for Your Business 223

Chapter 10: Zoho Projects: Managing Your Team's Timeline 225

It All Begins Here: Getting Started With Zoho Projects 226
Customizing Zoho Projects the Way You Like It 228
    Using the General Settings tab..229
    Using the Company Settings tab.......................................230
Creating a New Zoho Projects Project..230
    Welcome to the Project dashboard....................................231
    Adding users..232
    Getting busy: Adding tasks to a project.............................233
    Creating a task list 236
    A sense of progress: Creating project milestones 237
Using Your People Skills: Managing Your Users...............................239
    Changing roles..239
    Adding a new user 240
    Deleting a user...240
    E-mailing a project's users...240
Some Face Time: Setting Up Meetings with Zoho Projects...................241
Getting a Long-Term Overview with the Built-in Calendar 242
    Filtering the Calendar view...243
    Creating events from the calendar 244
Keeping Track of Time..245
    Logging time with the Timesheet 245
    Logging time with the Projects timer.................................246
Having Your Say Using Zoho Projects Forums 246
    Creating a forum post..247
    Adding a comment to a post 248
Generating Reports 248
Working with Documents 249

Chapter 11: Zoho Invoice: Billing Your Customers. 251

Getting Started with Zoho Invoice..252
    Setting up your company profile 253
    Adding your company logo 254
    Setting your currency and time zone 256
    Specifying tax information..257

Telling Zoho Invoice About Your Customers.................................257
Manually adding customers 258
Importing contacts 262
Editing customers and contacts 263
Deactivating and reactivating customers 264
Deleting contacts 264
Creating Your Inventory 265
Getting Paid: Selecting a Payment Gateway............................266
Customizing Your E-mail Notifications 267
Getting New Business: Creating and Sending Estimates 268
The Payoff: Creating and Sending Invoices............................271
Happy Days Are Here Again: Marking an Invoice as Paid 272

Chapter 12: Zoho CRM: ManagingYour Customers 275
Choosing the Right CRM Edition 276
Creating Your Zoho CRM Account 276
Getting a Look at the Zoho CRM Interface 278
Customizing Zoho CRM 279
Hiding tabs..279
Rearranging and renaming tabs 280
Adding and deleting components....................................280
Getting People Involved: Managing Users 282
Adding new users...282
Creating new roles 284
Assigning a role to a user..284
Creating a profile...285
All about Zoho CRM Modules 287
Welcome to the Marketing modules...............................287
Welcome to the Sales modules 288
Welcome to the Inventory and Ordering modules 288
Welcome to the Customer Support modules 289
Welcome to the Data Analysis modules........................290
Putting a Zoho CRM Module to Work 290
Dissecting a module 291
Creating a new record in a module................................292
Editing and deleting a record 293
Creating Custom Views..295

Part V: The Part of Tens.. 297

Chapter 13: Top Ten Zoho Help Resources 299
The Zoho FAQ 299
Zoho Forums 300
Zoho Writer FAQ..300
Zoho Notebook Help 300

Video on Zoho Sheet 301
Zoho Show FAQ 301
Zoho Projects Help 301
Zoho Invoice User Manual...301
Zoho CRM Help 302
Zoho CRM Blog 302

Chapter 14: Top Ten Online Zoho Tutorials 303

Zoho App Videos 303
A Guided Tour of Zoho 304
Zoho Projects Tutorial..304
Zoho Notebook Tutorial..304
Zoho Planner Tutorial 305
Zoho Sheet Tutorial..305
Creating Macros in Zoho Sheet...305
Zoho Writer Tutorial 305
Taking Zoho Writer Offline 306
Zoho CRM Tutorials 306

Index *307*

Introduction

*Z*oho — the free suite of online productivity applications — offers a fantastic set of resources for anyone with Internet access. You can use a state-of-the-art word processor, spreadsheet, database system, or any of many other applications that Zoho offers. Those applications are as powerful as any you'll find that you install on your computer.

And the best part is that Zoho is free (with the exception of some levels of advanced business computing). As a result, Zoho has taken off in a big way, gaining millions of users. Zoho is part of the *cloud* computing initiative, where applications and your data stay online. You can access those applications from anywhere there's an Internet connection, and you don't have to worry about installing new versions.

About This Book

This book is your guide to Zoho. As great as Zoho is on software, it's not quite so great on documentation.

Users will find the Zoho help files very spotty. Some applications have no help files at all, some only have frequently asked questions (FAQ) lists, and others rely on interactive forums.

That's where this book comes in. Here you find the documentation that's missing from Zoho. There's plenty of stuff here that you won't find anywhere else.

Foolish Assumptions

You won't need anything besides a browser and an Internet connection to use this book. Zoho will do the rest as far as the technical aspect goes.

On the other hand, this book assumes that you have a few basic skills: for example, the basics of working with a word processor. You don't have to be an expert at any of the applications in this book, but when it comes to basic skills that most people have already been exposed to — such as clicking the B icon to make text bold — I don't spend a lot of time on such details because nearly everyone already knows them.

In other words, this book is intended to bring you up to speed on Zoho without wasting a lot of time on basic office suite skills.

How This Book Is Organized

This book is organized into parts, with each part covering some area of Zoho. Here's what you find in this book.

Part I: Working with Documents

This part gets you going with Zoho, explaining how to create documents in depth. Here's what's in this part:

- ✓ **Zoho Writer** is Zoho's word processor, and it's nearly as powerful as any you'll find anywhere.
- ✓ **Zoho Show** is the app to use to create exciting slide shows that you can use when giving presentations.
- ✓ **Zoho Notebook** is Zoho's scrapbook, letting you clip Web pages, images, text, audio, video, and more from the Internet.

Part II: Scheduling and Communicating

In this part, you get a guided tour of Zoho's scheduling and communicating applications. Here's what's in this part:

- ✓ **Zoho Planner,** just like any other organizer, allows you to schedule your life. You can store addresses, to-do lists, appointments, and more.
- ✓ **Zoho Mail** is Zoho's deluxe e-mail system, and it gives you all the features you'd expect.

Part III: Managing Data

This part is for you if you like to crunch data. Here's what you find:

- ✓ **Zoho Sheet** is the Zoho spreadsheet application. Not only can you use it to do all you can on other spreadsheet applications, but you can also use formulas and functions to make super-powerful spreadsheets.

✔ **Zoho Reports** is the database system. Store your data in this application and view it many different ways, or use Structured Query Language (SQL) to work with that data.

Part IV: Using Zoho for Your Business

Zoho contains a number of applications designed for businesses, and here's what you find in this part:

✔ **Zoho Projects** keeps your team on track by coordinating a project's tasks and milestones among all team members.

✔ **Zoho Invoice** allows you to create invoices to bill your customers.

✔ **Zoho CRM** is the customer relationship management system you can use to track everything from potential customers to sales orders.

Part V: The Part of Tens

In this part, you see two collections of ten important resources available for Zoho: the top ten Zoho help resources and the top ten online Zoho tutorials.

Icons Used in This Book

The Tip icon marks tips and shortcuts that you can use to make everything you're doing with Zoho easier.

Remember icons mark the information that's especially important to know. To siphon off the most important information in each chapter, just skim through these icons.

The Warning icon tells you to watch out! It marks important information that may save you headaches. There are plenty of pitfalls with any applications as powerful as the ones you find in Zoho, so be sure to pay special attention to these warnings.

Where to Go from Here

Zoho is huge, and you don't need to start at any particular point. The same is true of this book: You can jump in anywhere you want. So pick a chapter and dive in! (Chapter 1 covers how to create your Zoho username and password, so that may be a good place to start.)

Part I
Working with Documents

The 5th Wave

By Rich Tennant

"I love the way Zoho Writer justifies the text in my resume. Now if I can just get it to justify my asking salary."

In this part . . .

This part gets you started with Zoho, covering the most essential applications for creating your own documents.

Zoho Writer is the Zoho suite word processor — a super-popular application that offers plenty of power.

Zoho Show enables you to create slide show presentations. You can add graphics, text, images, and more to your presentations and share them with an audience or online.

Zoho Notebook is the scrapbook of the Zoho suite. Notebook is a handy app with which you can collect just about anything you find online: text, images, video, audio, and even whole Web pages.

Chapter 1

Getting Started with Zoho

In This Chapter

▶ The Zoho advantage: Why it's right for so many people

▶ Signing up for Zoho

▶ Finding out about the Zoho apps covered in this book

*W*elcome to Zoho, your online productivity and collaboration suite of applications. Zoho is different from a traditional suite of productivity apps in that it works online (although you can work with some Zoho apps offline and synchronize them when you're back online, as you'll see). All the applications are available at www.zoho.com; all you have to do is to sign up with Zoho.

Zoho offers all the applications you would expect in a full productivity suite and more. It's got all the applications you see in application suites costing hundreds of dollars, but Zoho is free (although some applications charge you to go beyond the basic levels). Zoho gives you word processing, spreadsheets, mail, customer relations management, database, invoicing, presentation applications — and that's just the beginning. It's fair to say that Zoho has an application matching just about every popular type of application out there.

Zoho is all about *cloud computing* — that is, storing your data online for use with online applications. No longer do you need to be tied to older software that hasn't been updated on your computer. In fact, you don't even have to run the application on your computer at all — it runs in the "cloud." And that makes it easy to, among other things, share your data with co-workers online.

As you will see throughout this book, Zoho applications have a lot to offer. You can use them from anywhere with an Internet connection, share your data with others, and collaborate interactively. Best of all, you don't have to worry about buying new versions of Zoho as they come out because they're automatically updated online.

In this chapter, you take care of the first order of business: signing up for a Zoho account. Once you have a Zoho account, you're ready to start working with the applications. This chapter gives you a rundown of the Zoho applications covered in this book, explains what you can do with them, and points you to the chapters where you can find out more about them.

Signing Up for Zoho

To access all the Zoho applications, sign up for Zoho. Start at www.zoho.com, as you see in Figure 1-1.

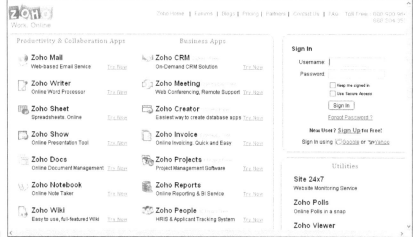

Figure 1-1:
Create
your Zoho
account
here.

Setting up your account

To enter the world of Zoho, you get a username and password which you need to use to sign in to every Zoho application. To get your username and password, follow these steps:

1. **Navigate your browser to www.zoho.com.**

2. **Click the Sign Up for Free! link you see at the right in Figure 1-1, opening the Create a Zoho Account page you see in Figure 1-2.**

3. **Enter the username you want to use.**

   Your username should be 6 to 30 characters long, and it can contain letters, numbers, underscores, and/or dots (.).

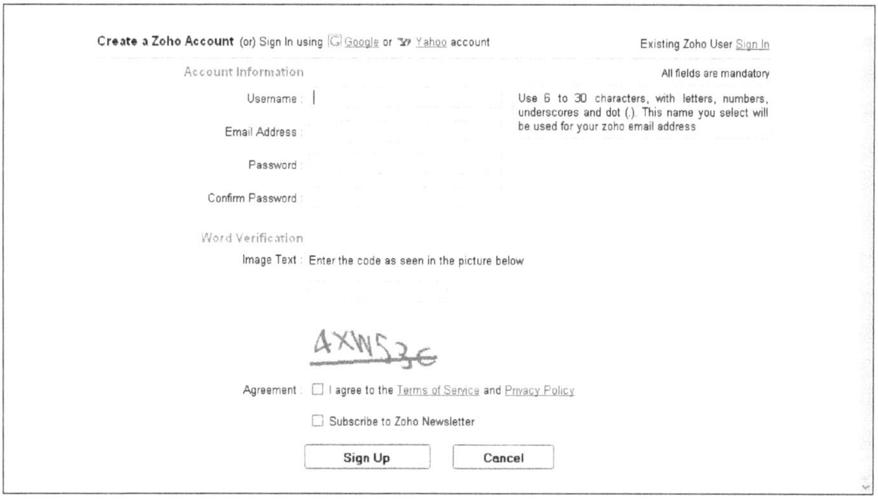

Figure 1-2:
The Zoho
signup
page.

Create a Zoho Account (or) Sign In using Google or Yahoo account   Existing Zoho User Sign In

Account Information   All fields are mandatory

Username : | Use 6 to 30 characters, with letters, numbers,
                                       underscores and dot (.). This name you select will
Email Address :   be used for your zoho email address

Password :

Confirm Password :

Word Verification

Image Text : Enter the code as seen in the picture below

4XWS36

Agreement : ☐ I agree to the Terms of Service and Privacy Policy

☐ Subscribe to Zoho Newsletter

[Sign Up]   [Cancel]

4. Enter a valid e-mail address.

Zoho will send a confirming e-mail to the address you enter.

5. Enter the password you want to use.

Your password should be 3 to 60 characters.

Don't use your Zoho username or e-mail address in your password. Zoho checks for that and will reject it.

6. Retype your password.

7. Enter the visual code you see into the text box just above the code.

If you get the visual code incorrect, Zoho will give you more chances by displaying another code (without erasing the information you already entered).

8. Select the check box for I Agree to the Terms of Service and Privacy Policy.

If you want to read the Zoho terms of service, click the Terms of Service and the Privacy Policy links.

9. (Optional) To subscribe to the Zoho newsletter, select that check box.

10. Click the Sign Up button.

If you entered all the information correctly, Zoho displays a new page with this message.

A verification email has been sent to steve@meadowridgetownhouses. com. Please click the link given in that email to confirm your registration. Note: If your registration is not confirmed, Zoho reserves the right to deactivate/delete it later without notice.

Just click Continue, and you should get an e-mail that reads something like this:

Hi username,

Thanks for registering with Zoho! To confirm your registration, please click here within 7 days of receiving this email, else the link will be expired.

If the above link doesn't work, please copy and paste the below URL on your browser.

https://accounts.zoho.com/confirm?DIGEST=Jkqxo8C5OMFe9Uvil7xnub1 T2H28*HIte2P*14e.nm*9qag41TWWxDVIk0BjjK.6FNEzdfLhUz_sn3hz3EMV GAsMb*9xrKGaQOGbG3nFWY-

If this email means nothing to you, then it is possible that somebody else has entered your email address either deliberately or accidentally from the IP address xxx.xxx.xxx.xxx, so please ignore this email.

Thanks,

Team Zoho

http://zoho.com

Your subscription: You are receiving this email because of your registration with Zoho that entitles you to receive this one time mail communication. If you wish to unsubscribe from Zoho, visit https:// accounts.zoho.com.

Zoho / AdventNet, Inc.

4900 Hopyard Rd, Suite 310 Pleasanton, CA 94588, USA

Phone: +1-925-924-9500 Fax: +1-925-924-9600

Signing in for the first time

You're almost done creating your Zoho account. To finish, follow these steps:

1. **Click the link in the confirmation e-mail (or copy the link and paste it into your browser's address bar).**

   A page appears in your browser asking for your password.

2. **Enter your password.**

3. Click Continue.

You see another page with a Confirmation Successful message.

4. Click the Continue Signing In button.

The Zoho Sign In page appears, as shown in Figure 1-3.

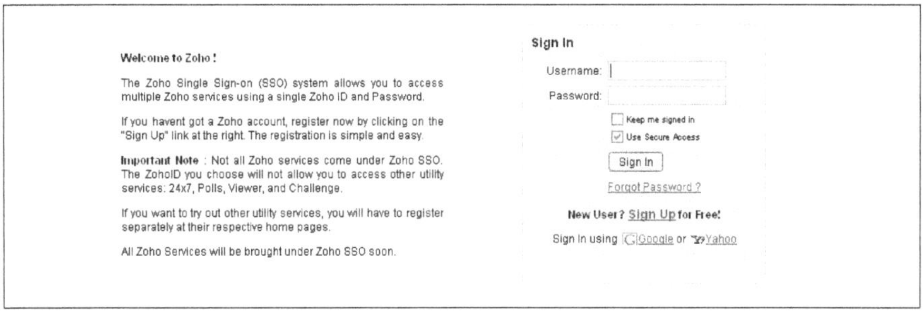

Figure 1-3:
The Zoho
Sign In
page.

5. Enter your username.

6. Enter your password.

7. Click the Sign In button.

Your Zoho Accounts page appears, as shown in Figure 1-4.

Congratulations! You're in!

Figure 1-4:
Your Zoho
Accounts
page.

From this point, click the links you see in Figure 1-4 to start any Zoho application: Writer, Sheet, Show, and so on.

However, after you have your username and password, I recommend that you go to each individual application's page — `http://writer.zoho.com` for Writer, or `http://sheet.zoho.com` for Sheet, for example — to start an application.

Here's why signing in directly from the app home page is better than going to the Accounts page and clicking an application's link. Zoho sometimes adds a navigation bar of links at the left of the application's page from which you can switch to other applications. That navigation bar takes up space, and usually pushes menus and buttons off the screen. Not optimal.

So, when you sign in at an application's home page, Zoho still asks for your username and password, but after you sign in, the application starts immediately.

Taking a Look at the Zoho Apps Covered in This Book

After you become an official Zoho user, take a look at what's available in Zoho. Zoho offers a ton of apps, but, unfortunately, I don't have space to cover them all here. Here are the ones I do talk about in this book.

Writer: Your word processor

Writer is the Zoho word processor extraordinaire, offering nearly all that word processors that cost hundreds of dollars have to offer. You can see Writer at work in Figure 1-5.

To start Writer, navigate to `http://writer.zoho.com`, enter your username and password (see the first part of this chapter for how to open a Zoho account), and click the Sign In button. That's all it takes.

With Writer, you can enter and format text, align page elements, insert images and hyperlinks, create tables, and work with templates. Additionally, you can use Writer to publish to the Web, share documents with others, and work offline. And as an organizational tool, you can add additional information with tags.

Read all about Writer in Chapters 2 and 3.

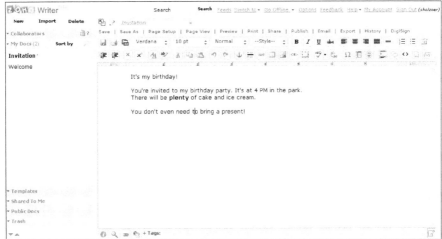

Figure 1-5:
Zoho Writer
at work.

Show: Your presentation manager

Show is your presentation manager, letting you create and show slides to your audience (much like Microsoft PowerPoint). You can see Zoho Show at work in Figure 1-6.

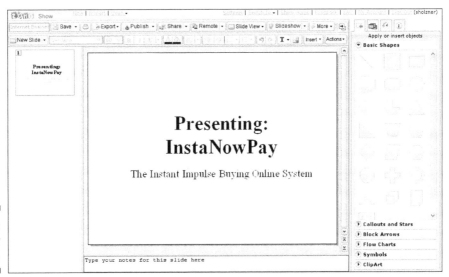

Figure 1-6:
Zoho Show
at work.

To start Show, navigate to `http://show.zoho.com`, enter your username and password, and click the Sign In button. With Show, you can create presentations by adding slides, using text and images, and adding shapes. You can also work with notes, share your presentations with others, and view presentations online.

Read all about Show in Chapter 4.

Notebook: Your online scrapbook

With Zoho Notebook, you can collect text, images, video, audio, and other items that you upload or that you clip from the Web. It's a great scrapbook application that allows you to collect items from all over and store them in one place. You can see Zoho Notebook at work in Figure 1-7.

Figure 1-7:
Zoho
Notebook
at work.

To start Notebook, navigate to `http://notebook.zoho.com`, enter your username and password, and click the Sign In button. Zoho Notebook allows you to add all sorts of content (videos, text, images, and audio), add shapes and pages, use Web clipping, and share your notebook.

Read all about Notebook in Chapter 5.

Planner: Your online organizer

Ever have a paper organizer? You know, one of those heavy collections of tabbed papers that pages keep falling out of? Now you can take your organizer online, with Zoho Planner. You can keep track of events, addresses, meetings — just about everything in your busy life. You can see Zoho Planner at work in Figure 1-8.

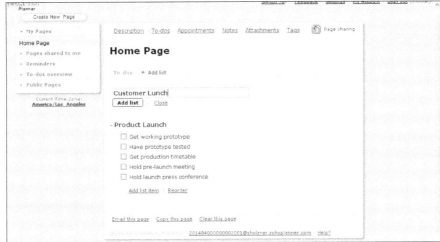

Figure 1-8:
Zoho
Planner
at work.

To start Planner, navigate to `http://planner.zoho.com`, enter your username and password, and click the Sign In button. With Planner, you can create a to-do list, add and edit items in a list, add appointments, get reminders, keep track of addresses, and share pages.

Read all about Planner in Chapter 6.

Mail: Your communication center

Many online application suites offer mail programs, and Zoho is no exception. You can send and receive mail, send and receive attachments, embed HTML in your mail, and more with Zoho Mail.

You can see Zoho Mail at work in Figure 1-9.

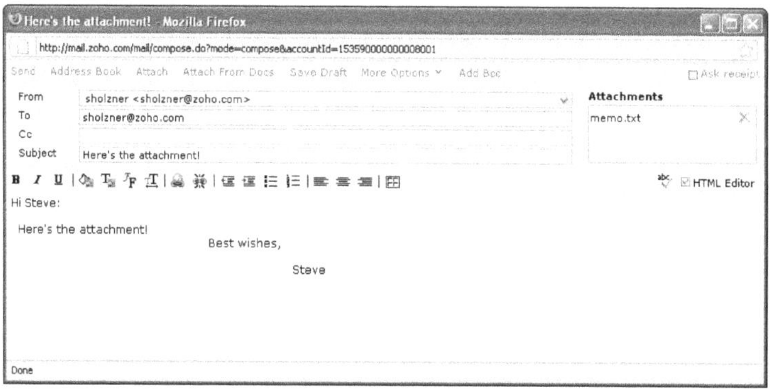

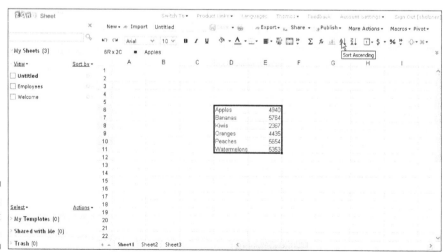

Figure 1-9:
Zoho Mail
at work.

To start Mail, navigate to `http://mail.zoho.com`, enter your username and password, and click the Sign In button.

Read all about Mail in Chapter 7.

Sheet: Your spreadsheet

You'd expect a serious application suite to have a powerful spreadsheet program, and Zoho does: Sheet.

Sheet is as feature rich as applications you could pay hundreds of dollars for, but it's completely free. You can enter or import your data, sort or filter it, and apply functions and formulas, all with ease. You can see Sheet at work in Figure 1-10.

Figure 1-10:
Zoho Sheet
at work.

To start Sheet, navigate to `http://sheet.zoho.com`, enter your username and password, and click the Sign In button. Use Sheet to create, import, and format spreadsheets; enter and sort data; add and delete rows and columns; use formulas and functions; create pivot tables; export to other programs; handle external data; and share spreadsheets with others.

Read all about Sheet in Chapter 8.

Reports: Your database

Zoho even sports a database application: Zoho Reports. As strong of a database system as Microsoft Access, Reports allows you to sort and filter your records, as well as execute full SQL (Structured Query Language) statements, just as you'd expect from a professional database application. You can see Zoho Reports in Figure 1-11.

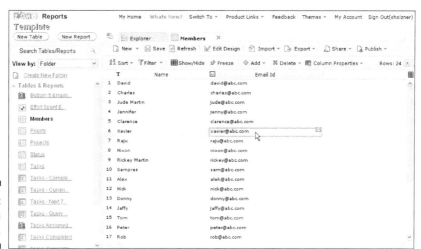

Figure 1-11:
Zoho
Reports.

To start Reports, navigate to `http://db.zoho.com`, enter your username and password, and click the Sign In button. Use Zoho Reports to create a database from scratch or by importing, enter records, work with tables and edit their design, sort and filter records, execute SQL statements, choose from different views, and share your data online.

Read all about Reports in Chapter 9.

Projects: Your team scheduler

If you manage a team and want to keep on schedule with your projects, Zoho Projects offers a great solution. You can set up timelines, meetings, appointments, and tasks; assign tasks to people; and share everything interactively. You can see Zoho Projects at work in Figure 1-12.

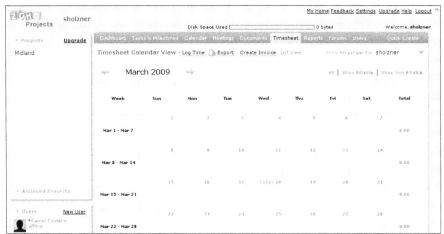

Figure 1-12: Zoho Projects at work.

To start Projects, navigate to `http://projects.zoho.com`, enter your username and password, and click the Sign In button. Use Zoho Projects to work with the Projects dashboard; track time; create projects and milestones; add users and tasks, assign tasks and roles to users, and manage users; use the built-in calendar and schedule meetings; work with, upload, and organize documents; tag data; use forums; and generate reports.

Read all about Projects in Chapter 10.

Invoice: Your billing application

When it comes to collecting what customers owe you, Zoho Invoice is right there with you. From creating invoices to sending them out, Invoice gets the job done. You can see Zoho Invoice at work in Figure 1-13.

To start Invoice, navigate to `http://invoice.zoho.com`, enter your username and password, and click the Sign In button. Use Zoho Invoice to set your company profile, currency type, time zone, tax information, and logo; create an invoice; add and delete customers; and manage inventory.

Read all about Invoice in Chapter 11.

CRM: Your customer relationship management system

This is the big one, the whopper of the bunch. Zoho CRM is the biggest of the Zoho applications, and you can sign up and pay for multiple levels. Or, you can opt for a free level.

CRM stands for *customer relationship management,* and with Zoho CRM, you can keep track of just about every marketing and sales task there is. This application mimics CRM applications that sell for thousands of dollars.

You can track leads, potential leads, customers, sales orders, purchase orders, inventory, and much more. You can see Zoho CRM at work in Figure 1-14.

To start CRM, navigate to `http://crm.zoho.com`, enter your username and password, and click the Sign In button. Use Zoho CRM to customize your CRM; create records, forecasts, profiles, and custom views; add users; track inventory, marketing trends, and sales by sales rep; manage users and customers; and work with modules.

Read all about CRM in Chapter 12.

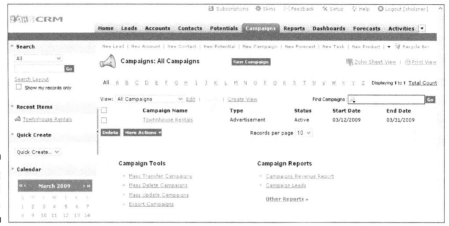

Chapter 2

Zoho Writer: Getting It Down in Print

In This Chapter

▷ Getting to know Zoho Writer

▷ Creating your first document

▷ Entering and formatting text

▷ Working with templates

▷ Inserting images and hyperlinks

▷ Creating tables

▷ Tagging your documents

*W*hen you think of a word processor, you probably think of a dedicated piece of software loaded on your laptop or desktop computer. You open the application; your computer grinds around for a while; the word processor starts; and then you use the word processor to create, edit, save, and even spellcheck your documents. Word processors are indeed handy tools — as long as everyone's on the same page, so to speak.

Zoho Writer is here to change the landscape of word processing apps. And that's what this chapter is all about.

Signing In and Starting Zoho Writer

Time to see just how easy it is to work in Zoho Writer. To start, navigate your Web browser to `http://writer.zoho.com` to open the Zoho Writer home page. Enter your username and password. Then click the Sign In button, which takes you to Writer, as shown in Figure 2-1. (If you haven't signed up for a Zoho account, see Chapter 1 for details.)

Document tab   Toolbar tabs   Format toolbar

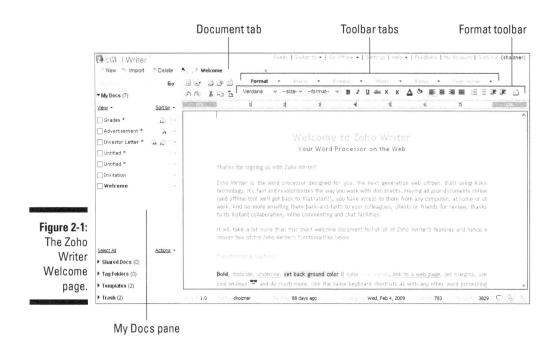

Figure 2-1:
The Zoho
Writer
Welcome
page.

My Docs pane

When you open Zoho Writer for the first time, you see its Welcome page, as shown in Figure 2-1. That Welcome page is actually a Writer document, and it's already saved in your My Docs pane, as you can see in Figure 2-1. The Welcome document gives you an overview of some of the features that Writer offers, mentioning some standard items (such as bulleted lists and tables) and also what makes Writer different (such as sharing documents online).

Taking a Quick Tour of Zoho Writer

Take a look at Writer in Figure 2-1, replete with its many buttons and menus and links. Before jumping headfirst into Writer, though, take a moment to follow a guided tour of the Writer window so when I talk about the so-and-so toolbar or the such-and-such tab, you'll know what I mean.

Document management

Start with the buttons you see at upper left in Figure 2-1. These buttons are the basics of document management, like in any word processor.

- ✔ **New:** Create a new document. Go figure.
- ✔ **Import:** Import documents in a variety of formats, including simple text.
- ✔ **Delete:** Guess.

Below these three buttons, you find a Search field. Enter the text you want in the Search field and then click the Go button.

General functions

The next group of buttons (under Welcome on the Document tab) handles some general Writer functions:

- ✔ **Save:** Saves your current document. If no name is associated with the document, Zoho Writer asks you to name it before saving it.
- ✔ **Save As:** Saves your current document, giving it the name you choose.
- ✔ **Print:** Prints the current document.
- ✔ **Export:** Exports the current document.
- ✔ **Document properties:** Displays a dialog box with statistics about your current document, such as the number of words and characters.

Toolbars

Writer has many toolbars that don't appear until you need them. You can see a full toolbar by clicking one of the tabs shown in Figure 2-1 and described in Table 2-1. For example, when you click the Format tab, Writer displays the full Format toolbar, as shown in Figure 2-1. Or if you click the down arrow on a tab, you can see a menu of toolbar options.

Table 2-1	Toolbar Tabs
Tab/Toolbar	*Why You Can Do with It*
Format	Format the text you've selected. For example, apply bold, italic, underline, and so on.
Insert	Insert images, spreadsheets, Web pages, and so on into your document.
Review	Review your document with features such as Spellcheck, Thesaurus, and Find and Replace.
Share	Share your document with options such as Share, Publish, and Publish to Web.
View	Change the document view: Normal View, Print Preview, and HTML View.
Page Setup	Change the page setup with such items as Header, Footer, and Page Layout.

Left pane

Now take a look at the pane on the left in Writer. This pane has a number of bars that, when clicked, expand. By default, as shown in Figure 2-1, the My Docs bar is clicked, and you can see the My Docs view, which lists your documents. Here's an overview of the bars available to you in the left pane:

- ✔ **My Docs** lists your documents, and you can open a document just by double-clicking it.

- ✔ **Shared Docs** lists documents that people have invited you to share or take a look at. Read about sharing in Chapter 3.

- ✔ **Tag Folders** lists the tags in your documents.

- ✔ **Templates** lists the templates you can use as the basis of a document. *Templates* specify font size and style, line spacing, and so on. Templates can also contain boilerplate text, such as for an invoice form. Get the scoop on templates later in this chapter.

- ✔ **Trash** holds the documents you delete until you deliberately empty the Trash.

The Writer links

Next, check out the set of links at the top of Writer, above the writing space. Here's what they do:

- **Feeds:** Click to see sharing information for documents shared with your collaborators. For example, if you're sharing a document with someone else, you can see the history of all shared actions here.

- **Switch To:** Click to switch to another Zoho application, such as Notebook.

- **Go Offline:** Click to work offline with up to 25 of your documents. See Chapter 3 for more information on going offline.

- **Settings:** Click to customize Writer in various ways, such as arranging tabs.

- **Help:** Clicking this link won't provide you with detailed help in the sense you might find it for other software. Instead, this provides access to a set of FAQs (frequently asked questions lists), forums, and blogs. Clicking the down arrow next to the Help link opens a menu with these items:

  - *FAQ:* The Frequently Asked Questions list

  - *Zoho API:* The application programming interface specification for developers

  - *Template Library:* A set of good templates for you to use as the basis of your documents

  - *Zoho Writer Forums:* Forums in which you can ask questions, and general users (and sometimes Zoho staff) will answer

  - *Zoho Blogs:* A list of blogs from Zoho staff

  - *Keyboard Shortcuts:* A list of keystroke shortcuts for common actions, such as saving a document

- **Feedback:** If you want to suggest something to Zoho, or send in a compliment or complaint, just click this link.

- **My Account:** Click to access a page with information about your Zoho account.

- **Sign Out:** Click when you're ready to exit Zoho. It's recommended that you click this link each time you finish editing in Zoho Writer to log you out. This is a security measure: When you log out, you need to supply your username and password to log in again, which means that someone sitting down at your computer after you've left won't be able to continue with your Zoho session without authorization.

Many of the preceding links are the same in other Zoho applications.

Document tabs

Underneath the links at the top of the Writer page is a set of document tabs you use to move between all the documents that you have open. In Figure 2-1, only one tab is available: the tab labeled Welcome, which corresponds to the Welcome document in Zoho Writer.

To close a tab, just click the X at right on the tab.

The button with the arrow to the left of the Welcome tab is the Maximize Editor button. Click it to make the editing space in Writer fill more of the screen, hiding unneeded bars. Screen space is at a premium in Web browsers, and there's a lot of clutter in Zoho Writer you might be able to do without. If so, just click the Maximize Editor button to get more breathing space. The Maximize Editor button toggles to become the Minimize Editor button when the editor is maximized. To make the editor return to its original size, click the Minimize Editor button.

Now, however, it's time to create your first document in Writer!

Creating, Saving, and Naming Documents

Creating a new document in Writer couldn't be easier. Just click the New button (upper left). A new document named Untitled is created and opened, as you can see in Figure 2-2.

Note what happens: The new document is opened in its own tab — Untitled — as you can see in Figure 2-2. You can still access the Welcome page if you like; just click its tab.

And note that the new document, Untitled, appears in the left pane, as you can also see in Figure 2-2. The Welcome document is also visible in the left pane, as you can see in Figure 2-2. Clicking Welcome opens that document again.

The main action takes place in the *editing space* — that blank space just waiting for your words that you see in Figure 2-2. To enter text into your new document, click the body of the blank document. A flashing text cursor — an upright bar, also called the *insertion point* — appears. That's where the text you type will be inserted.

Your new document

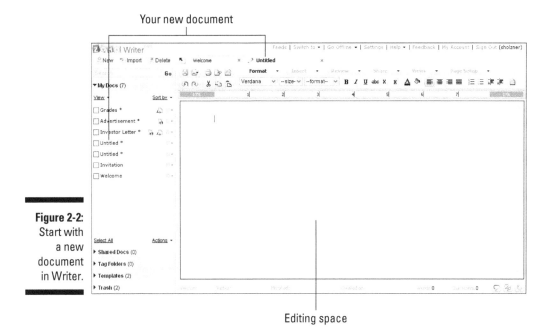

Figure 2-2:
Start with
a new
document
in Writer.

Editing space

After your text is in place, save the new document and give it a name:

1. **Click the Save button (the button with a diskette on it).**

   A Save As dialog box opens, as shown in Figure 2-3, asking you for the name of the new document.

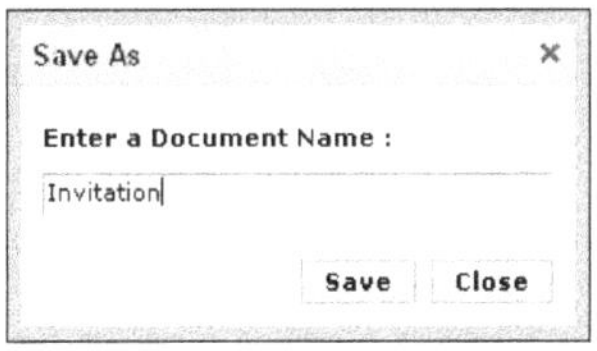

Figure 2-3:
Name your
new doc.

2. **Enter the name of the new document in the text field and then click OK.**

   For my example, I used Invitation, as you can see in Figure 2-3. Then in my new document, I entered text for an invitation to a birthday party.

   After you click OK, the document is saved (using the name you speci-fied) and a pop-up box appears briefly at the bottom right telling you the document was saved and how many words are in it.

After your document is given a name and saved, it gets its own tab. It also shows up in the left pane, as you see in Figure 2-4.

The saved document

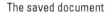

Figure 2-4:
A saved
document.

After you name a document, Zoho won't ask you for its name when you click the Save link: It will just save the document.

When you save a document using Save As instead of Save, a new copy of the document is made and saved — and the tab for the original document still stays open. That way, you can save a copy of your document under a new name.

To save a document under a new name, follow these steps:

1. **Click the Save As button (the button with a diskette and pencil on it).**

   A drop-down menu opens under the Save As button with two items in it.

2. **Choose one of the following options:**

   • *New Document:* Choose the New Document menu item to make the dialog box from Figure 2-3 appear. Enter a name for the document, and then click OK.

   • *Template:* Choosing the Template menu item allows you to save the document as a template. I talk about this in the upcoming section, "Creating your own template."

To rename a document, double-click its tab, and enter the new name for the document. That's all it takes.

Formatting Tips and Tricks in Writer

Many formatting commands and actions in Writer work just like many other word processing applications, but in this section, you run down some techniques and nuggets that will help your productivity and creativity. After all, formatting applies not only to text but also to how the elements in your document look — and the whole document, itself.

Saving time with keyboard shortcuts

When you're typing away, sometimes you might not want to stop, grab the mouse, click a toolbar tab, and then select a button from the toolbar that appears. Well, you're in luck — Writer contains many keyboard shortcuts for common actions, including those in Table 2-2.

Table 2-2	Keyboard Shortcuts
Actions	*Shortcut*
Save file	Ctrl+S
Undo last action	Ctrl+Z
Redo last action	Ctrl+Y
Formatting	
Bold toggle for selection	Ctrl+B
Italic toggle for selection	Ctrl+I
Underline toggle for selection	Ctrl+U
Line break in a document	Shift+Enter
Justify left	Ctrl+L
Justify center	Ctrl+E
Justify right	Ctrl+R
Justify full	Ctrl+J
Add link to the text	Ctrl+K

(continued)

Table 2-2 *(continued)*

Actions	Shortcut
Selection	
Select whole document	Ctrl+A
Select text from beginning of line to cursor position	Shift+Home
Select text from cursor position to the end of line	Shift+End
Navigate	
Go to the beginning of line from the current cursor position	Home
Go to the end of line from the current cursor position	End
Move to the top of the document	Ctrl+Home
Move to the end of the document	Ctrl+End
Up one screen	Page Up
Down one screen	Page Down

Aligning page elements

When you insert new page elements (such as an image or a table), or just write a paragraph or text or add a title, you might want to alter its position. One easy way to do that is to align the page element by using the justification buttons in Zoho Writer.

You can also add elements to Writer layers if you want more fine control over positioning such elements in your document. For more on layers, go to

http://blogs.zoho.com/writer/layers-embedding-documents-and-more

To set the justification of page elements, use the appropriate button on the Format toolbar (click the Format toolbar tool to see the Format toolbar). Select the element and then click the appropriate button. Your choices are left, center, right, and *full* (stretched between left and right with variable spacing between words).

Here's the nub, though. Say you import an image of a birthday cake into an invitation that already has text. (Read how in the upcoming section, "Inserting images in Writer.") The image left-aligns, but you want to center-align it in the invitation. Good enough. Click the cake image to select it, and then click the Justify Center button. You see the result in the top half of Figure 2-5.

Ruler width

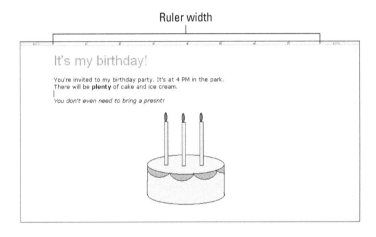

Figure 2-5:
Center-align
an image.

Hmm. In Figure 2-5, you might think that instead of centered, the image is too far left. In fact, Zoho did its job and centered the image *in the page* — but the page width is wider than you might expect.

You can check the page width by taking a look at the ruler, which appears at the top of the writing space in Writer. As shown in the top half of Figure 2-5, the page width — shown by the white space of the ruler — extends from the right margin all the way to nearly the left edge of the page.

To adjust the page width, simply use the mouse to drag the edges of the ruler. For example, check out the invitation with a new (and more appropriate) page width in the bottom half of Figure 2-5 (where the title has also been centered).

Making your text look pretty

You have many ways to customize the appearance of your text with the Format toolbar (click the Format tab to see the Format toolbar). Here are some of the possibilities:

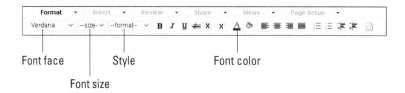

Font face   Style   Font color

Font size

✓ **Choose a different font.** You might like other fonts better than the default font in Writer (Verdana). First, select the text you want to change, and then choose the new font from the Font Face drop-down list box.

✓ **Change the font size.** Frequently when you format text, you want to set the *size* of that text. For example, you probably want to make title text stand out more than the rest of your text. With Writer, selecting a new font size is a snap. Just select the text you want to change and then choose the new size (in points) from the Font Size drop-down list box.

If you don't see the font size that you want in the drop-down list box, just type the size you want (in points) in the text box at the top of the drop-down list box and then press Enter.

✓ **Select a font color.** Say you want some red text in your document. To color text, select the text you want to color and then click the Font Color button. From the color palette that opens (see Figure 2-6), just double-click that color in the dialog box. The new color is applied to the text you selected.

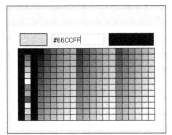

Figure 2-6:
The Font
Color
palette.

Be careful about using red text if you're going to spellcheck your document because Writer marks misspellings in red.

✔ **Use a style:** A *style* is a collection of formats, and using styles ensures consistency throughout your document. Zoho offers a number of styles from the Style drop-down list box.

As of this writing, Zoho Writer offers only 13 styles (6 of which correspond to the HTML `<font>` element's `size` attribute, which can range from `1` to `6`).

You can also add your own CSS (Cascading Style Sheet) to a Zoho Writer document if you want to use your own pre-created styles. To attach a style sheet to your document, select the Insert Style Sheet item from the Style drop-down list box and enter your style sheet file location. You'll need to edit the HTML of the document directly (in particular, you have to set the `style` attribute of text you want to style) to use the styles in your style sheet.

Putting a hex on your colors

If you don't see the color you want in the color palette dialog box, you can enter the hex code for the color directly into the text box in the dialog box, such as the value #FF3366. These color values are the same hex values that browsers use, and they're composed of three color triplets — rrggbb — where rr is the red color value (00–ff), gg is the green color value (00–ff), and bb is the blue color value (00–ff). To create your own color values, you can use online utilities, such as the color picker at www.pagetutor.com/colorpicker/index.html.

Inserting Elements in a Writer Document

You're not limited to just using text in a Writer document. You can also add images, links, tables, and more. Here's how easy it is.

Inserting images in Writer

You can juice up your Writer documents by adding images easily: Just click the Insert Image button on the Action toolbar. For example, say you want to add an image of a birthday cake (`cake.jpg`) to a birthday invitation. Here's how:

1. **Click the Insert toolbar tab and then click the Image button on the Insert toolbar.**

   The Insert Image dialog box opens, as shown in Figure 2-7.

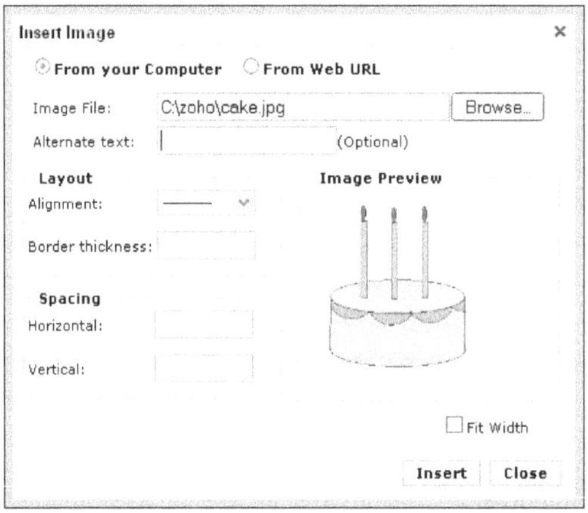

Insert Image   ✕

  ⦿ **From your Computer**   ○ **From Web URL**

  Image File: C:\zoho\cake.jpg   Browse…

  Alternate text: | (Optional)

  Layout   **Image Preview**
  Alignment: ──── ⌄

  Border thickness:

  Spacing
  Horizontal:

  Vertical:

                                   ☐ Fit Width

                                   Insert   Close

Figure 2-7:
The Insert
Image
dialog box.

---

2. **Find the image you want to embed.**

   To upload an image from your machine, click the Browse button and navigate to your image.

   To preview an image, click the Preview button, and your image will appear in the dialog box, as shown in Figure 2-7.

3. **After you make your choice, click Insert to place the image into your document.**

   If you don't want to insert the image at this time, click Cancel.

   Your new image is inserted into your document at the location of the text cursor. You can see what the cake looks like in the document shown in Figure 2-8.

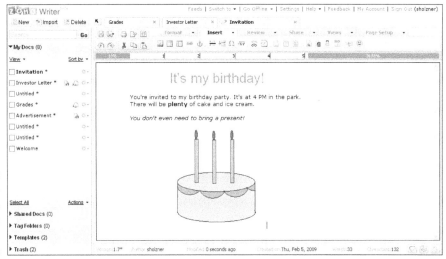

Figure 2-8:
A newly
inserted
image.

Inserting a hyperlink

You can also insert a hyperlink into a Writer document. For example, if you reference an online article in your text, you can link to the article in case the reader wants more information. To insert a hyperlink, follow these steps:

1. **Place the text cursor in the document where you want the new hyperlink to appear.**

2. **Click the arrow on the Insert toolbar tab and choose the Insert/Modify Link from the drop-down menu.**

   The Insert/Modify Link dialog box appears, as shown in Figure 2-9.

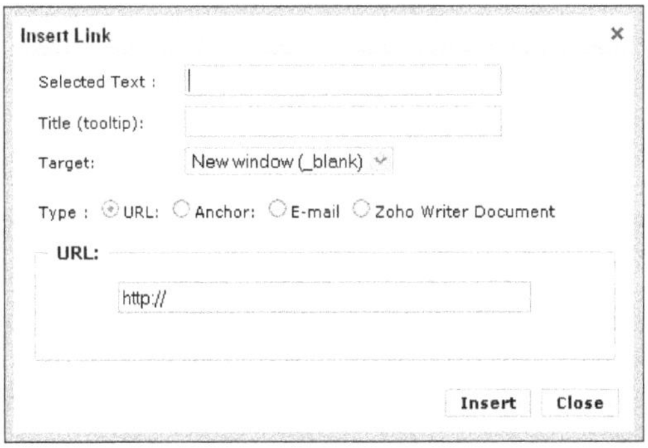

Insert Link   ✕

Selected Text :

Title (tooltip):

Target: New window (_blank) ∨

Type : ⊙ URL: ○ Anchor: ○ E-mail   ○ Zoho Writer Document

URL:

        http://

                                        Insert   Close

Figure 2-9:
The Insert/
Modify Link
dialog box.

3. **Fill in these fields:**

   - *URL:* The URL that the hyperlink should link to

   - *Anchor:* The anchor for the URL (typically given at the end of an URL, following a # sign

     If you don't know what that means, you don't need to fill anything in this field

   - *Selected Text:* The text you want to appear in the document for the link

   - *Title (tooltip):* The text you want to appear in a tooltip when the user moves the mouse over the link

   - *Target:* The hyperlink's target

     Specify whether you want the linked-to page to replace the current page or to appear in a new browser window.

4. **Click Insert to insert the new hyperlink, or click Cancel to close the dialog box without inserting the link.**

   You can see a new hyperlink in the example advertisement in Figure 2-10. Note that by default, hyperlinks appear underlined and blue. They change to green after they're clicked.

Figure 2-10:
A new
hyperlink.

Creating and Refining Tables in Writer

To create a table in Writer, start by clicking the Insert Table button. A sample grid appears, as you can see in Figure 2-11. You click the cell that corresponds to the lower-right cell of your table, and Writer creates that table for you; see Figure 2-12.

Insert Table

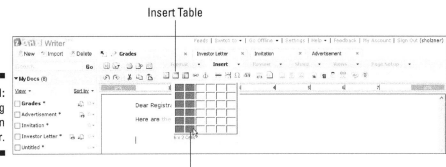

Figure 2-11:
Creating
a table in
Zoho Writer.

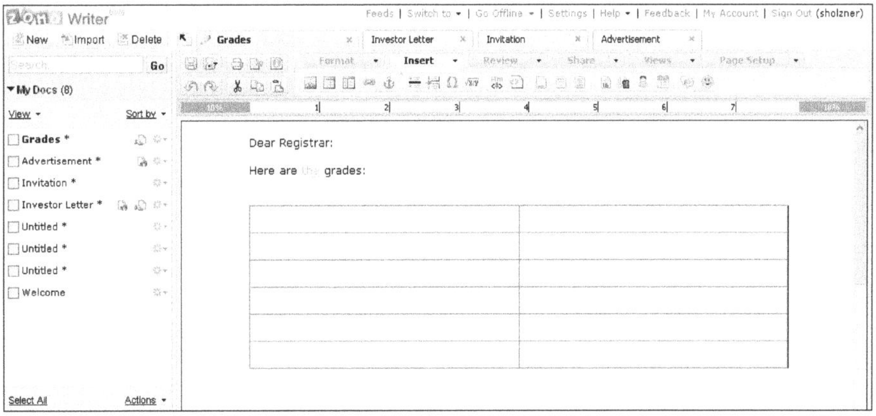

Lower-right cell of your table

Figure 2-12:
A new table
in Zoho
Writer.

If the table is wider than you need, click the table to display a set of *sizing handles* — white squares that you can drag — and then drag the sizing handles to resize the table how you want. Release the sizing handle, and the resized table snaps into position.

To add a new row or a column to a table, simply right-click the table, as shown in Figure 2-13, select the Table Operations item, and then choose the Insert Row After or Insert Column After menu option. You can see many other standard table formatting options on this menu, such as deleting rows and columns and justifying text.

To enter text into a cell in a table, just click that cell, and then type your text. Proceeding cell by cell, you can enter what you want. You can format table headers by formatting the text in them as bold and making their font size larger.

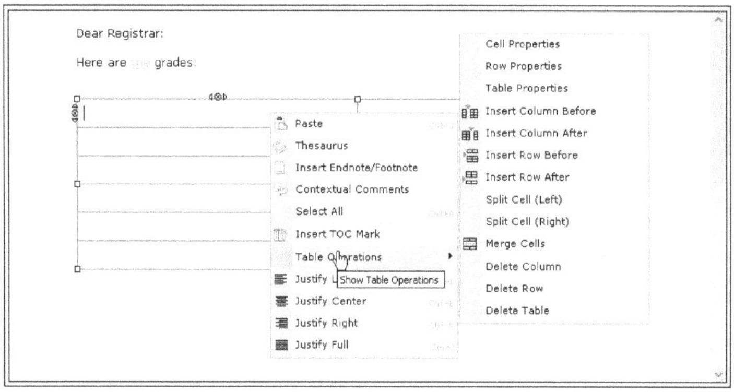

Figure 2-13:
Format
your table
with these
choices.

To access more sophisticated table formatting options, open the Table Properties dialog box. Right-click your table, select Table Operations, and then choose the Table Properties menu item. The Table Properties dialog box appears, as shown in Figure 2-14.

Figure 2-14:
The Table
Properties
dialog box.

Use the various sections of the Table Properties dialog box to customize the appearance of your table by setting the properties (the width and number) of the various borders.

All the Full Facts: Getting Your Document's History

Say you change the formatting in your document. Maybe you remove the rules from a table but want to put them back. Fortunately, Zoho Writer keeps a history of your document, and you can easily revert to an earlier version of your document.

Every time you save a document, Writer saves it with a new version number. To see the previous versions — and perhaps revert your document to one of them — click the Review tab to display the Review toolbar. Then click the History button, which opens the History section shown in Figure 2-15.

Click to return to editing   History section

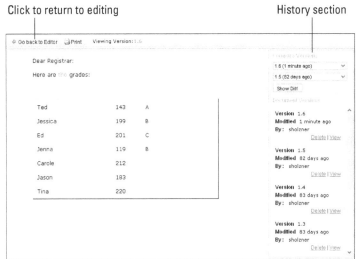

To look through previous versions, just click them in the History section.

To return to editing your document from the History page, click the Return to Editor link shown in Figure 2-15.

Organizing Your Documents with Tags

Zoho Writer allows you to tag documents to make it easy to organize those documents. *Tags* are words that mark a certain document. For example, you might tag the document containing a Grades table as *Grades*.

Follow these steps to tag your document:

1. Click the Tags button at the bottom right of the document.

This opens the Tags section, as you can see in Figure 2-16.

2. **Enter the tag name and then click the Add button.**

   To create a new folder for the tag in the Tags Folder section of the left pane, click the tag and choose the Add as Folder menu item. This adds a new folder for the tag, and you can open the folder by double-clicking it in the Tag Folders section of the left pane. Doing so shows all the documents with that tag, as you can see in Figure 2-17.

Tags   Folder name

Like a Cookie Cutter: Templates

Templates are just like cookie cutters: You use a template as the basis for a document. Templates can contain all kinds of styles, ready for use, such as headings, body text, and margins. When you create a new document from that template, those styles automatically become available to you.

Even better, templates aren't restricted to styles. Templates can also contain *boilerplate text* — that is, standard text — that appears when you create a new document from the template.

Including boilerplate text is also useful for letters that just need tweaked with a product or person's name, or that contain strict legal language.

Finding and downloading a template

Zoho Writer maintains a library of templates for you to choose from at `http://writer.zoho.com/templates.htm`. Either navigate to the URL via your browser or choose the library from the Help drop-down menu in Writer. Either path opens the Template Library, as shown in Figure 2-18.

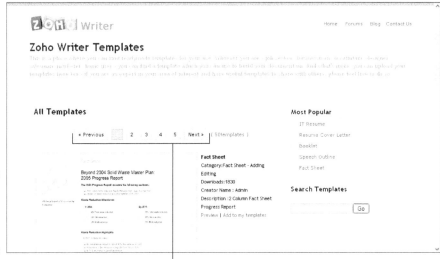

Figure 2-18:
The
Template
Library.

Preview templates

As you can see in Figure 2-18, the first template shown is a generic fact sheet template. Move from template to template by clicking the boxed numbers. You find resume templates, cover letter templates, speech outline templates, and so on.

If you don't feel like previewing each template one by one to find what you want, use the Search Templates feature to search the descriptions of all the templates in the Template Library. Or, check out the Most Popular templates. As of this writing, the most popular template is the IT Resume template. Go figure. Just click the template to preview it in full.

After you choose a template, download it. Every template you open to preview has an Add to My Templates link. Just click that link to add the template to your own collection of templates. You can see the template added to the Templates section of the left pane.

Using a template

Say you want to create a new document based on the IT Resume template. To do that, just follow these steps:

1. **Open the Templates section in the left pane.**

2. **Click the template you wish to use.**

   A preview of the template opens, as you can see in Figure 2-19.

Click to create document from this template

Figure 2-19:
A template
preview.

At this point, decide whether to create a document based on this template as-is or with an edited template.

If you're going for Door #1, follow these steps to create a document from the template you chose:

1. **Click the Use This Template link at the top of the template preview.**

   This creates a new Writer document based on the template.

2. **In the template that opens, edit the boilerplate text.**

Hmm. Maybe you don't want to edit all that text every time you create a new document from the template. Time for Door #2.

You can easily edit the templates you work with in Zoho Writer. Just follow these steps:

1. **Open the Templates section in the left pane and then click the template you wish to edit.**

2. **In the template that opens, click the Edit Template link.**

3. **Make your edits to the template (including styles and fonts) as you would to any Writer document.**

4. **Click the Save Template link.**

    This saves the new version of the template with the same template name.

Clicking the Save Template link saves the new version of the template. When you preview it (by clicking it in the Template section), you see that the changes were indeed made and saved to the template.

You customized a Zoho Writer template. Nice.

Creating your own template

So you don't want what's behind Door #1 or Door #2. You want just the right template for your needs. Say you run a bird shop and need a business letter telling customers a rare bird arrived. Or you might be a scientist who needs a template useful for applying for government grants. You can certainly create your own templates in Zoho Writer.

You don't have to create a template to use a document as boilerplate for other documents. You can just open the document and make changes, saving the result each time.

I see two big advantages to creating your own templates:

- ✔ **You can share the template, as a template, with other users.** Read more about this in the next section, "Exporting a template to the Template Library."

- ✔ **The template appears in the Templates section of Writer, not in the My Docs section.** The Templates section is usually a lot less crowded than the My Docs section, making templates more readily accessible to be used as boilerplate.

Saving an open document as a template is simple:

1. **Click the Save As button (the button with a diskette and pencil on it).**
2. **Choose the Template menu item.**
3. **Enter the name for your template in the Save as Template dialog box.**
4. **Click OK.**

   The new template appears in the Templates section of the left pane.

Exporting a template to the Template Library

Like your template so much that you want to share it with other Zoho users that you don't even know? Export your template to the Template Library.

For any open template, all you need to do is click the Export to Template Library link that appears at the top of the preview. In the Template Library Details dialog box that appears, just fill in the details about your template and then click the Export button.

Chapter 3

Zoho Writer: Publishing, Sharing, and Working Offline

In This Chapter

▷ Adding comments in your documents

▷ Publishing your documents

▷ Sharing documents

▷ Sharing with groups

▷ Working offline

*I*n Chapter 2, you find out how to create Zoho Writer documents. But there's a lot more in Zoho Writer to cover and use to its full potential. This chapter explains how to add comments to, publish, and share documents, as well as work offline.

One thing I love about a Zoho Writer document is the freedom of sharing your document with collaborators — simultaneously! Not only that, but you can collaborate in real time. And as I mention in Chapter 2, you don't have to worry about whether the new computer supports the same word processor, or even the same *version* of that word processor. Zoho seamlessly meshes everyone's contributions into the same document without conflicting edits.

Of course, because this is Zoho, you can work on the document without having to be at your desk or having to connect to your business's intranet or wiki. Win, win, win.

Having Your Say with Comments

Sometimes, you want to add text *about* your text. For example, you might want to pass a document along to folks and ask them questions about some of your text, or ask questions about some of the text in one of their documents.

Adding a comment to text is simple. Just follow these steps:

1. **Select the text that you want to comment on; then click the Add Comment button on the Insert toolbar.**

   This opens the Add Comment dialog box that appears in Figure 3-1.

Figure 3-1:
Adding a
comment.

2. **Enter the text for the comment and then click Add (or click Cancel to cancel the operation and not add the comment).**

   Take a look at Figure 3-2, which is the first draft of a letter to the investors of a company.

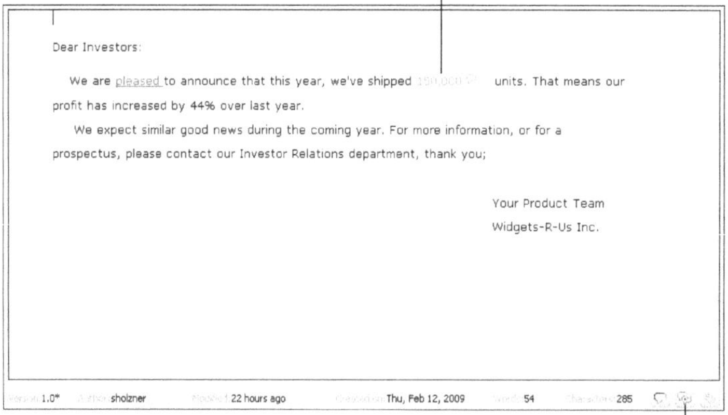

Embedded comment

Dear Investors:

We are pleased to announce that this year, we've shipped 150,000 units. That means our profit has increased by 44% over last year.

We expect similar good news during the coming year. For more information, or for a prospectus, please contact our Investor Relations department, thank you;

Your Product Team
Widgets-R-Us Inc.

Figure 3-2:
A document
with a
comment.

1.0"   sholzner   22 hours ago   Thu, Feb 12, 2009   54   285

Contextual Comments

The 150,000 in *150,000 units* is highlighted in orange (trust me on that one), and there's a little comment icon next to it (like a speech bubble in a cartoon). Both items indicate that there's a comment there. When you click the comment icon, the comment text pops up, as you can see in Figure 3-3. To dismiss the Comments dialog box, click the X button at the upper right.

Figure 3-3:
Read a
comment in
a document.

Comments are useful as notes to yourself, of course, but the real use for comments in Zoho Writer becomes apparent when you share a document, which I cover in the upcoming section, "What's Mine Is Yours: Sharing Documents."

To view all comments in a document at once, open the Comments pane, which displays all a document's comments at the same time on the right side of the screen. You can open the Comments pane by clicking the Contextual Comments button at the extreme lower right of the editing space.

Getting the Word Out: Printing and Publishing to the Web

You can print Writer documents just like any other document. Of course, all printers are different, so I won't get into that. Just use the Print button.

You can also share documents by publishing them on the Web directly. Zoho makes your documents accessible from any browser, if you want. This is a nice feature of Zoho Writer because you can automatically publish your documents as Web pages, hosted by Zoho for you.

Here's how:

1. **Open the document you want to publish on the Web.**
2. **Click the Publish button on the Share toolbar.**
3. **Choose the Public Info item from the drop-down menu that opens.**

   Writer displays the warning you see in Figure 3-4.

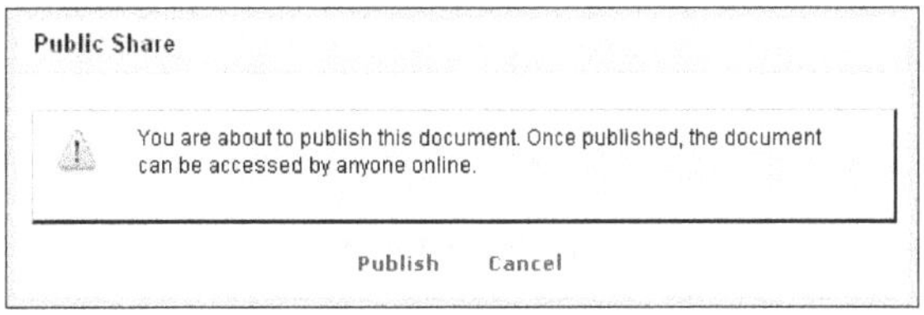

Figure 3-4:
The public
document
warning.

Public Share

You are about to publish this document. Once published, the document can be accessed by anyone online.

Publish   Cancel

4. **Click the Publish button to publish your document on the Web, or click Cancel to cancel.**

    In the Public Share dialog box that opens, Writer gives you a small HTML script (as you see in Figure 3-5) to embed into a Web page that will display your document.

    Note the Allow Others to Give Comments check box at the bottom of the figure. Select that check box if you want people to leave comments on your Web page.

Public Share   ×

Document Public URL: Advertisement

Embed Document on your webpage/blog

    <script src="http://writer.zoho.com/public/sholzner
    /Advertisement/script"></script>

☑ Allow others to give comments

Close

Figure 3-5:
The
publishing
script.

Here's a sample script (the `src` attribute points to a JavaScript script that does the actual inserting of the document):

```
<script
src="http://writer.zoho.com/public/sholzner/Advertisement/script"
>
</script>
```

To embed this script in a Web page, open the Web page's source file and paste the preceding `<script>` element where you want your Writer document to appear.

When you embed this script in a Web page and navigate to that Web page with your browser, you see your document, as shown in Figure 3-6. Note the Comments link at lower left — viewers of your page can leave comments by clicking that link and entering their comments.

Congratulations! You published your document to the Web.

You can also publish a document to a blog if you select the Publish button's Publish to Blog option from the drop-down menu. You'll be asked for your blog host, as well as your username and password.

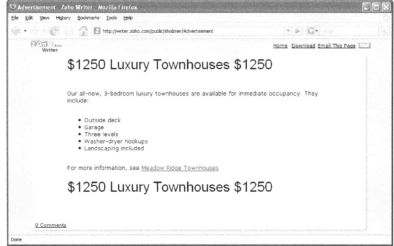

Figure 3-6:
The published document.

What's Mine Is Yours: Sharing Documents

Sharing documents is one of Zoho Writer's big plusses, and it's not too much to say that many companies use online applications like Writer in preference to desktop applications because online applications let you share documents with other people — *collaborators* — easily.

How easily? Take a look.

Inviting collaborators

To share a document, follow these steps:

1. **Open the document in Zoho Writer.**

2. **Click the Share button on the Share toolbar.**

   The Share This Document dialog box opens, as shown in Figure 3-7. Make sure that the Invite tab is selected.

Share This Document

Invite   Shared Details

Read Only Members :

Individuals: Add Contacts **Groups:**   Add Groups

Read / Write Members :

Individuals: Add Contacts **Groups:**   Add Groups

Invitation Message:

Select Invitation Language: English ⌄   Edit Invitation Mail >>

Share   Close

Figure 3-7:
Share a
document.

3. **Enable document sharing with other Writer users by selecting one of the following options:**

  • *To let people share the document but only view the document:* Enter their e-mail addresses, separated by commas, in the Read Only Members field for Individuals.

  • *To let people share the document by allowing them to view and edit the document:* Enter their e-mail addresses, separated by commas, in the Read/Write Members field for Individuals.

4. **Click the Edit Invitation Mail button to create an e-mail message to send to the people you want to invite; see Figure 3-8. Enter a subject line and craft your message here.**

Share This Document

Invite   Shared Details

Read Only Members :

Individuals: Add Contacts **Groups:**   Add Groups

Read / Write Members :

Individuals: Add Contacts **Groups:**   Add Groups

Invitation Message:

Select Invitation Language: English ⌄   << Hide Editing

Share   Close

Subject:
Document Shared to You on Zoho Writer

Message:(400 Characters max)

Hi User,
Steve has shared a document with you on Zoho Writer named
'Investor Letter'|

sholzner

Figure 3-8:
Customize
your
invitation
e-mail.

5. Click the Share button to send your invitation by e-mail.

The Share This Document dialog box displays (in the Shared Details tab) the people with whom you're sharing the document, as shown in Figure 3-9.

```
Share This Document

    Invite      Shared Details

Email/Zoho ID                          Permission      Action
   nlconner                            View/Edit       Change | Remove






                    <                                                    >
                                       Close
```

Figure 3-9:
See your collab-orators.

The Share This Document dialog box also lists the permissions for each col-laborator. Here's how you can customize permissions for your collaborators:

✔ **To change the permission for a collaborator:** Click the Change link at the right. The permission toggles between View Only and View/Edit when you click this button.

✔ **To delete a collaborator:** Click the Remove link.

The people you invited — your prospective collaborators — will receive an e-mail like this:

```
Hi User, Steve has shared a document with you on Zoho
Writer named 'Investor Letter'
--------------------------------------
Click here to view the document shared by sholzner
writer.zoho.com/Home.do?shrDocId=Investor-
         Letter&author=sholzner
```

When a collaborator clicks the link, he's asked to log into Zoho, and a dialog box appears, asking whether to open your document.

When collaborators edit a shared document

When a collaborator is editing your document, that document is highlighted with a yellow background (and you can't edit the document), so you know that changes might appear. See Figure 3-10. (If you don't like the changes, you can always revert to an earlier version using the document's history. See Chapter 2 for more the history feature.) Note that Writer does not have a revision marks feature like you'd find in other word processors like Microsoft Word.

Comment icon

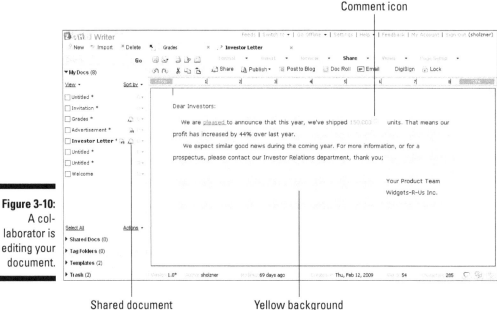

Figure 3-10:
A collaborator is editing your document.

Shared document

Yellow background

Collaborators can answer comments from other editors. (See "Having Your Say with Comments," earlier in the chapter.) For example, if a collaborator wants to respond to your comment, "Is this right?" in Figure 3-11, he just clicks the Add Comment link and types his response, as shown in Figure 3-11.

When the collaborator stops editing the document and signs out, the background of the document returns to normal (not yellow).

When you click the comment icon, you can see the collaborator's return comment, as shown in Figure 3-11, offering a correction. To delete a comment, right-click the comment icon and choose the Cut menu item.

Figure 3-11:
Read a col-
laborator's
comments.

Communicating with a document's collaborators

Can you get in touch with your collaborators interactively, while they're editing your document? Certainly.

To send a message to the collaborators who are currently editing or viewing
your document, click the Collaborators button, which is the third from the
right at the lower right in the browser, and type your message into the message box in the Collaborators pane; see Figure 3-12.

When you finish typing your message, press Enter. Your message is then visible
to all collaborators who have your document open, as shown in Figure 3-12.

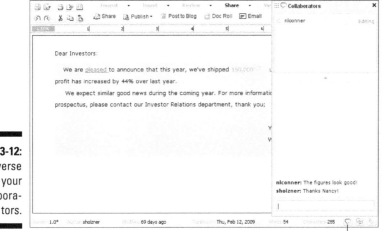

Figure 3-12:
Converse
with your
collabora-
tors.

Click to open Collaborators pane

The Collaborators pane holds your back-and-forth conversation, much like an IM interface. In this way, you can exchange messages with your collaborators, chatting with them.

Your collaborators get a link to your document in the invitation, but your collaborators can also access your document again by opening the Shared Docs section to see a list of the documents that they're sharing. Clicking any document opens that document for editing or viewing.

Collaborating with groups of collaborators

Besides sharing documents with individuals, you can share documents with whole *groups* of Writer users. To share a document with a group, you have to create a group first. To do that, follow these steps:

1. **With the to-be-shared document open in Writer, click the Share button on the Share toolbar to open the Share This Document dialog box. (Refer to Figure 3-7.)**

2. **Click the Add Groups link.**

   This opens the Groups List dialog box, shown in Figure 3-13.

Figure 3-13: The Groups List dialog box.

3. **Click the Create New Group link in the Groups List dialog box to open the Create Your Personal Group dialog box, as shown in Figure 3-14.**

4. **Fill in the following fields:**

   • *Group Name:* The name you want to give your new group

   • *Description (Optional):* A description of your new group

   • *Members Mail IDs:* The e-mail addresses of the individuals you want to invite to the group

   Use a comma to separate multiple e-mails.

- *Enter a Short Message:* The message you want to send with the invitation to join the group

- *Select Invitation Language:* The language for the invitation (English, Chinese, or Japanese)

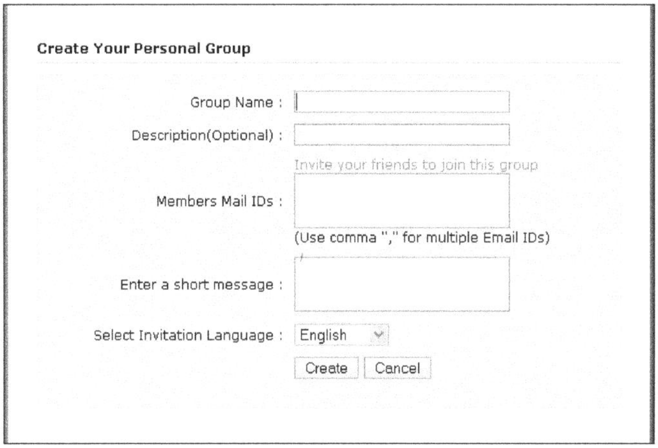

Create Your Personal Group

Group Name :

Description(Optional) :

Invite your friends to join this group

Members Mail IDs :

(Use comma "," for multiple Email IDs)

Enter a short message :

Select Invitation Language : English

Create   Cancel

Figure 3-14:
Create a
group here.

5. **Click the Create button.**

   A summary dialog box opens, as shown in Figure 3-15, showing your new group.

Groups   Create New Group

Logo **Group Name** **Description**   **Members**   **Actions**

      Group One   5   Invite Edit Delete

Figure 3-15:
The Groups
summary
dialog box.

6. **Close the Groups summary dialog box.**

   You created a new group of collaborators.

Inviting a group of collaborators to share a document

After you create a group, you can invite its members to share a document. To do that, follow these steps:

1. **With the document that you want to share open in Writer, click the Share button on the Share toolbar.**

2. **In the Share This Document dialog box that opens, click the Add Groups link.**

3. **In the Groups List dialog box that opens (refer to Figure 3-13), click the name of the group you want to share the document with; then close the Groups List by clicking the X button at the upper right.**

4. **Click the Share button in the Share This Document dialog box to share the document with the group.**

   All the members in the group get an e-mail invitation. Now you can share a document with a whole group at once.

Managing groups

After you create your groups, it's important to know how to manage those groups: inviting new members, editing your group member list, and even deleting a group.

To invite new members to a group, follow these steps:

1. **With the document that you want to share open in Writer, click the Share button on the Share toolbar.**

2. **Click the Add Groups link.**

3. **In the Groups List dialog box that opens, click the My Groups link.**

4. **Click the Invite link (refer to Figure 3-15) for the entry for the group to which you want to invite new members.**

   This opens the Invite Friends dialog box; see Figure 3-16.

5. **Enter the e-mail addresses of the group members you're inviting, and also enter a short message.**

6. **Click the Invite button.**

7. **Close the Summary dialog box that opens.**

8. **Close the Groups List dialog box and then the Share This Document dialog box.**

Groups » Group One » **Invite Friends**

Members Mail IDs :

(Use comma "," for multiple Email IDs)

Enter a short message :

Select Invitation Language : English

Invite   Cancel

Figure 3-16:
The Invite
Friends
dialog box.

Editing the members of a group works much the same way. *Note:* Editing
just lets you delete members of the group — you can't set permissions
individually by member.

1. **Open the document that you want to share and then click the Share
   button on the Share toolbar.**

2. **Click the Add Groups link.**

3. **Click the My Groups link in the Groups List dialog box, opening the
   Groups List dialog box.**

4. **Click the Edit link for the group you want to edit.**

5. **In the Edit Group dialog box that opens, click the Edit Group Details
   link.**

6. **In the Groups dialog box that opens (see Figure 3-17), make the edits
   you want to the group and then close the dialog box.**

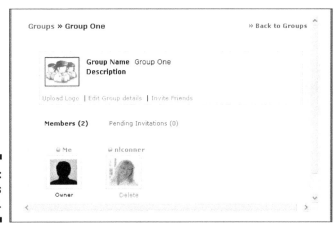

Figure 3-17:
The Groups
dialog box.

7. Close the Summary dialog box that opens, and then close the Groups List dialog box and the Share This Document dialog box.

Deleting a group works just the same except that you click the Delete link for the entry for the group you want to delete.

Importing and Exporting Documents

You can import documents easily to Writer — just click the Import button at the upper left in Writer to open the Import Document dialog box, as shown in Figure 3-18.

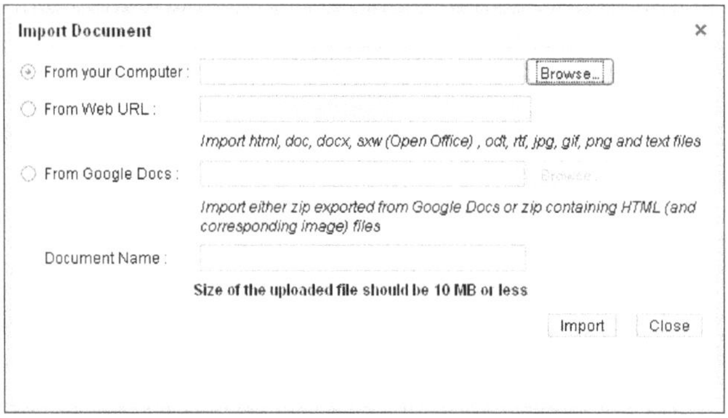

Figure 3-18: The Import Document dialog box.

> **Import Document** ✕
>
> ⦿ From your Computer : [   ] [Browse...]
> ⚬ From Web URL : [   ]
>   *Import html, doc, docx, sxw (Open Office) , odt, rtf, jpg, gif, png and text files*
> ⚬ From Google Docs : [   ] [Browse...]
>   *Import either zip exported from Google Docs or zip containing HTML (and corresponding image) files*
> Document Name : [   ]
>   **Size of the uploaded file should be 10 MB or less**
>   [Import] [Close]

To import a document, click the Browse button, select the document in the File Upload dialog box that opens, click the Open button, and then click the Import button.

You can import these file types:

- ✔ **DOC:** Microsoft Word document, pre–Word 2007
- ✔ **DOCX:** Microsoft Word Document, Word 2007 or later
- ✔ **ODF (ODT):** OpenOffice.org document
- ✔ **PDF:** Portable Document Format document
- ✔ **LaTeX:** LaTeX document

✔ **SXW:** Star Office document

✔ **RTF:** Rich Text Format document

✔ **TXT:** Text document

✔ **HTML:** HTML document

Now what about exporting documents? Although you can edit, print, customize, and work with your document online, sometimes you need to have a physical file for your document, like when you need to pass the document to someone who doesn't know about Zoho.

After you create (and potentially collaborate on) a document, you can access it and share it outside Writer by exporting it. When you export a document, Writer sends it to your browser, which downloads it.

 To export a document, click the Export button shown in the margin. You see a drop-down list of the export file types from which to choose — these types are the same as the allowed formats for importing a document.

After you choose the export file type, Writer sends your document to your browser, and a dialog box from your browser opens, like the one in Figure 3-19.

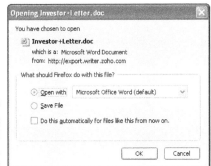

Figure 3-19:
A download
dialog box.

If you ask your browser to download the document and open it, it'll open in the application on your computer best suited to that type of document. For example, you can see a Writer document opened in Microsoft Word in Figure 3-20.

The comments in the document are repeated faithfully in the Microsoft Word version of the document, as you can see in Figure 3-20.

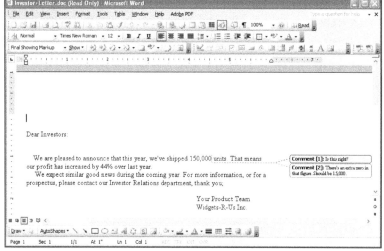

Figure 3-20:
A down-
loaded
document
opened in
Microsoft
Word.

Taking It off the Internet: Working Offline

With the help of a package from Google named Gears, you can run Zoho Writer offline. In a nutshell, if you're somewhere the Internet isn't — say, stuck on a plane, with no connectivity — you can still work with Zoho Writer.

Installing Gears from Google

The first step is to install Gears. Your system needs to meet these requirements:

OS	*Browser*
Windows XP or Vista	Internet Explorer (IE) 6 or higher
Windows XP or Vista	Firefox 1.5 or higher
Windows XP or Vista	Google Chrome*
Mac OS X 10.2 or higher	Firefox 1.5 or higher
Linux	Firefox 1.5 or higher
Windows Mobile 5 or higher	Internet Explorer 4.01 or higher

*Chrome has Gears built in, so you don't need to follow the remaining installation instructions.

If your system meets these requirements, go to `http://gears.google.com`, the Gears homepage. Then follow these steps to install Gears:

1. **Click the Install Gears button on the Gears home page.**

2. **On the Terms and Conditions page that opens, click the Agree and Download button.**

3. **Save the `GearsSetup.exe` file:**

   • *IE:* Click Save in the dialog box that appears.

   • *Firefox:* Click Save File.

   If you're using Internet Explorer, you might get a security bar at the top of the page, blocking the download. Click the security bar and then select the Download File item.

4. **Run the downloaded `GearsSetup.exe` file and follow the directions.**

5. **Close your browser and restart it before using Gears with Zoho Writer.**

Using Writer with Gears

To set up Writer to work with Gears, follow these steps after you install Gears:

1. **Sign in to Zoho Writer.**

2. **Click the Go Offline link at the top of the Zoho Writer page.**

3. **In the Gears Security Warning dialog box that appears, select the I Trust This Site Allow It to Use Gears check box.**

4. **Click the Allow button in the Gears Security Warning dialog box.**

   Gears will transfer up to 25 of your most recent documents to your computer.

To download more than 25 documents, click the down arrow next to the Go Offline link and select the number of documents to download.

Now, when you click the Go Offline link, up to 25 documents will be downloaded for you to work on. ***Note:*** You won't have to go through the I Trust This Site process after the first time.

You're ready to work offline. To do that, navigate your browser to `http://writer.zoho.com/offline`. That's all it takes. Now you can work with documents, opening them as usual, in Writer, even though you're offline. When you're done, there's no need to sign out from Zoho; after all, you're not signed in. Just close your browser.

Synching your offline documents with Writer online

Synchronizing your offline documents with your online documents is a snap. The next time your computer has access to the Internet, navigate your browser to `http://writer.zoho.com/offline`. That's right: to the *offline* address.

Zoho Writer displays its Synchronization Summary dialog box (see Figure 3-21), listing the online documents that are out of date and need to be refreshed using your offline versions. To upload your offline documents (as new versions of those documents, as kept track of by Writer), click the Synchronize button.

Figure 3-21: Synchronizing documents.

Synchronization Summary

Following document(s) have been modified offline. Select the documents to be Synchronized.

	Document Name	Offline Version	Online Version	Version after Sync	Remarks
☑	Agenda 10/28	1.4	1.4	1.5	Local copy modified
☑	Cover letter	1.6	1.7	1.8	Local copy modified

Note: In case of a conflict between the Offline version and the current Online version of a document, Zoho Writer will just upload the offline document as a new version. Users have to take care of manually merging the document, incase its required.

Synchronize   Cancel

Chapter 4

Zoho Show: Lights, Camera, Action!

In This Chapter

▷ Creating presentations

▷ Adding slides

▷ Using text and images

▷ Adding shapes

▷ Sharing presentations

▷ Viewing presentations online

Presentation software has become hugely popular. Want to present your idea to a group of investors? Create a presentation. Want to present your company's profits for the last quarter? Create a presentation. Want to show shareholders how your organization works? Create a presentation.

Presentations are comprised of slides, one after the other, that you present to your audience. Zoho Show is perfect for this purpose, helping you create and share your slide shows; add text, images, clip art; and more.

I take a look at Zoho Show in this chapter. It's easy to use and allows you to create professional presentations in a snap. And you can easily share those presentations with others — which is a good thing, because that's the whole idea behind presentations.

Creating a Presentation

To sign in to Zoho Show, go to `http://show.zoho.com`, enter your user-name and password, and then click the Sign In button. (See Chapter 1 for information on signing up for a Zoho username and password.) From here, you can either create a new presentation or import an existing presentation, as I describe in the following sections.

Creating a new presentation

The Zoho Show welcome page is where you create a new presentation. Follow these steps:

1. **Click the Create New button at the upper left, opening the page you see in Figure 4-1.**

    On the Create New Presentation page, you can name your presentation and customize it to some extent.

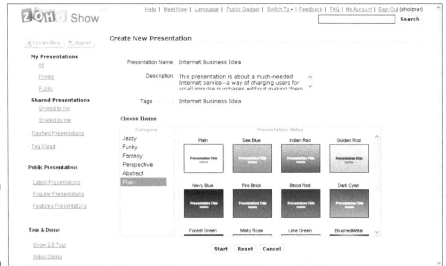

Figure 4-1:
Creating a presenta-tion.

2. **Enter a descriptive name for your new presentation in the Presentation Name text box.**

3. **(Optional) Change the prepopulated tag in the Tags field.**

    When you enter a presentation name in Step 2, Show also copies that text into the Tags field. Show *tags* (which work just the same way as Writer tags; covered in Chapter 2) are descriptive keywords that you can search on, finding matching presentations.

4. **Choose a theme category from the Category pane on the left.**

    Selecting a theme allows you to specify the background of the slides you'll use in the presentation. As you can see in Figure 4-1, you can pick from six categories of themes in Show, ranging from Jazzy to Funky to Plain.

5. **Select one of the slide themes on the right.**

    When you select a category, you see a group of themes that you can select from.

6. **After you specify your presentation's name, description, tags, and theme, click the Start button to open and start editing your new presentation (which I get to after discussing how to import presentations).**

Importing an existing presentation

Another option is to import a presentation into Show. The presentation types you can import are Microsoft PowerPoint (PPT, PPS documents) or OpenOffice.org (ODP, SXI documents).

To import a presentation, follow these steps:

1. **Click the Import button (at the top left of the welcome page), opening the page you see in Figure 4-2.**

Figure 4-2:
Importing a presentation.

2. **You can import a local document on your computer or a presentation on the Web. Just select the appropriate option and then either browse to the document or enter the URL.**

   Presentation documents that you import should be 10MB or smaller, according to Zoho.

3. **Enter a name for the presentation, a description, and tags.**

4. **Choose from two import options: read/write mode or read-only mode.**

   If you don't want to make inadvertent changes to the document, select read-only mode.

5. **When you're all set, click the Import button to import your presentation, opening it in Zoho Show.**

Welcome to Zoho Show

When you click the Start button to create a new presentation, or click the Import button to import an existing presentation, you see the presentation in Zoho Show, as shown in Figure 4-3, where I just created a new presentation.

Getting to know the interface

Spend a few moments taking a look at Zoho Show. The left pane holds an overview of the slides in your presentation. All your slides are displayed here, and clicking one lets you open that slide in the *editing area* — your workspace — located in the center of Zoho Show.

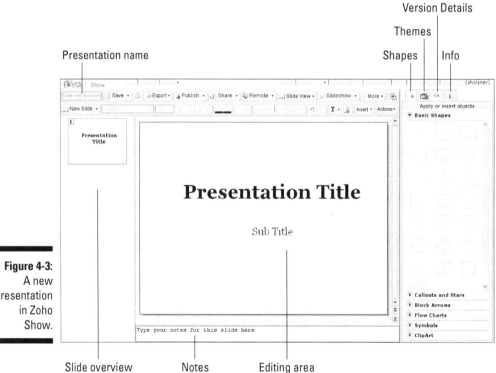

Figure 4-3:
A new
presentation
in Zoho
Show.

To the right is a set of four stacked tabs:

- ✔ **Shapes:** A vast collection of shapes and callouts, including clip art for you to use. For the lowdown on shapes, see the section "Adding shapes," later in this chapter.

- ✔ **Themes:** Contains the Show themes you can use in your presentation. To find out more about themes, see "Changing themes on the fly," later in this chapter.

- ✔ **Version Details:** Displays the version of your presentation.

- ✔ **Info:** Presentation name, description, tags, and so on.

Note the space for notes for this slide: the Type Your Notes for This Slide Here text box at the bottom of the window. You can add notes for each slide in this section; the notes will be visible only to you when you play the presentation, allowing you to create your own speech scripts, if you like.

The slide in the editing area is ready for you to edit and format. But before you jump in and start editing this slide, take a look at a crucial Show concept: *views.*

Understanding presentation views

When you start working on a presentation, you see toolbars, tabbed controls, and so on that you use to edit and work on your slides.

However, when you want to actually show your presentation to your audience, you don't want toolbars or menus showing. You just want to see slides. For this reason, you can use different views to see your presentation. From the Slide View drop-down menu, you can choose from these three options when editing your presentation:

- ✔ **Normal View:** This view — the view you see in Figure 4-3 — is what Show starts with. You edit your slides, add new slides, and create your presentation in this view.

- ✔ **Master View:** Use Master View to customize aspects of your presentation across all slides at once. When you enter Master View, you see two slides — title master and slide master — and editing the styles in those slides lets you edit the styles across all slides.

- ✔ **Sorter View:** This view gives you an overview of all your slides at once, allowing you to arrange and sort your slides. This view is particularly useful when you have many slides to work with.

One other viewing option is Slideshow. This is the view that your audience will think of because this is how you display your slides in a slide show. For more on this view, see the section "Showtime! Presenting Your Presentation," later in this chapter.

Customizing Your Presentation

In Normal View, your first slide looks similar to what you see in Figure 4-3. Suppose that you want to present a new Internet business idea called InstaNowPay. You might change that slide to read like this:

> Presenting: InstaNowPay
>
> The Instant Impulse Buying Online System

In the following sections, you find out how to add slides, text, bullets, and shapes to your presentation.

In Show, all text and images are *objects*. To delete an object, you just have to right-click it and then choose Cut Object from the menu that appears.

Adding slides

To add a new slide to your presentation, follow these steps:

1. **Click the New Slide button (upper left in Show) and then choose Create Slide.**

   If you want to create a slide just like the first slide in the presentation, choose Duplicate Slide after you click the New Slide button.

   The Create New Slide dialog box appears, as shown in Figure 4-4.

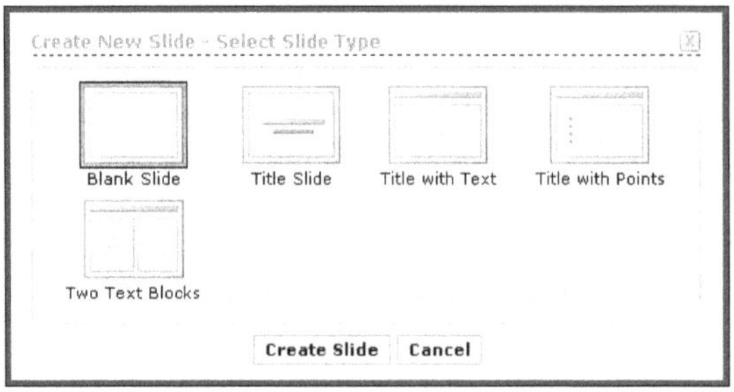

Figure 4-4:
The Create
New Slide
dialog box.

Create New Slide – Select Slide Type

Blank Slide   Title Slide   Title with Text   Title with Points

Two Text Blocks

Create Slide   Cancel

2. **Choose one of the following new slide types:**

   - *Blank Slide:* An empty slide.

   - *Title Slide:* A slide that has a text box for a title.

   - *Title with Text:* A title slide that also has a text box for text.

   - *Title with Points:* A title slide with a box for entering bullet points. Figure 4-5 shows what the new Title with Points slide looks like.

   - *Two Text Blocks:* A slide with two text blocks below the title.

3. **Click the Create Slide button.**

   That creates a new slide, which is added to your presentation.

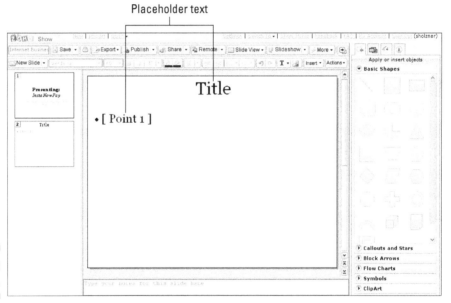

Placeholder text

Figure 4-5:
A new slide.

Here are a few other tips for working with slides:

- ✔ To sort slides, click the View button, select Sorter View, and then drag the slides around as you want them.

- ✔ To delete a slide, right-click it in the left-hand pane and select Delete.

- ✔ To save your presentation, click the Save button.

Adding text

Your new slide is ready to have some text added. So how do you edit the slide to make changes, customizing it with the text you want? Follow these steps:

1. **Click the placeholder text that you want to replace.**

   A text box appears.

   For example, if you click the placeholder text *Presentation Title* in Figure 4-3 (earlier in the chapter), the text box shown in Figure 4-6 appears.

Formatting toolbar   Text box

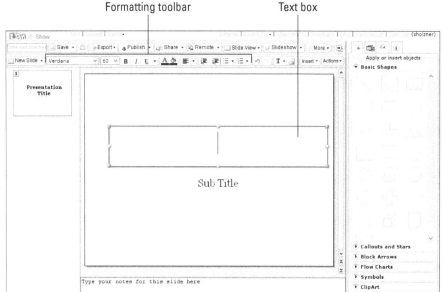

Figure 4-6: Editing a presentation title.

2. **Enter your text into the text box.**

3. **When you're finished, click outside the text box.**

   The text box disappears, and the new title appears in the style of the original title.

4. **Click the Save drop-down button and then choose Save from the menu that appears.**

If you want to format the text you entered, use the buttons on the Formatting toolbar, as shown in Figure 4-6. These formatting buttons are similar to what you use in Zoho Writer (see Chapter 2).

Now suppose you want to add additional text but don't have a placeholder for it. In this case, you need to insert a new text box on your slide, as described in the following steps:

1. **Click the Insert button.**

2. **Choose Text Box from the drop-down menu that appears.**

3. **Choose one of the following options:**

   - *Title Box 1:* A box for a title

   - *Sub Title Box:* A box for a subtitle

   - *Title Box 2:* A box for a small title

   - *Text Box:* A box for text

   After you make your selection, a new text box appears on your slide.

4. **Click the new text box and use the *sizing handles* (those small black squares on the edges of the title's box) to position the text box where you want it.**

5. **Enter your text.**

Working with bullets

If you select the Title with Points option when creating your slide, placeholder bullet text already appears on the slide (refer to Figure 4-5). If you don't have any preformatted bullets on your slide but you want to add them, follow these steps:

1. **Click the Insert button.**

2. **Choose Text Box⇨Bullet Box from the drop-down menu that appears.**

   This creates a new bullet box.

3. **Click the new bullet box and use the sizing handles to position the box where you want it.**

Now you're ready to add your bulleted text. To do so, just click the placeholder text and start typing; press Enter to separate each bullet. Show adds a new bullet for every line, as you see in Figure 4-7.

Here's how to get fancy and give your bullets sub-bullets. Create the new sub-bullets, select them, and then click the Increase List Level button on the Formatting toolbar. To "outdent" bullets, click the Decrease List Level button.

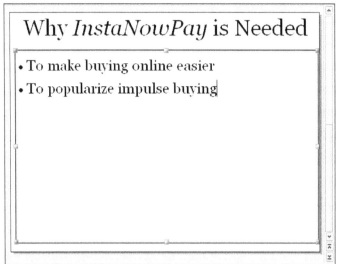

Figure 4-7:
The new
bullets.

Adding shapes

Show comes with many built-in shapes for you to use. Just take a look at the palette of shapes at the right in Figure 4-8. There are endless uses for shapes in slides — stars to emphasize text, flowchart shapes to show how a process works, boxes to set off text, and so on. In the following sections, you get an overview of what shapes are available in Show and find out how to insert them into your presentation.

Inserting a shape

To see how to put these shapes to work, say, for example, that the text in your slide indicates that there should be a button. (See Figure 4-8 for an example.) Hmm. There is no button — but you can make one with a shape. Show offers 22 basic shapes, as you can see at the right in Figure 4-8, and they're just waiting to be put to work.

Follow these steps to add a shape to your slide:

1. **Select a shape from the collection of shapes at the right and then drag it the desired location on the slide.**

   For an overview of all the types of shapes that are available, see "Exploring shape categories," later in this chapter.

2. **Using the sizing handles (see Figure 4-9), resize the shape as desired.**

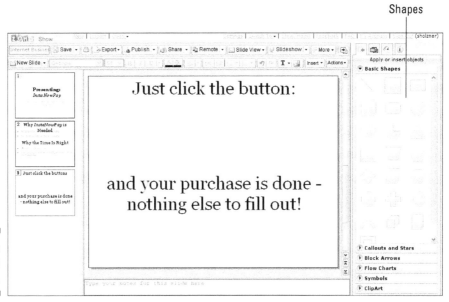

Figure 4-8:
Add a shape
to this slide.

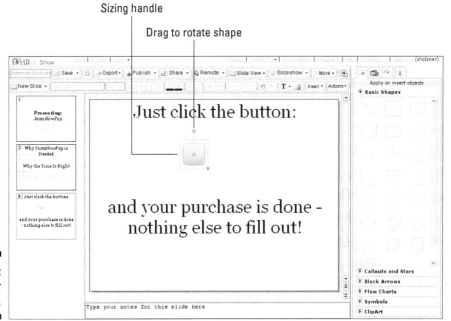

Figure 4-9:
Resize your
shape.

To rotate the shape, drag the top handle clockwise or counterclockwise. See Figure 4-10 to see how I made the shape bigger.

Just click the button:

and your purchase is done - nothing else to fill out!

Figure 4-10:
The new
button
shape.

Adding text to a shape

You can also put labeling text into the new shape, making it look as though a button has a caption. To add a text box to a shape, follow these steps:

1. **Click the Insert button.**

2. **Choose Text Box⇨Text Box from the drop-down menu that appears.**

   This creates a new text box.

3. **Click the new text box and use the sizing handles to resize and position the box where you want it inside the shape.**

4. **Click in the text box and enter the new text you want to display, as shown in Figure 4-11.**

Exploring shape categories

In addition to the Basic Shapes collection shown in Figure 4-8, you can also add shapes from these categories:

✔ **Callouts and Stars:** Want to add some pizzazz to your presentation? Try making it talk — with callouts. In Show, *callouts* are small "speech bubbles" like what you see in cartoons, and you can find them in the Callouts and Stars section of the shapes palette in Show.

Say, for example, that you need a talking cat. Start with a cat image from the ClipArt section (read about this shortly), and then drag a speech bubble from the Callouts and Stars section to the slide, as shown in Figure 4-12. To add text to the speech bubble, just follow the steps in the preceding section.

Figure 4-11:
Add text to
a shape.

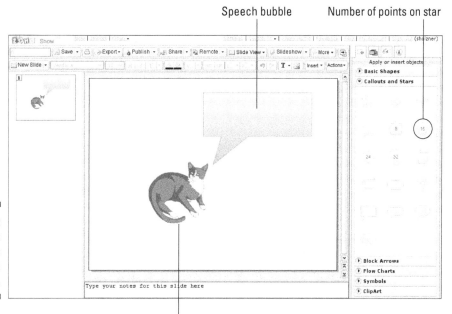

Figure 4-12:
Use a shape
to add a
speech
bubble.

The numbers (8, 16, 24, and so on) in some of the shapes you see on the right in Figure 4-12 tell you how many points each of those star shapes have.

✔ **Block Arrows:** Another type of shape you can use in slides are arrows, which you can access from the Block Arrows palette. Arrows are particularly useful in slides that show progressions of some kind, from point A to point B, or even to point C and D and so on. If you're illustrating a process of some type, arrows are a good choice.

You can see an example slide using an arrow in Figure 4-13.

Figure 4-13:
Add arrows
to a slide.

✔ **Flow Charts:** Flow charts are very popular in presentations because you often find yourself trying to illustrate the steps you want people to understand. In the Flow Chart category, you find shapes that you can use to create a flow chart. Then if you want to connect your flow chart boxes, use the Block Arrows shapes in Show, as you see in Figure 4-14. Nice.

Compare the arrows in the Block Arrows palette to the arrows in Figure 4-14: Some don't appear in the palette. For example, there's only one curved 90-degree arrow, and it goes from south to east. How did I get the others in the slide with the flow chart? Sure, you can rotate shapes with the rotation handle, but what about creating an east-to-south arrow? There's no way to do that without flipping an image, and you can't do that with the rotation or sizing handles. Here's the trick: Flip shapes by right-clicking them, choosing Properties, clicking the Flip & Rotation bar in the dialog box that opens, and then clicking the Flip Horizontal or Flip Vertical button as needed.

Flow Chart shape

Block Arrow shape

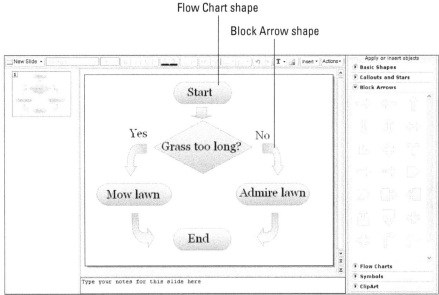

Figure 4-14:
Add arrows
to a flow
chart.

- ✔ **Symbols:** In this catch-all category, you can find shapes such as a moon, lightning bolt, heart, and flower.

- ✔ **ClipArt:** One of the most exciting new additions to Zoho Show is the ClipArt category, which you can find in the ClipArt section on the right of Show.

  Zoho actually does a good job of providing you with many different clip art choices, so the chances you'll find something you can use are good. The ClipArt categories range from Animals to Plants to Transport.

Don't see the shape you want? Create it by assembling it from more basic shapes. There's even a line shape that you can rotate and resize to create any line-based shape you like.

Setting a solid fill color for shapes

After you add a shape to your slide, you're not locked in to the current color or border. For example, the default color for shapes in Show is gold, which is nice, but it gets to be a little monotonous. Say that you want to change a star's color to solid (a *fill*) red instead of a shaded gold. To do that, follow these steps:

1. **Right-click the shape whose fill you want to change.**

2. **Choose Properties to open the Properties dialog box.**

3. **Make sure that the Fill Color bar is selected.**

4. **Select the Solid Fill radio button, which collapses the dialog box so that it asks for only a single fill color, as shown in Figure 4-15.**

5. **Click the color box under Fill Color, opening a color picker window.**

6. **Click the color you want.**

7. **If you're happy with it, click the X button in the upper right of the Properties dialog box to close it.**

Click to open color picker

Figure 4-15:
Change
the fill
color in the
Properties
dialog box.

A shady business: Setting a shape's gradient

Shapes can often look snazzier if you give them a *gradient fill* — when their fill color varies smoothly across the shape from one color to another. The default fill for shapes in Show is a gradient from gold to white, proceeding upward.

Here's how to make the gradient fill go from one color to another, from side to side:

1. **Right-click the shape whose fill you want to change.**

2. **Choose the Properties menu item to open the Properties dialog box. Make sure the Fill Color bar is selected.**

3. **Select the Gradient Fill radio button.**

4. **Click the color box in the Fill Color 1 box, opening the color picker.**

5. **Select the shade you want to use and then click OK.**

6. **Click the color box in the Fill Color 2 box, opening the corresponding color picker.**

7. **Click the shade you want to use from the color picker and then click OK.**

8. **Select the direction for the gradient in the Gradient Direction section, as shown in Figure 4-16.**

   After you make your selection, a new gradient appears in your shape. Feel free to try several gradient directions until you find the one you want.

Figure 4-16:
Select the
gradient
direction.

9. **If you're happy with it, click the X button in the upper right of the Properties dialog box to close that dialog box.**

Click the Presets button in the Properties dialog box to choose from 45 preset gradient color schemes.

Setting a shape's border

By default, Show shapes have a 1-pixel (px) border, but you can change that. All you need to do is follow these steps:

1. **Right-click the shape whose border you want to change.**

2. **Choose Properties to open the Properties dialog box.**

3. **Make sure that the Border bar is selected, opening the Border section in the Properties dialog box.**

4. **Select the new width of the border in the Border Thickness drop-down box.**

You can select between solid and dashed borders for Show shapes. Just select Solid or Dashed from the Border Style drop-down list box in the Border section of the Properties dialog box. You can also set the color of the border in the same section of the Properties dialog box.

Changing themes on the fly

Although you select a theme when you create a presentation, you're not locked into that. At any time, you can change the theme, which includes the color and background used for slides.

To change a presentation's theme on the fly, just click the Themes tab at the upper right in Show; see Figure 4-17.

Themes tab

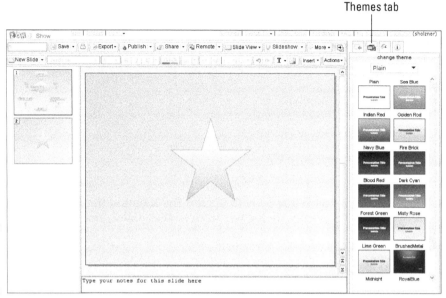

Figure 4-17:
Change a
theme here.

The Themes tab includes a drop-down list box that lists the categories of themes, ranging from Funky to Plain. To select a different theme, just click the new theme, which immediately makes it active in the presentation.

Being able to change the theme on the fly allows you to experiment with themes, selecting the one that works best for you.

Adding images

Clip art and shapes are fine, but they won't be specific enough for some of your purposes. For example, what if you need to display an image of your company's exalted founder? Or a projected new building? Clearly, you need to be able to insert images into a presentation.

To insert images, just follow these steps:

1. **Click the Insert button and then choose Image from the drop-down menu.**

2. **In the Insert Image dialog box that appears, click the Browse button, navigate to the image file you want to upload, select it, and then click OK.**

   The image appears in the Insert Image dialog box, as shown in Figure 4-18.

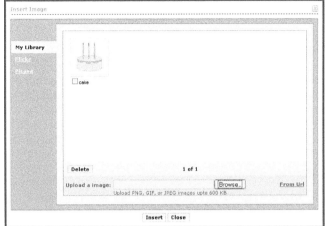

Figure 4-18:
Upload an
image to
insert it.

3. Click the image in the Insert Image dialog box to select it.

4. Click the Insert button to insert the image into the slide, as shown in Figure 4-19.

Figure 4-19:
An inserted
image.

Sharing Presentations with Other Show Users

As you'd expect, you can share Show presentations with other Show users online. You can let others view your presentation, or let them view and edit it: The choice is up to you. Here's how to share a presentation online, which gives others access to your presentation:

1. **Open the presentation you want to share.**

2. **Click the Share button.**

3. **Choose Invite from the drop-down menu that appears.**

   The Share This Document dialog box appears, as shown in Figure 4-20.

Share This Document	[X]
Invite Shared Details	
Read Only Members:	
Individuals: Add Contacts Groups: Add Groups	
Read / Write Members:	
Individuals: Add Contacts Groups: Add Groups	
Share Options:	
☐ Notify me, whenever a shared user modifies this presentation	
Invitation Message	
Select Invitation Language Default ▼ Edit Invitation Mail >>	
Share Close	

Figure 4-20: Set presentation sharing here.

4. **Enable sharing — and permissions — for other Show users by entering their e-mail addresses. Choose between assigning users as Read Only Members or Read/Write Members.**

   Separate the names with a comma.

   Show lets as many read-only people view your presentation at a time as you like, but only one person can edit it at a time.

5. **(Optional) Select the Notify Me check box if you want to receive an e-mail whenever a user edits the presentation.**

6. **(Optional) Click the Edit Invitation Mail button to edit the e-mail message sent to the people you want to invite.**

7. **Click the Share button to send invitations by e-mail to everyone you want to share the document with.**

   The Share This Document dialog box displays the Zoho IDs of the people you invited.

8. **Click the Close button to close the dialog box.**

Showtime! Presenting Your Presentation

With your presentation all set, it's time to show it to your audience. You can do that in person or remotely. Very cool.

Showing your presentation in person

To show your presentation in person, just open the presentation you want to show and follow these steps:

1. **Click the Slideshow button and then select one of the following options:**

   • *From Beginning:* Start your slide show from the beginning.

   • *From Current Slide:* Start your slide show from the current slide.

   • *Select Slide Number:* Start your slide show from a selected slide.

   Show opens a new browser window, displaying your presentation, as you see in Figure 4-21.

2. **To move from slide to slide in your presentation, click the arrows at the bottom of the screen.**

   You can also enter the number of the slide you want to view in the text box at left on the bottom of the screen.

3. **When you're done, just close the browser window.**

Note that you see only your slides in this window: no theme options, no overview of the slides, no toolbars — nothing like that. Presumably, your slide show is ready to go at this point, and all you want your audience to see are the slides.

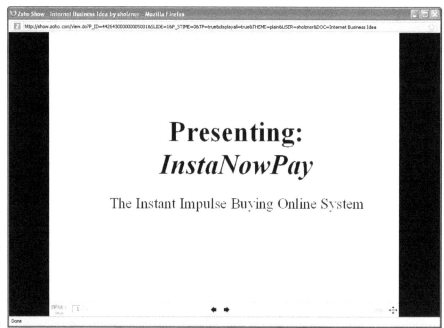

Figure 4-21:
Showing a
presenta-
tion.

You can also have your slides show themselves, moving to the next slide after a set number of seconds. To do that, click the More button (above the editing window), select the Slide Show Time item, enter the number of seconds you want between slides, and then click OK.

Controlling your presentation remotely

If you can't get everyone together to view your presentation in the same room, you can present your presentation on the Web. Just follow these steps:

1. **Open the presentation you want to display on the Web.**

2. **Click the Remote button and then choose Make Remote from the drop-down menu that appears.**

   The Play This Presentation Remotely dialog box opens.

3. **Click the Make Remote & Continue button.**

   The Remote URL dialog box appears, as shown in Figure 4-22.

   Show tells you the URL that participants will navigate to in this dialog box.

Figure 4-22:
Set remote
viewing
here.

4. **Enter the e-mail addresses of the people you want to invite, separated by commas.**

5. **(Optional) If you want to edit the invitation message, select the Invitation Message (optional) check box. In the text area that opens, enter your invitation message.**

6. **Click Start.**

   Show opens a new browser window for the remote presentation.

You might want to e-mail the remote URL to your audience because relying on Show to invite them can sometimes take an hour or more.

Now you wait for your audience to show up. When they do, their names appear at the upper right of the window. When your audience is fully assembled, you can start your presentation by clicking the Start Remote link in the middle of your window. The presentation starts, as shown in Figure 4-23.

Here are some tips for controlling your presentation:

✔ **To navigate through the presentation:** Use the arrow buttons at the top of the window.

✔ **To show your notes for each slide:** Click the Show Notes button at the top of the window. Remember that by default, they'll be visible only to you.

✔ **To show your presentation full-screen:** Press F11.

✔ **To chat with participants:** Enter your text into the message box at the lower right and then press Enter. Your message, along with any answers, will appear in the chat area in the middle, on the right. See Figure 4-23.

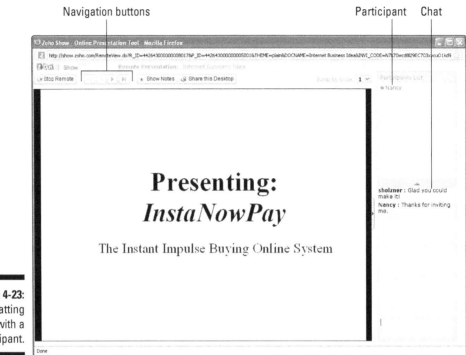

Figure 4-23:
Chatting
with a
participant.

✔ **To stop the remote session:** Click the Stop Remote button at the upper left.

✔ **To share what's on your desktop with participants:** Click the Share This Desktop button. When you share your desktop, everything on your computer screen is visible to the users you're sharing with, so if you minimize the browser, those folks can see what's going on on your screen.

Chapter 5

Zoho Notebook: Organizing and Storing Content

In This Chapter

▶ Creating a notebook

▶ Adding content

▶ Embedding documents

▶ Adding shapes

▶ Adding pages

▶ Web clipping

▶ Sharing a notebook

*Z*oho Notebook is a handy application with which you can collect and organize just about any content that you'd want to work with — the online equivalent of a scrapbook. You can paste text, Web pages, audio files, RSS, and more using Notebook.

Notebook is well suited for all kinds of uses. For business, you might maintain business-related clippings about your business or your clients. You can collect varying types of information about ongoing projects and keep such information well organized by project. You might even maintain a notebook of data on other companies (um, in case you have to find a new job).

Notebook also excels at personal use, of course. You can use it to store hundreds of recipes in a notebook, store information about your favorite stars, or store information about a new big-ticket item, such as a car or even a house, so you can comparison-shop.

All of which is to say that Notebook is designed to be an organizer. The Web has billions of content items in hundreds of formats, and often it can seem a chaotic place. That's where Notebook comes in — it's a unique application that lets you get on top of hundreds of bits of information that might otherwise be scattered.

Getting Started with Notebook

To sign in to Zoho Notebook, go to `http://notebook.zoho.com`, enter your username and password, and then click the Sign In button. (See Chapter 1 for details on creating a Zoho account.) Signing in brings up Zoho Notebook, as you can see in Figure 5-1. Notebooks are organized into pages, and your first blank page appears, as shown in Figure 5-1.

Current book title

Toolbar | Link bar

Page tab

Figure 5-1:
Signing in
to Zoho
Notebook.

In the following sections, I give you the lowdown on some of the basic tasks you need to know to get started with Notebook: renaming and saving your notebook and adding new pages.

Renaming and saving your notebook

The default name for your first book, as you can see on the top tab in Figure 5-1, is New Book 1 — not exactly the most descriptive title for a notebook on your Hawaii trip, for example.

To change the name of the current book, double-click the tab that reads New Book 1, which opens the Rename Book dialog box, as shown in Figure 5-2.

Enter the new name for the book — for example, The Hawaii Trip — and then click the Rename button. When you do, the dialog box disappears, and the book's tab shows the new name.

When you change the name of a book, Notebook saves it automatically for you.

If you want to save your book manually, click the Save button on the toolbar and then select Save from the drop-down list that appears. Zoho Notebook saves your book immediately, using the name you gave it.

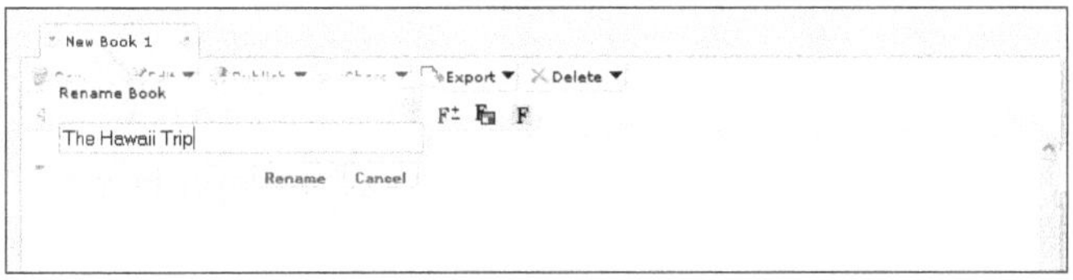

Figure 5-2:
Rename
your
book with
something
meaningful.

New Book 1

Rename Book

The Hawaii Trip

Rename   Cancel

Growing your notebook: Adding pages

Most Zoho notebooks contain multiple pages, so take a look at how to add new pages. You can add these types of pages to a notebook:

- ✔ Blank
- ✔ Text
- ✔ Writer
- ✔ Sheet
- ✔ Web

The links for creating these pages are located in the upper left of Notebook:

- ✔ **Blank page:** To insert a new blank page, just click the Add Blank Page link at the top of the left-hand pane. Doing so inserts a new page into your notebook and opens that page.

  You keep pages separate and access the page you want with the tabs on the right of Notebook.

✔ **Text page:** A text page is just that — a page into which you can enter text. To add a new text page to your notebook, just click Add Text Page.

✔ **Writer or Sheet page:** You can easily add new pages that are made up of Writer (see Chapter 3) or Sheet (see Chapter 8) documents. This is different from inserting Writer or Sheet documents as items in a page — this inserts a whole new page corresponding to a Writer or Sheet document.

To insert a Writer or Sheet document as a new page, click Add Writer Page or Add Sheet Page, respectively. In the dialog box that opens, click either the New tab to create a new page or the Existing tab to import an existing page. Then click the Insert button.

✔ **Web page:** You can add whole Web pages as pages to your notebook. That's a great idea in case you're collecting, say, house listings, or online recipes, or doing some research on a medical procedure, or studying competing companies, and so on.

To add a Web page to your notebook, click Add Web Page. In the dialog box that opens, enter the URL of the Web page to add as a new Notebook page. Then click the Create button.

For example, you can see an online newspaper front page added as a Notebook page in Figure 5-3.

To delete a page, just open that page, click the Delete button on the toolbar, and then choose Page from the drop-down menu that appears.

Tabs

Figure 5-3:
A Web
page as a
Notebook
page.

Adding Stuff to Notebook

What good would a scrapbook be without the ability to add stuff to it? You can add all kinds of items to Zoho Notebook — images, text, video, and so on, and this section takes a look at that.

To access this functionality, you click the links in the left-hand pane of Notebook.

Adding text to a page

Say that you recently returned from a trip and want to produce a notebook about it for your co-workers. You might start by creating a title on the first page: The Hawaii Trip.

The simplest way to add text to a Notebook page is to click the Add Text link in the left-hand pane, opening the text box you see in Figure 5-4. Just click the text box to make a text cursor appear; then start typing your text.

Figure 5-4: Add text to a text box.

The text box in Figure 5-4 has an editing toolbar with buttons displaying the same icons that Writer does for text formatting (see Chapter 1). For example, to enlarge the text, select the text in the text box and click the Font Size icon (the icon with two *T*s on it), opening a drop-down list box. Click the largest text size, which makes your text that size.

To position the text box where you want your text to appear in the page, just drag the text box by its *title bar* (the top bar in the text box). After the text box is where you want it, as shown in Figure 5-5, just click outside the text box. That causes the text box to disappear — but the text remains.

Figure 5-5:
Positioning
a text box.

When you drag the text box, the editing toolbar disappears. To get it back, just click the Edit button on the toolbar.

As I discuss in the preceding section, you can insert text into a Notebook page using a text box. But why do you have to go to all the trouble of using a text box? Why can't you just type the text into the page directly?

The answer is that Notebook takes data in many formats, so text isn't the default. You can draw shapes or lines, or drag images around a page, so it doesn't make sense to have a text cursor automatically appear when you click a page. (For more on drawing shapes, see "Adding Shapes," later in this chapter.)

However, there's no denying that if you want to enter text into a Notebook page, it would be easier to simply click the page, have a text cursor appear (much as it would in Zoho Writer — see Chapter 1), and then just type your text.

In fact, you can make Notebook work in exactly that way. That is, you can put it into *text mode* so that clicking a page displays a blinking text cursor at the location of the click, and then you can just type your text. And it'll even display a text toolbar at the top of the page.

To put Notebook into text mode, click the Text tool button. (It's marked with a capital L, on the drawing shapes toolbar in the lower right of the window.) You know you're in text mode when the text toolbar is at the top of the page and a text cursor is where the mouse cursor usually is.

To enter some text into the page, just click the page and start typing — it's that simple.

To get back to the original page mode (and remove the text toolbar), click the Select tool button at right in Notebook.

Adding images

Zoho Notebook lets you add images to notebook pages, as you'd expect. To insert an image into a page, follow these steps:

1. **Click the Add Image button in the left-hand pane, opening the Add Image dialog box, as shown in Figure 5-6.**

Figure 5-6:
The Add Image dialog box.

The Add Image dialog box is open to the Collection tab, which displays any images you've added to your Notebook collection.

2. **Click the Upload tab.**

If you want to load an image from a URL instead of from your computer, click the From URL tab instead of the Upload tab, enter the URL of the image into the text box that appears, and then click the Insert button.

3. **Click the Browse button, opening the Upload dialog box; navigate to and select the image you want to upload.**

4. **Click Open.**

The Upload dialog box closes and inserts the file path and name in the Upload text box.

5. **Click the Insert button.**

Zoho uploads the image and inserts it into the notebook page in an image box, as you see in Figure 5-7.

Of course, you're not limited to a single image. You can add as many as you like. After all, what's a scrapbook without images?

Adding an image to a page also adds the image to your image collection, which makes it easy to insert the image into other pages.

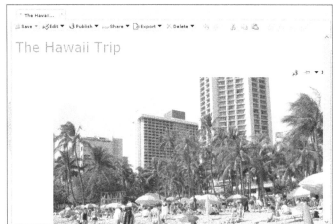

Figure 5-7:
A new image in an image box.

Adding video

Here's one advantage Zoho Notebook has over traditional, paper notebooks — you can add and play video clips. To get them into your notebook page, just follow these steps:

 1. **Click the Add Video button in the left-hand pane, opening the Add Video dialog box you see in Figure 5-8.**

    Contrary to what you might expect, Zoho Show doesn't let you upload videos in any format. In fact, it doesn't let you truly upload videos at all. They have to be hosted elsewhere, such as on YouTube.

 2. **Get the video's "embed" code.**

    If you uploaded a video to a video-sharing site like YouTube, you need to get the *embed code* (that's an HTML `<object>` tag, most commonly) that Notebook can use to display your video. YouTube and other sites display the embed code in the page with the video, so getting that code is usually not too difficult. The embed code for the Hawaii sample video is:

    ```
    <object width="425" height="344"><param name="movie" value="http://
        www.youtube.com/v/WmTaJQD6HzY&hl=en&fs=1"></param><param
        name="allowFullScreen" value="true"></param><param
        name="allowscriptaccess" value="always"></param><embed
        src="http://www.youtube.com/v/WmTaJQD6HzY&hl=en&fs=1"
        type="application/x-shockwave-flash" allowscriptaccess="always"
        allowfullscreen="true" width="425" height="344"></embed></
        object>
    ```

TIP

If you have a Webcam, you can click the Record tab you see in Figure 5-8 to record a new video on the spot.

Figure 5-8:
The Add
Video dialog
box.

3. **Paste the embed code of the video into the Add Video dialog box and then click Insert.**

   The video opens in a video box, as shown in Figure 5-9.

   After you insert your video on the page, you can move or resize it, as described in the section "Arranging content on the page," later in this chapter.

Figure 5-9:
The video in
a video box.

Adding audio files

Don't have a video but have an MP3 audio file instead? You can add it to your book as well. For example, you might want to add a favorite podcast to your notebook.

To add an audio file to a notebook page, follow these steps:

1. **Click the Add Audio link at the left in Notebook.**

   The Add Audio dialog box opens, as shown in Figure 5-10.

Figure 5-10:
The Add
Audio
dialog box.

2. **Choose one of the following options, represented by the tabs in the Add Audio dialog box:**

   • *From URL:* If your audio file is on the Web, enter its URL here.

   • *Upload:* If your audio file is on your computer, you can upload it from this tab.

   • *Collection:* If you've already uploaded audio files, they'll be here in the collection, waiting to be inserted again.

   • *Record:* You can record audio files if you have the appropriate equipment (that is, a sound card and a microphone).

3. **After you enter the URL or the file path and name, or select a file from the collection, or record a file, just click the Insert button.**

   Notebook displays your audio file with the player shown in Figure 5-11.

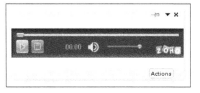

Figure 5-11:
The Add
Audio
player.

Adding HTML

Don't like the text styles available to you? Think you could do better than Notebook in picking background colors? Want to display page elements specific to a particular browser, like the Microsoft Internet Explorer <marquee> display element?

You're in luck. You can insert your own HTML directly into a notebook page. To do that, just follow these steps:

1. **Click the Add HTML link at the left in Notebook.**

2. **Enter your HTML in the Add HTML dialog box, as shown in Figure 5-12.**

   In this example, I'm adding an HTML <h1> header.

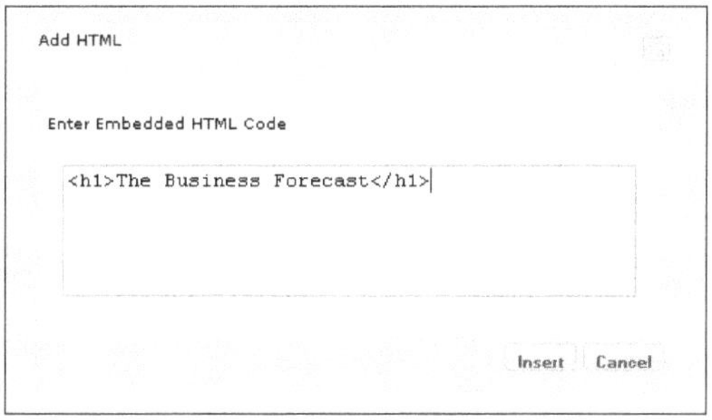

Add HTML

Enter Embedded HTML Code

```
<h1>The Business Forecast</h1>
```

Insert   Cancel

Figure 5-12: The Add HTML dialog box.

3. **Click the Insert button.**

   Your HTML appears in a text box.

You can even add HTML controls, such as buttons and check boxes, to a page this way — and then add some JavaScript to make those controls active. For example, you might hide an image until a button is clicked.

Adding a URL

Another useful Notebook feature is the ability to *clip* other Web pages and embed them into your notebook. And you can have as many page clips in a notebook page as you want. That's particularly useful if you're doing research on the Internet because nothing brings a collection of URLs to life as much as actually seeing the pages they represent, all at once.

So if you're doing research on cars, or trying to decide what computer to buy, or doing just about anything you can do on the Internet, keep this one in mind. You can create page clippings and embed them into a notebook page with ease.

Just follow these steps to add a URL to your notebook page:

1. **Click the Add URL link at the left in Notebook.**

2. **Enter your URL in the Add URL dialog box that appears.**

3. **Click the Insert button.**

   This opens the page referenced by your URL and displays the page in a box.

4. **Size the box and drag it where you want the other page to be displayed in your notebook page.**

5. **Click outside the box to dismiss it.**

Adding RSS feeds

RSS, also known as really simple syndication, has become more popular in recent years. RSS offers feeds from various sources, and if you connect to an RSS feed, you can see an often-updated list of articles from that source that you can check as often as you like. RSS presents you with a list of titles of new articles, and if you like one of those article titles, just click it to read the whole article.

Zoho Notebook can act as an RSS reader, letting you read RSS feeds — and it's easy to implement. When you have RSS feeds coming into your page, you see a clickable list of articles from the RSS source.

To use RSS, you need an RSS source, and most news outlets publish their stories in RSS format these days. Just look for the orange RSS or XML button on a page and click it. Clicking the RSS or XML button will display either a URL for the RSS feed (which is what you want for Notebook) or an XML document. If you get an XML document, don't try to paste that into Notebook — copy the URL from the browser's address bar instead.

Armed with the URL for the RSS feed, you're ready to start reading RSS using Notebook. Just follow these steps:

1. **Click the Add RSS link.**

2. **Enter the RSS URL into the text box in the Add RSS dialog box.**

3. **Click the Insert button.**

   This opens a box with the RSS feed that your URL references.

4. **Size the box and drag it where you want RSS feed displayed in your notebook page.**

5. **Click outside the box to dismiss it.**

For example, you can see an RSS feed in a Notebook page in Figure 5-13. Now you can open your notebook and take a look at the RSS feeds from various sources at a glance — very convenient indeed.

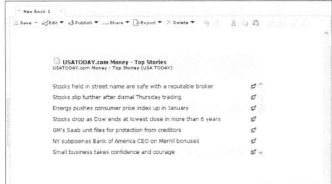

Figure 5-13: An RSS feed in Notebook.

Embedding Documents

Zoho Notebook lets you embed all kinds of documents, just as you'd expect from a scrapbook. For example, what about that recipe in plain text format? No problem. Or that Zoho Sheet spreadsheet of your club's expenses? No problem at all.

Embedding a non-Zoho document

Notebook allows you to insert your own files into your pages. It doesn't display the contents of the file, even if it's a type Notebook knows how to handle easily, such as an image file. It just displays a file icon with the name of the file. To open the file, you have to double-click it, and then your browser will offer to either download or open the file for you.

Embedding files like this is a good idea when you have file types that aren't easily handled by browsers; for example, Microsoft Access documents (MBD documents) or Excel spreadsheets (XLS) that you want to embed.

To insert a file into Notebook, follow these steps:

1. **Click the Add File link.**

2. **Select one of the three tabs that indicate how you want to get your file:**

   • *From URL:* Enter the URL of the file.

   • *Upload:* Enter the path and filename, or click the Browse button to browse to the file on your computer.

   • *Collection:* Select a file that you have uploaded.

3. **Click the Insert button.**

   This opens a box that displays a file icon with the name of the file.

Adding a Zoho Sheet or Writer document

As you might expect, you can also embed Zoho Writer (see Chapter 2) or Sheet (see Chapter 8) documents in Notebook pages.

Embedding a Writer or Sheet document isn't hard. Here's what you do:

1. **Click the Add Sheet or the Add Writer link.**

2. **Select one of the two tabs that indicates how you want to get your document:**

   • *New:* Create a new Writer or Sheet document.

   • *Existing:* Select an existing Writer or Sheet document.

3. **Click the Insert button.**

   This opens a box that displays your document. For example, you can see a birthday invitation (Writer document) embedded in Zoho Notebook in Figure 5-14.

Adding a Show document

You can also add Zoho Show documents (see Chapter 4) to Zoho Notebook pages. That can be very useful if you have multiple Show presentations that you want to give to the same audience, because you can organize them into the same Notebook.

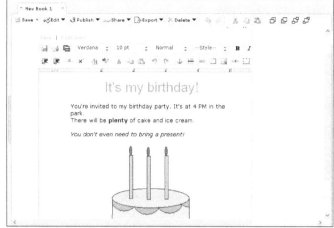

Figure 5-14:
An
embedded
Writer
document.

Follow these steps to embed a Show document:

1. **Click the Add Show link.**

2. **Select an existing slide show from the Add Show dialog box that appears.**

3. **Click the Insert button.**

   This opens a box that displays your document.

Playing the presentation is similar to playing the presentation in Show. Just click the arrows at the bottom of the embedded Show document, or enter a slide number in the text box in the bottom left of the embedded Show document.

You can move forward from page to page in an embedded Show document by clicking the current slide.

Adding Shapes

You know how you can cut out shapes and add them to scrapbooks? You can add shapes to Notebook as well for all kinds of reasons — decorations, call-outs, diagrams, speech bubbles, and more. You can create your own shapes or use the ones that come with Notebook.

Drawing shapes

Zoho Notebook contains a number of tools for drawing your own shapes, and these tools are

- ✔ Line
- ✔ Freehand
- ✔ Rectangle
- ✔ Circle (actually draws ellipses)

You can find these tools, shown in Figure 5-15, at the lower right of the Zoho Notebook window. Clicking one of these tools makes the corresponding tool-bar appear at the top of the Notebook window.

Select

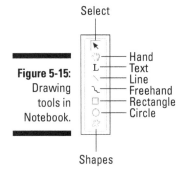

Figure 5-15:
Drawing
tools in
Notebook.

Hand
Text
Line
Freehand
Rectangle
Circle

Shapes

By default, the ellipses and rectangles you draw are filled in with Zoho's pre-ferred color — gold. You can change the fill color with the Fill Color button in the Circle and Rectangle tools' toolbars (second button from the right).

Just click the Fill Color button, click a color from the color box that appears, and then click OK. This sets the fill color used for the current figure and any similar figures from then on (unless you happen to reset the color).

You can see the results of working with the Line, Freehand, Circle, and Rectangle tools in the abstract art example shown in Figure 5-16.

Because you can draw all over a Notebook page, the drawing tools are great for connecting embedded items or annotating them.

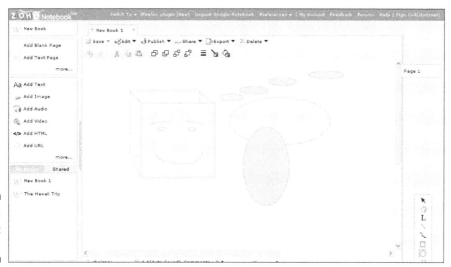

Figure 5-16:
An abstract
art example.

Copying, pasting, and deleting shapes

It's often the case that you need to copy a shape. You can draw two of the
same shape, but that can mean sizing them exactly the same, which can be a
little iffy if you're just using the mouse.

To copy a shape and paste it, just follow these steps:

1. **Click the Select tool button at the lower right in Notebook. (Refer to
   Figure 5-15.)**

2. **Right-click the shape you want to copy and then choose Copy from the
   menu that appears.**

3. **Right-click the page, away from any shape.**

4. **Choose the Paste menu item to paste a copy of the shape.**

   The newly pasted shape appears in a box with sizing handles around it.

5. **Drag the newly pasted shape where you want it.**

To delete a shape, click the Select tool. Right-click the shape you want to
delete, and then choose Delete from the menu that appears.

Inserting shapes

Like Zoho Show, you can insert a variety of shapes into Zoho Notebook documents. There aren't nearly as many shapes available in Notebook as there are in Show, but you still have plenty of shapes to work with. You can access the shapes with the Shape tool at the lower right in Notebook. Clicking the Shape tool displays a menu of shapes, as shown in Figure 5-17.

Figure 5-17:
Notebook
shapes.

When you click the Shape tool, the Shape toolbar appears at the top of the Notebook window. You can use this toolbar to customize the shapes you draw, setting the stroke width (used to draw the edges of the shape) and the fill color as well as selecting what shape you want to draw. Here are some popular shapes:

✔ **Callouts:** These are the speech balloons that you use to add a speech or an annotation to Notebook content. You can use callouts in conjunction with text in Notebook to create annotations.

✔ **Arrows:** This popular shape is great for connecting items in a page to show a relationship or logical flow. You can see an example in Figure 5-18.

Figure 5-18:
Using
arrows in
Notebook.

✔ **Flowcharts:** Put arrows with flowchart shapes to create flowcharts, which are useful to show the logical flow of a procedure. The Shapes menu includes many flowchart shapes that you can arrange on a page.

Editing shapes

By default, arrows in Notebook point up, not down. However, you can change how shapes are drawn by using the Drawing toolbar, which appears when you click the Shapes tool. For example, say you want to draw down-pointing arrows instead of up-pointing arrows. Use the Flip Type button on the Drawing toolbar, as shown in Figure 5-19.

Flip Type button

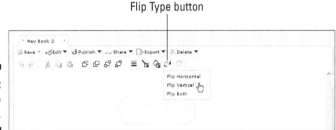

Figure 5-19:
The Flip
Type button.

To draw a down-pointing arrow, follow these steps:

1. **Click the Shapes tool button. (Refer to Figure 5-15.)**

2. **Select the up-pointing arrow.**

3. **Click the Flip Type button on the Drawing toolbar that appears at the top of the page.**

4. **Choose the Flip Vertical item from the Flip Type drop-down menu.**

5. **Draw the down-pointing arrow by dragging the mouse.**

   You can see the resulting arrow in Figure 5-20.

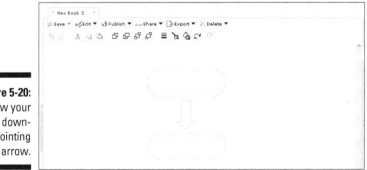

Figure 5-20:
Draw your
own down-
pointing
arrow.

Finessing Content: Arranging, Fixing, Freeing, and Stacking

As you might expect, you can arrange your content in all kinds of ways in Notebook, just as in any scrapbook. This section takes a look at your options for arranging content.

Arranging content on the page

After you add content to your page, you can rearrange it to your liking by moving and resizing it:

- **Move content.** Drag the box to the location where you want to display the image in the notebook page.
- **Resize content.** Move the mouse over the lower-right corner of the box until the mouse cursor turns into a double-headed diagonal arrow. Click the mouse, and resize the content as you like it.

After you position the content where you want it, click outside the image box to remove the image box but leave the content. This positions and sizes your content as you want it in the notebook page.

Fixing and unfixing content

Having gone to a lot of trouble to arrange the content on a Notebook page, you probably want to make sure it's not moved inadvertently.

In Notebook, you can move content simply by clicking and dragging it — and in pages dense with content, it's easy to click the wrong item. But you can fix content in place easily with Notebook by *pinning* it. And it can't be moved until it's unpinned.

To pin content, just follow these steps:

1. **Click the Select tool button at the lower right in Notebook.**
2. **Right-click the content you want to pin in place.**

3. **Choose Pin from the menu that appears.**

   To unpin content, choose the Unpin menu item.

Stacking content

Notebook pages can get kind of crowded with items, which you might find yourself stacking one on top of the other. Sometimes, admittedly, stacking is intentional, like when you create a complex figure (such as a drawing of a house) from a number of simpler shapes.

You can use Notebook to set the *stacking order* of items on a page. When you right-click an item, you see the following four menu items in the menu that appears, as shown in Figure 5-21, and you can use them to set stacking order:

- ✔ Send Backward
- ✔ Bring Forward
- ✔ Send to Back
- ✔ Bring to Front

For example, take a look at the three rectangles in Figure 5-21, where they are stacked atop each other.

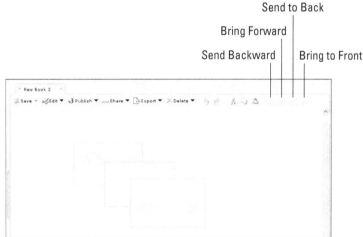

Figure 5-21:
Three stacked rectangles.

Now say that you want to bring the bottom rectangle to the front — that is, stack it on top of the other two rectangles. Just follow these steps:

1. **Click the Select tool button at the lower right in Notebook (the button with an arrow showing).**

2. **Right-click the bottom shape.**

3. **Choose Bring to Front.**

And that's it. Now the bottom rectangle is on top, as you can see in Figure 5-22.

Figure 5-22:
Restacked
rectangles.

If you just want to bring the back rectangle forward one step — so it is still stacked under the top rectangle — you would follow the preceding steps but choose Bring Forward in Step 3.

Deleting content

Deleting content on a page is simple — just select the content and click Delete.

Clipping on the Web (For Firefox Users Only)

You can add snapshots of whole Web pages, or sections of them, to your notebook if you have the Firefox browser and use the Zoho Notebook *Helper*, which is a plugin for the Firefox browser only.

To install the Zoho Notebook Helper plugin in Firefox, follow these steps:

1. **Click the Firefox plugin link at the top of the Notebook window, open-ing the Firefox add-ons in a new Firefox tab.**

2. **Click the Add to Firefox button.**

3. **Click the Install Now button in the Software Installation dialog box that opens.**

4. **In the Add-ons dialog box that opens, click the Restart Firefox button to restart Firefox.**

5. **Click the Restart button in the Restart Firefox dialog box that opens.**

6. **Close the Add-ons dialog box.**

With the Zoho Helper plugin installed, you can *snap* (take a snapshot of) a Web page and add it to your notebook, as described in the following sections.

This procedure takes a snapshot of the Web page — that is, an image — but it doesn't preserve the Web page and all the links in it.

Snapping a whole Web page

To snap a whole Web page with the Zoho Notebook Helper plugin, follow these steps:

1. **In Notebook, open the page to which you want to add the snapshot.**

   You must have Zoho Notebook open to the page you want to add the snapshot to use Zoho Notebook Helper.

2. **In Firefox, choose File⇨New Tab and then navigate to the Web page you want to work with.**

3. **Right-click the Web page and choose Snap Page to Zoho Notebook.**

4. **Enter a name for the new page in the dialog box that opens and then click OK.**

Snapping part of a Web page

You can also record just a region of a Web page as well, instead of the whole thing. To take a snapshot of just a region of a Web page, follow these steps:

1. **Follow Steps 1 and 2 in the preceding section.**

2. **Right-click the Web page and choose Snap Region to Zoho Notebook.**

3. **Resize and move the shaded window that appears to the region you want to snap.**

4. **Click the camera icon at the upper right in the shaded window to snap the region.**

5. **Enter a name for the new page in the dialog box that opens and then click OK.**

Getting Others Involved:
Sharing a Notebook

You can also share notebooks with other users, as you can in other Zoho applications. To share a notebook, follow these steps:

1. **Click the Share button on the Notebook toolbar.**

2. **Choose the item you want to share (Book, Page, or Object) from the drop-down menu that appears.**

   This opens the dialog box you see in Figure 5-23.

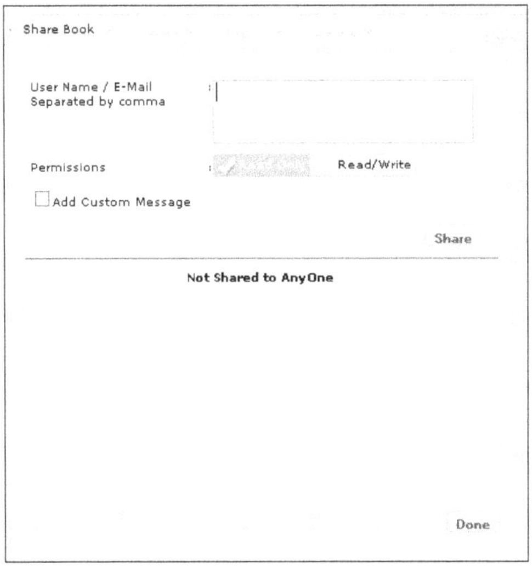

Share Book

User Name / E-Mail
Separated by comma

Permissions   Read/Write

☐ Add Custom Message

Share

Not Shared to AnyOne

Done

Figure 5-23:
The sharing
dialog box.

3. **Fill in the following options:**

   • *User Name/E-Mail Separated by Comma:* Enter the usernames or e-mail addresses of the people you want to share with, separated with commas.

   • *Read-Only or Read/Write:* Click the appropriate button to indicate the type of permission you want to give the people you're sharing the notebook with.

   • *Add Custom Message:* Select this check box to add a custom message.

4. **Click the Share button and then click Done.**

When users with read/write privileges share with you, you get a notification with a small dialog box that appears at the lower right in Notebook. They can make changes to your notebook items just as you can.

You can access any items shared with you by clicking the Shared tab at the lower left in Notebook.

Part II
Scheduling and Communicating

The 5th Wave
By Rich Tennant

"He saw your laptop and wants to know if he can check his Zoho Mail."

In this part . . .

*I*n this part, I take a look at the scheduling and communicating applications available in Zoho.

Zoho Planner is your online organizer. Use this app to keep track of appointments, addresses, meetings — just about anything you need to manage your busy life.

Zoho Mail is a powerful online mail application that gives you all you'd expect: handling, sending, receiving, and forwarding e-mail; working with attachments — and some extras you might not expect.

Chapter 6

Zoho Planner: Organizing Your Life

In This Chapter

▸ Creating a to-do list

▸ Adding items to a list

▸ Editing items in a list

▸ Adding appointments

▸ Getting reminders

▸ Adding notes

▸ Sharing pages

*U*se Zoho Planner to help keep you on track by creating lists of items that you want to get done. These lists can contain anything you want, from steps for planning a product launch to lists of groceries to pick up.

Zoho Planner is for people who want to take their lists online. If you're tired of dozens of scraps of paper floating around, now you can collect your lists in one place. It's a natural for people who use Zoho a lot because they're already on the site, and switching to Zoho Planner is simple.

You can also share a planner, of course. That means you can make multiperson lists — say, when you're planning some company-wide event, such as a shareholder's meeting, and are trying to line up speakers.

And you can also ask Planner to remind you through e-mail of upcoming items on your list so you don't even have to sign in to Planner to keep up to date.

Starting Planner

To sign in to Zoho Planner, go to `http://planner.zoho.com`. The signing-in process is the same as for any Zoho application: Enter your username and password, and then click the Sign In button. (To get a Zoho username and password, see Chapter 1.)

Signing in to Planner brings up the Planner Home Page, as shown in Figure 6-1.

Click to start a list

Figure 6-1:
The Zoho
Planner
Home Page.

Zoho Planner shares a lot in common with other Zoho applications. Note the bar of links at the upper right; these are the same links you find in any Zoho application. Use these links to view your account, make preference settings, switch to other Zoho apps, and more.

A central workspace contains your lists (currently labeled Home Page), and the left pane displays shared pages and reminders, and more.

Creating a To-Do List

The base task in Planner is creating to-do lists. Say you're in charge of a product launch for your company, and you want to add items to your Product Launch to-do list. Here's how to start a to-do list:

1. **On the Home Page of Planner, click the To-Dos link, opening the dialog box shown in Figure 6-2.**

2. **Enter a name for the new list.**

3. **Click the Add List button.**

New list name

Figure 6-2:
Start a to-do
list here.

4. **In the page that opens, enter the first item in your list in the To-Do Description field.**

5. **Click the Add List Item button.**

   Planner adds the first item to the list, as shown in Figure 6-3, and keeps open the To-Do Description field to accept a new list item.

6. **Keep building your list, repeating Steps 4–5.**

7. **When you're finished, click the Close link, closing the To-Do Description field and completing your list, as shown in Figure 6-4.**

List items appear in the order you enter them.

New list item   Add list items here.

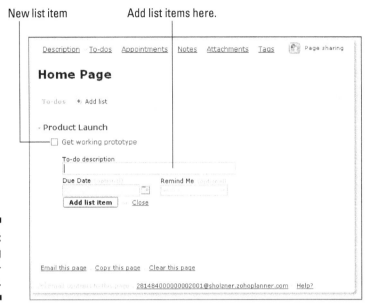

Figure 6-3:
Building
your to-
do list.

New list

Figure 6-4:
The com-
pleted list.

To add additional lists, click Add List. Then just repeat the preceding steps. In a nutshell, you open a new list, give it a name, populate it, and save it. See Figure 6-5.

And, Planner lets you collect all your lists and make them accessible from a single location — the Planner Home Page.

With multiple lists, things can get a little crowded on your Planner Home Page, but you can fix that by collapsing a list. (See Figure 6-5.) To collapse a list, just click the down arrow in front of the list, and the list collapses to just one line, showing the list's name. To open the list again, just click the same arrow (which toggles to a right arrow).

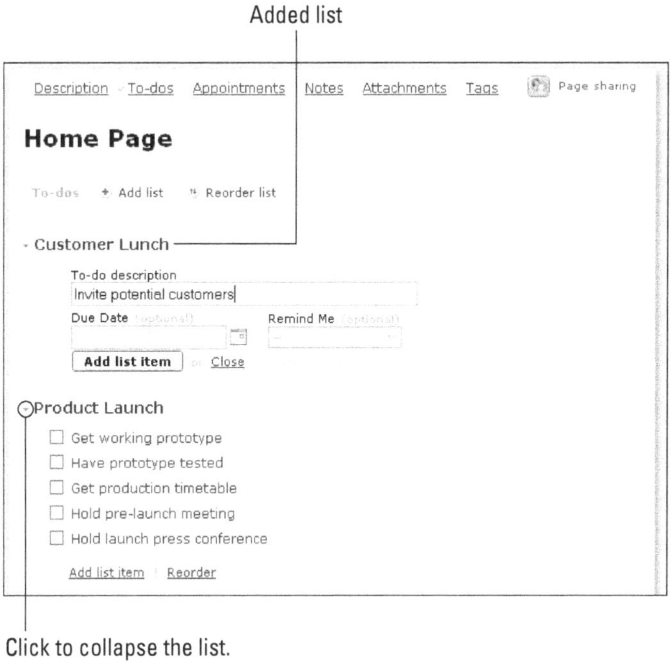

Added list

Description To-dos Appointments | Notes Attachments Tags   Page sharing

Home Page

To-dos   + Add list   ⅛ Reorder list

- Customer Lunch —————

To-do description
Invite potential customers

Due Date (optional)   Remind Me (optional)

Add list item or Close

⊙Product Launch
☐ Get working prototype
☐ Have prototype tested
☐ Get production timetable
☐ Hold pre-launch meeting
☐ Hold launch press conference

Add list item · Reorder

Figure 6-5:
Add as
many lists
as you want.

Click to collapse the list.

Amending a To-Do List

Lists are meant to be helpful tools. Nothing spells progress like checking off completed items. And, what good is a list if you can't edit it to update it? Here's how to keep a to-do list current.

Checking items off a list

Of course, the goal of a to-do list is to complete the tasks on the list. Planner can keep track of which tasks you have completed and which ones are still to come.

After the first task is completed, it's time to check it off your list. To check an item off a list, click the to-do list's name in the left-hand pane of the Planner Home Page. Then, select the check box for the to-do item. Easy.

The selected list item is moved to the Completed section at the bottom of the list, as you see in Figure 6-6.

Click to reorder the list.

Figure 6-6:
Mark a list
item as
completed.

Completed item

Click to hide completed items.

To hide the completed items in your list, click the red X to the right of Completed.

Suppose, though, that you need to take an item off the completed part of the list and move it back to the to-do list. That seems easy enough: Just deselect the completed item's check box in the Completed list. However, when you do, Planner doesn't remember where in your list the item first appeared, so it puts the item you moved from the Completed list at the bottom of the to-do list. Keep reading to see how to put your list back in the order you want.

Reordering a to-do list

If you need to reorder a list — such as moving the bottom list item to the top — just follow these steps:

1. **Click the Reorder link at the bottom of the list.**

2. **Move the mouse over the item you want to move until the mouse cursor changes to a cross-shaped, four-headed arrow.**

3. **Drag the list item to its new location in the list.**

4. **Click the Save Order link at the bottom of the list.**

Adding a new list item

Say you need to add a new item at the end of the list. Easily done. Just follow these steps:

1. **Click the Add List Item link at the bottom of a list.**

2. **Enter the new list item in the To-Do Description field.**

   Figure 6-7 shows an example.

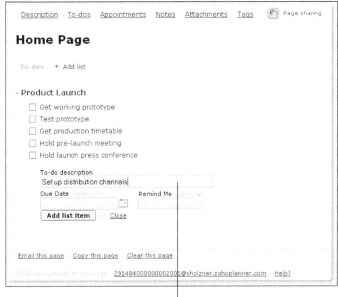

Figure 6-7:
Add a new
list item.

Added list item

3. **Click the Add List Item button.**

4. **Click the Close link.**

   The new list item is added to the end of the list.

If you now need to reorder the list, see the preceding section, "Reordering a to-do list."

Editing and deleting a list item

Say that you need to change an item in your list. To edit a list item, just follow these steps:

1. **Let the mouse cursor rest over the item you want to edit.**

   A pencil icon and an X icon appear at the end of the item.

2. **Click the pencil icon to open the Edit dialog box.**

3. **Enter the new description — that is, text for the list item — in the Description field.**

4. **Click the Save List Item button.**

   The new version of the list item is written to the list, replacing the old version of the item.

You can also delete list items as well. Deleting items from a list is simple. Just follow the steps for editing a list item. However, click the X button at the end of the list item. (See Step 1.) Then, click OK in the dialog box that opens.

Setting Due Dates for List Items

To help stay organized, you can not only order your to-do lists, but also set *due dates* for list items: that is, dates by when list items have to be completed. Follow these steps to place a due date on a list item:

1. **Hover the mouse over the list item you want to add a due date to, making the pencil and red X icons appear.**

2. **Click the pencil icon, opening the list item for editing.**

3. **Click the box next to the text box for the Due Date, opening a calendar control.**

4. **Click the date you want to set as the due date for the list item.**

   See Figure 6-8.

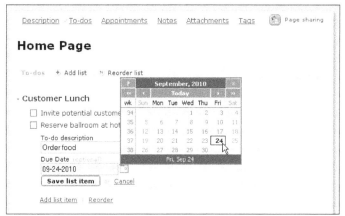

Figure 6-8:
Use the
calendar
to set a
due date.

5. **Click outside the calendar control to close it.**

The due date for the list item appears next to the item, as shown in
Figure 6-9.

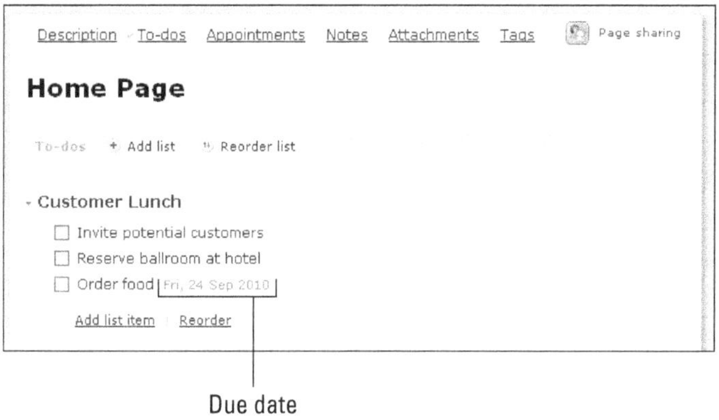

Figure 6-9:
A new due
date for a
list item.

Due date

Setting Reminders

Hmm. Yup, you can display a due date for a list item, but maybe you don't
want to open Zoho Planner every day to check on your lists. It would be great
if you could have Planner to tell you about upcoming due dates.

Lucky for you, telling Planner to remind you of an upcoming due date is simple. Here's how:

1. **Hover the mouse over the list item you want to add a reminder to, making the pencil and red X icons appear.**

2. **Click the pencil icon, opening the list item for editing.**

3. **Open the Remind Me drop-down list box, presenting the list shown in Figure 6-10.**

   You can set the due date

   - One day before

   - On the same day

   - When the due date expires (on *expiry*)

   - Every day between now and the due date

4. **Choose the reminder type you want.**

5. **Click the Save List Item button.**

   Planner will remind you of upcoming due dates, e-mailing you automatically.

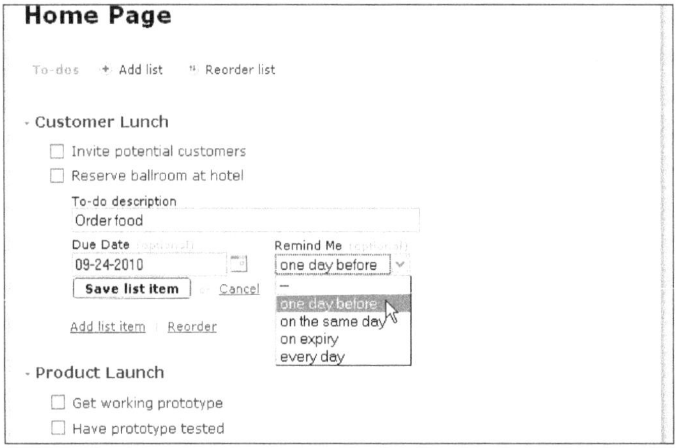

Figure 6-10:
Set a
reminder
here.

Home Page

To-dos   + Add list   Reorder list

· Customer Lunch

☐ Invite potential customers
☐ Reserve ballroom at hotel

To-do description
Order food

Due Date
09-24-2010

Remind Me
one day before ⌄

[Save list item] Cancel

―
one day before
on the same day
on expiry
every day

Add list item   Reorder

· Product Launch

☐ Get working prototype
☐ Have prototype tested

Zoho Planner doesn't offer very flexible reminder timeframes. For example, there is no "three days before" or "five days before" option. If you want to be reminded of a due date more than one day in advance, you have no other option than to be reminded daily between now and the due date.

Scheduling Appointments

Besides to-do lists, Planner can keep track of your appointments. Consider listing your appointments in Planner because it's accessible from any place you have an Internet connection. Planner can also automatically schedule recurring appointments for you.

Setting your time zone

Here's one thing to keep in mind, especially if you ask Planner to keep you reminded of an appointment: The default Planner time zone might not be the same as yours.

The default time zone for Planner is America/Los_Angeles. To change that, follow these steps:

1. **In the left pane, look for Time Zone Setting. Beneath that is the default: America/Los_Angeles. Click that link.**

   The Time Zone Setting dialog box opens, as shown in Figure 6-11.

Figure 6-11:
Set a new
time zone.

2. **Select your time zone from the drop-down list.**

3. **Click the Save Time Zone button.**

   Your new time zone appears under the Current Time Zone title on the Planner Home Page.

TIP

To return to the Planner Home Page, click the My Pages link at the upper left. Then click the Home Page link.

Creating your first appointment

Here's how to schedule your first appointment in Zoho Planner. (To see how to add additional appointments, see the upcoming section, "Adding more appointments.")

1. **On the Home Page, click the Appointments link, opening the dialog box shown in Figure 6-12.**

2. **Enter the new appointment in the Appointments field.**

3. **To set the date for the new appointment, click the calendar control to the right of the Scheduled On field.**

4. **Click the appointment's date in the calendar.**

5. **Set the time for the appointment, using the three drop-down lists (hour, minutes [in 5-minute intervals], and a.m. or p.m.) next to the Scheduled On field.**

6. **(Optional) Select a reminder time, using choices from the Remind Me drop-down list. Your choices range from the time of the appointment to one day in advance.**

   I take a look at scheduling recurring appointments and shared e-mail IDs shortly.

7. **Click the Add Appointment button.**

   Figure 6-13 shows a new appointment.

Hour, minute, and time of day

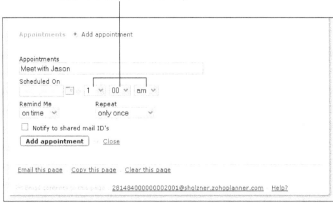

Figure 6-12: Create a new appointment here.

Figure 6-13:
Setting an
appoint-
ment.

New appointment

Adding appointments and lists to your Planner Home Page can make it a little crowded. Here's an easy way to see just your to-do lists: Click the To-Dos Overview link in the left pane, and then click the All My To-Dos link that appears. All your to-do lists appear on their own page.

Setting a recurring appointment

Sometimes, certain appointments need to be scheduled over and over: a weekly meeting, for example. Planner lets you handle this kind of task easily. To make an appointment a recurring one, follow these steps:

1. **Hover the mouse over the appointment you want to make recurring until the pencil and red X icons appear at the right.**

2. **Click the pencil icon to open the appointment for editing, as shown in Figure 6-14.**

Figure 6-14:
Set a
recurring
appoint-
ment.

3. **Open the Repeat drop-down list box to reveal your "how often?" choices. You can choose from a number of set hours, every day, every week, every month, or every year.**

4. **Click the Update Appointment button.**

When you make an appointment a recurring appointment, Planner displays a small icon — two arrows in a circle, chasing each other's tail, like a refresh button in a browser — to indicate that the appointment recurs.

If you set up a reminder for a recurring appointment, Zoho sends that reminder via e-mail each time the appointment recurs.

Adding more appointments

When you first click the Appointments link (to create your first appointment), Planner opens its Appointment field as well as controls with which you create that appointment. After you create this first appointment, though, those controls don't appear automatically. To add new appointments, just follow these steps:

1. **Click the Appointments link, opening the Appointments section of the Planner Home Page.**

2. **Click the Add Appointment link in the Appointments section (which displays your existing appointments) to open the dialog box shown in Figure 6-15.**

New appointment

Figure 6-15: Creating more appointments.

Existing appointment

3. Fill in the name of the new appointment, set its time, and so on.

4. Click the Add Appointment button.

   The new appointment appears directly beneath any existing appointments.

Editing and deleting appointments

To edit the details of an existing appointment, just follow these steps:

1. Click the Appointments link to open the Appointments section of the Planner Home Page.

2. Hover the mouse over the appointment whose details you want to edit until the pencil and red X icons appear to the right of the appointment name.

3. Click the pencil icon to open the appointment for editing.

   The Add Appointment button (see the preceding section) toggles to Update Appointment.

4. Edit the appointment's details.

5. Click the Update Appointment button.

To delete an existing appointment, hover the mouse over the appointment, click the X, and click Yes in the dialog box that appears.

Recording More Details with Planner Notes

Just like with any good planner, there's a space for notes in Zoho Planner. Notes are just what they sound like. They're written text — not appointments or to-do items. You cannot add timers/reminders to notes.

You might suddenly be struck with inspiration on that business idea you were trying to crack, or think of something you want to suggest for your daughter's application letters to college, or any of a million other things.

Here's how to add a note to Zoho Planner:

1. On the Home Page, click the Notes link, opening the dialog box shown in Figure 6-16.

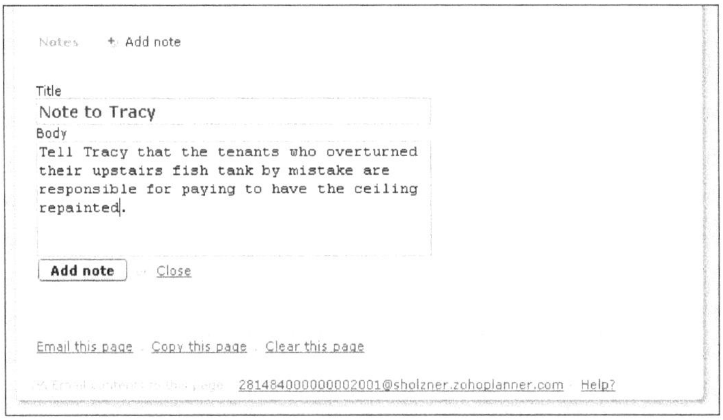

Figure 6-16:
Create a
new note.

2. **Enter the title of the new note in the Title field.**

3. **Enter the text of the new note in the Body field.**

4. **Click the Add Note button.**

   The new note appears on the Home Page; see Figure 6-17.

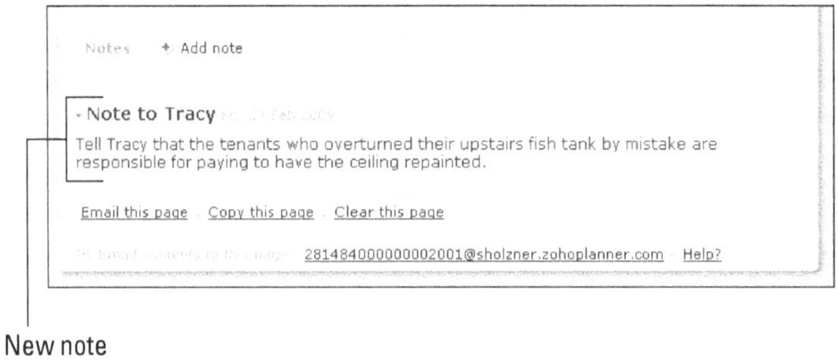

Figure 6-17:
A new note.

New note

Here are some additional ways to work with Planner notes:

✔ **To add another note:** Click the Add Note link in the Notes section of the Home Page (the section where your notes appear), fill in the title and body of the new note, and then click the Add Note button.

✔ **To edit a note:** Hover the mouse over the title of a note until the pencil and red X icons appear. Click the pencil icon, make your edits when the title and body text boxes appear, and then click the Save Note button.

✔ **To delete a note:** Hover the mouse to make the icons appear, but click the red X icon instead. Then click OK in the confirmation dialog box that appears.

Adding Attachments

Zoho Planner has another advantage over paper planners: the capability to handle attachments. Paper planners can't upload files, but Zoho Planner can.

Uploading an attachment

Say, for example, that you have a very important memo that you want to keep track of, and you want to upload it to your planner. Not a problem.

Uploading an attachment starts by clicking the Attachments link in Planner, which opens the controls you see in Figure 6-18. You can upload any file type that your browser allows.

Then do the following to upload an attachment:

1. **Click the Browse button, opening the File Upload dialog box.**

2. **Select the file you want to upload.**

3. **Click the Open button.**

   The File Upload dialog box closes.

4. **(Optional) Enter a description in the Description field, as shown in Figure 6-18.**

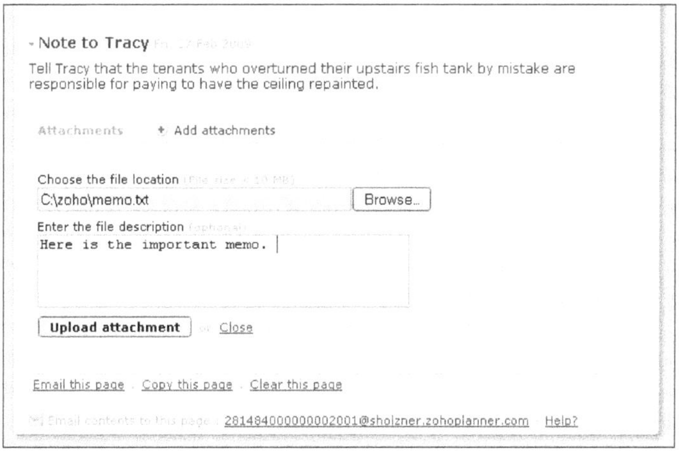

Figure 6-18: Adding an attachment.

5. **Click the Upload Attachment button.**

The attachment is uploaded and displayed as an icon, as shown in Figure 6-19.

Figure 6-19:
A new
attachment.

Click to open the attachment.

Opening an attachment

To open an attachment, just click its link (which is visible in Figure 6-19). That's all you have to do, and your browser does the rest.

When you click the link:

- ✔ **Internet Explorer** opens the attachment in a new window.

- ✔ **Firefox** opens the attachment in a new tab.

If the attachment is of a type that your browser doesn't know how to handle, it asks you whether you want to download the attachment.

Adding more attachments

When you first click the Attachments link, the Attachments section opens and displays the Browse button and the Description box (refer to Figure 6-18). Here's how to get those controls back again when you want to upload another attachment. Just follow the preceding steps, but click the Add

Attachment button in the Attachments section. The Attachments upload controls (the Browse button and the description box) appear. Then proceed with browsing and uploading.

There is no limit to the number of attachments you can upload.

Deleting an attachment

You probably don't want all your attachments to hang around forever. For example, if an attachment concerns an upcoming meeting or event that's over, here's how to do a little housekeeping and get rid of the attachment:

1. **Scroll down the Planner Home Page until you come to the Attachments section that holds your attachments.**

2. **Hover the mouse over the icon of the attachment you want to delete, or over the link to the attachment (right next to the icon).**

3. **Click the red X that appears.**

4. **In the confirmation dialog box that opens, asking whether you really want to delete the attachment, click OK.**

   And that gets rid of your attachment.

After you delete an attachment, it's deleted on the Zoho site, and there's no way to get it back again using only Planner. If you want to restore the attachment, you have to upload it again, so delete with care.

Creating a New Page

After you add lists, appointments, notes, and attachments, your Planner Home Page will start to look a little crowded. To keep things tidy, add more pages to your planner. Here's how:

1. **Click the Create New Page button at the upper left of Zoho Planner.**

2. **Enter the name of your new page in the Name Your New Page text box that appears, as shown in Figure 6-20.**

   For example, name it for a new project you want to keep track of or for the person whose information will be contained in it.

Figure 6-20:
Create a
new page.

3. **Click the Create button.**

   The new page is created and added to your My Pages list at the left in Planner, and Planner opens your new page, as shown in Figure 6-21.

   Your new page is all fresh and clean, ready for lists and appointments.

New page

Figure 6-21:
A new page.

Move between pages in Planner by opening the My Pages section in the left pane (open by default) and clicking the name of the page you want to open.

Even More Organization: Adding Tags to Planner Items

Say you create pages to help keep Planner organized. If it's hard to remember just what page to jump to — after all, is that to-do list you're looking for on the Eastern Division page or the Urgent page? — Planner comes to the rescue by giving you an additional layer of organization. You can tag pages and then search for pages by using tags.

One way to make sure you stay on top of your planner's organization is to use tags. Like with other Zoho applications, *tags* are words or phrases that you connect with your data to make that data easily searchable.

Adding a tag to a page

To use tags, just follow these steps:

1. **Open the Planner page you want to add a tag to.**

2. **Click the Tags link at the top of the page.**

   The Tags section of the page appears. A text box for the new tag opens, as shown in Figure 6-22.

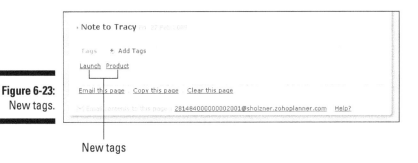

Figure 6-22: Creating a tag for a page.

3. **Enter the text of your new tag or tags.**

4. **Click the Save Tags button.**

   The text box closes; the tag you added to the page shows up (in this case, two tags, Product and Launch, because Planner treats each word as a separate tag) in the Tags section, as shown in Figure 6-23.

Figure 6-23: New tags.

New tags

To add more tags, repeat the preceding steps but click the Add Tags link at the top of the Tags section, which opens the text box for a new tag. Add the name of the tag, and then click the Save Tags button. Using this technique, you can add as many tags as you want.

Searching for a page with tags

To search for all pages with a particular tag, just go to the Tags section of a page: All tags appear as hyperlinks in that section. To see a list of all pages with a particular tag, just click that tag.

A list of pages with that tag opens, as shown in Figure 6-24. To open one of those pages, just click the name of the page (which is a link to that page).

Figure 6-24:
See pages
with the
same tag.

Sharing Planner Pages

Like with other Zoho applications, you can share Planner pages with others, which is handy if you're trying to schedule a meeting that involves several people. The folks you share pages with can modify appointment times, or add items to to-do lists, freeing you from having to do all the work yourself.

Inviting someone to share a page

To share a Planner page with someone, just follow these steps:

1. **Open the page you want to share.**

2. **Click the Page Sharing link at the upper right of the page, opening the sharing section shown in Figure 6-25.**

3. **In the Private Sharing section, enter the e-mail address of the person with whom you wish to share the page. Here is where you also set permissions for that person; choose whether to enter the address in the Read Only or Read/Write field.**

Figure 6-25:
Sharing
a page.

4. **Click the Share button.**

5. **Click the Close link to close the Sharing section.**

   That sends an e-mail invitation to the person you want to share your page with, and the person can click the hyperlink in the e-mail to open your page.

When someone shares your page

People you invite can share your page by clicking the link sent to them in your e-mail invitation (see the preceding section) or by clicking the name of your page in their Pages Shared To Me section in the left pane of Planner.

When someone shares your page, her Zoho username appears at the left in your version of Planner, as shown in Figure 6-26, in the Shared User's Chat section.

If you gave a user read/write privileges and he makes a change to your page, you won't see anything special except the new text the user adds. The portion of your page that person is editing doesn't turn yellow, like it does with Zoho Writer. (Read about Writer in Chapters 2 and 3.)

There's no special indication that your page is being edited by someone else. Items just appear and disappear.

Figure 6-26:
Someone
sharing your
Planner
page.

Someone sharing your page

Chatting with someone sharing your page

You can also chat with people sharing your page. Just click the person's name in the list of people sharing your page under the Shared Users Chat title.

Clicking a person's name opens a chat box, as shown in Figure 6-27. Enter your comment into the text box in the chat box and then press Enter to make your comments appear in the other person's chat box.

That person can reply, using the same method.

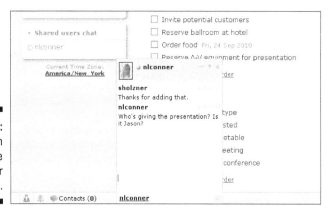

Figure 6-27:
Chat with
someone
sharing your
page.

Chapter 7

Zoho Mail: Your Communication Center

In This Chapter

- Signing up
- Composing e-mail
- Reading e-mail
- Marking e-mail
- Handling attachments

*W*hat would an online suite of applications be without e-mail? Zoho is up to the challenge here with Zoho Mail, a powerful e-mail program that gives you all you'd expect, including the ability to

- ✔ Create, send, and receive e-mail
- ✔ Handle attachments
- ✔ Mark e-mail as spam
- ✔ Organize your e-mail with folders and labels
- ✔ Maintain a list of contacts
- ✔ Search your e-mail *en masse*

All this is available for free; all you need is your Internet connection and a browser.

Getting Started with Zoho Mail

Here's some good news: If you have a Zoho username and password (see Chapter 1), you already have a Zoho Mail account. And your e-mail account is `username@zoho.com`, where `username` is your username. It's that simple — Zoho Mail has already been set up and is waiting for you.

To sign in to Zoho Mail, go to `http://mail.zoho.com` and enter your username and password. Then click the Sign In button, bringing up your Zoho Mail home page, which looks like Figure 7-1.

Current folder

Available folders   Toolbar

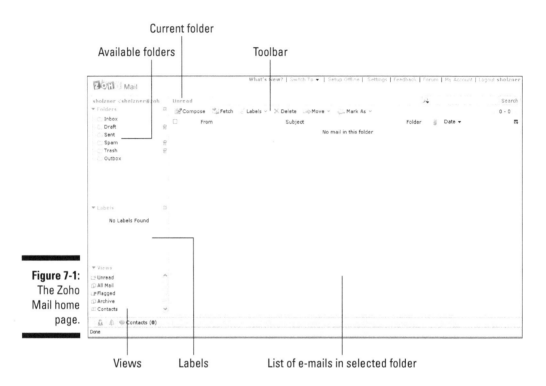

Figure 7-1:
The Zoho
Mail home
page.

Views   Labels   List of e-mails in selected folder

Zoho Mail gives you a number of folders for organizing your mail, as you can see in the upper left of Figure 7-1:

- ✔ Inbox
- ✔ Draft
- ✔ Sent
- ✔ Spam
- ✔ Trash
- ✔ Outbox

I discuss these folders in detail throughout the chapter.

Composing Your Zoho E-Mails

Start with one of the most common tasks in Zoho Mail — composing an e-mail. After logging in to Zoho Mail, you're ready to start writing your own e-mails.

To compose an e-mail, just follow these steps. Some of this is familiar from other e-mail programs, so I cover common tasks, like cc'ing recipients, relatively quickly:

1. **Click the Compose button on the toolbar.**

   A dialog box opens, as shown in Figure 7-2.

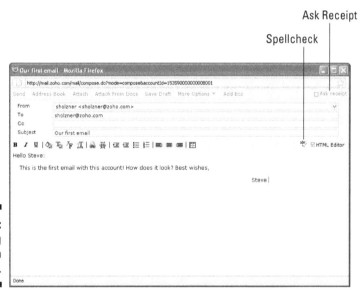

Ask Receipt

Spellcheck

Figure 7-2:
Composing an e-mail in Zoho Mail.

2. **Enter the e-mail address of the recipient in the To field.**

   If you have more than one recipient, separate the e-mail addresses with commas.

3. **(Optional) To send a copy of the e-mail to someone, enter that person's e-mail address in the Cc box.**

   If you have multiple recipients, separate their e-mail addresses with commas.

4. **(Optional) If you want to *blind carbon copy* (bcc) someone (that is, send a copy of the e-mail to someone without letting the other recipients know), click the Add Bcc link. Then in the Bcc field (which appears below the Cc box), enter the e-mail addresses of anyone you want to bcc.**

Again, if you have multiple recipients here, separate their e-mail addresses with commas.

5. **Enter the subject of the e-mail in the Subject field.**

6. **Enter the text of the e-mail in the large text box at the bottom of the dialog box.**

You can use the toolbar buttons in the dialog box to add bold or italics, set font size, add links, insert tables, and so on, just as you can in Zoho Writer (see Chapters 2 and 3).

7. **(Optional) Spellcheck your message by clicking the Spell Check button on the toolbar, shown in Figure 7-2.**

Zoho Mail runs a spellcheck on your e-mail's text and highlights all the words it doesn't know with a yellow background and red foreground text.

8. **Click Send to send the e-mail and close the dialog box.**

And that's it. You sent your first Zoho e-mail. Nice.

By default, the e-mail you compose is in HTML, which lets you see images and headers, as in a browser. You can alternate between creating HTML e-mails and plain-text e-mails by clicking the HTML Editor button at the extreme right when you're composing your e-mails.

There are a couple more options when it comes to sending e-mail that I take a look at in this chapter, such as working with attachments and address books. For now, though, I focus on a few other options: getting a return receipt for your e-mails when your recipient gets them, setting a priority level, and adding a signature. Additionally, you find out how to keep track of the e-mail you've sent with the Sent folder.

Not quite ready to send your e-mail? Click the Save Draft button that appears in the Compose window to save your e-mail. Saved drafts appear in the Draft folder in the left-hand pane.

Getting return receipts for your e-mails

You can request a receipt when someone receives your e-mail. It's something like sending a letter registered return receipt — you get notification of the delivery. That's handy to make sure that the person you're writing to actually got what you wrote.

You can request a delivery receipt with a single click. When you're composing the e-mail, just select the Ask Receipt check box (visible at the upper right in Figure 7-2).

Doing so means that the recipients are asked to confirm they got your e-mail (usually with a dialog box displayed by their e-mail program). If they click Yes or OK (depending on their e-mail program), you get a return e-mail that indicates your e-mail was delivered (the actual text of the return e-mail will differ by e-mail program). Having the recipient click OK or Yes is something like asking them to sign for a registered letter.

Note, however, that unlike with a real registered letter, they don't *have* to agree to send you a confirmation in order to get the e-mail. The recipient doesn't have to click OK or Yes (which means you get a receipt) to read your e-mail, so you can't count on getting such a receipt, even if your e-mail has been received.

Setting a priority level

You can also set the priority level of your outgoing e-mails. After all, some e-mails can wait, but others carry some urgency. To assign a priority level when you're composing an e-mail, follow these steps:

1. **Click the down arrow next to the More Options button in the Compose dialog box.**

2. **Click the arrow next to the Medium menu item.**

   New e-mails are set to Medium priority by default.

3. **In the new pop-up menu that appears, choose the priority level you want, from Highest to Lowest.**

   If your recipient's e-mail program displays priority, a flag matching the priority you set for the e-mail displays in his Inbox when he gets your e-mail.

Personalizing your e-mail: Adding a signature

You personalize the paper letters you send with your signature, and you can do something similar with Zoho Mail by adding a signature at the bottom of every e-mail. A Zoho Mail signature is not the same as an electronic signature.

An *e-mail signature* is a line or two of text that you'd like to tell the world. The signature is appended to the end of your e-mails, following a line of hyphens. Here's an example:

_____

Philosophers have more fun.

To add a signature to the end of all your e-mails, just follow these steps:

1. **At the top of the Zoho Mail page, click the Settings link.**

2. **Click the Personalize tab.**

3. **Click the Signature tab.**

4. **Enter the text for your signature into the text box.**

   Remember that your signature is added to the end of every one of your e-mails. So, for example, you might not want a signature that reads something like "PARTY UNTIL YOUR EARS FALL OFF!!" appended to all the cover letters you send out for your resumes when looking for a new job.

5. **To add your signature to the bottom of all e-mails, select the Add Customized Signature in All My Outgoing E-mails check box.**

6. **Click Save to save your new signature.**

   When you're done with the Personalize tab, click the Return to Mail link at right, closing the Settings tab.

Taking a look at your sent mail

After you send some e-mails, you can keep track of what you've sent in the handy Sent folder.

1. **Click the Sent folder icon in the Folders section of the left pane of Zoho Mail.**

   The current folder becomes the Sent folder, which opens in the main Zoho Mail page's box, as shown in Figure 7-3.

   Each e-mail is displayed as a single line in the Sent folder, and that line displays the e-mail's recipient, subject, and date. The e-mails are automatically ordered by date, with the most recent e-mails appearing toward the top.

Figure 7-3:
The Sent
folder of
Zoho Mail.

2. **To open an e-mail and read its contents, click the Subject of the e-mail.**

   The e-mail opens at the bottom of the main Zoho Mail box, as shown in Figure 7-4.

Figure 7-4:
Looking
at a sent
e-mail in
Zoho Mail.

You can sort e-mails by date by clicking the down arrow for the Date column header. When you do, the sort order switches to display the oldest e-mails first. Clicking the down arrow again toggles to restore the original sort order. To see all e-mails sent to a particular person, click that e-mail address in the To column, and Zoho Mail opens a new window showing all the e-mails sent to that person (one line per e-mail); click a subject to open the actual e-mail.

Receiving and Reading Your E-Mails

Sending e-mails is only half the fun — it's time to start receiving some e-mail.

Although Zoho Mail checks for new e-mail every few minutes, you can also manually check for e-mail. Just click the Fetch button in the toolbar. Zoho Mail immediately checks whether you have any e-mail and displays a brief pop-up (at the lower right of the browser window), indicating whether you have any new mail.

Zoho Mail has a special folder to hold the e-mail you get — the Inbox. Zoho Mail places your e-mail into this folder. Here's how to get your e-mail:

1. **Click the Inbox folder in the Folders section of the left pane of Zoho Mail.**

   The Inbox, shown in Figure 7-5, displays any e-mails you have received, with the most recent on top. As shown in Figure 7-5, there are two e-mails in the Inbox — the one I sent to myself earlier, and a welcome e-mail from Zoho Mail itself.

Figure 7-5:
The Zoho
Mail Inbox.

2. **To read an e-mail, click its Subject.**

   The e-mail opens in the bottom part of the window, as shown in Figure 7-5.

   You can also open e-mails in their own windows. To open an e-mail in a dedicated window (containing only that e-mail), click the Popout icon that appears between the From and Subject columns. The e-mail pops up in its own window.

When you first receive an e-mail, its entry (the line that indicates who it's from, the subject, and date) is in bold. After you read the e-mail, the entry reverts to plain text.

Want to see if any e-mails are waiting for you in a flash? Just take a look at the Inbox line in the Folders section of the left-hand pane. If you have any new e-mails, you see a number in parentheses next to the Inbox label indicating how many e-mails are waiting for you. For example, you can see a (2) in Figure 7-5. After you read the new e-mail, the number in parentheses is decreased by one automatically.

Replying To and Forwarding Your E-Mail

Say you just read an e-mail from a business colleague, and you want to send an answer back. Or, someone sent you an important report, and you want to send it to the other members of the committee you're on. Both replying to and forwarding e-mails are possible in Zoho Mail, as you'd expect.

Replying to an e-mail

It's simple to reply to an e-mail with Zoho Mail. Just follow these steps:

1. **In the Folders section of the left pane, select the folder that contains the e-mail you want to reply to.**

2. **Click the subject of the e-mail you want to reply to.**

   The e-mail opens at the bottom of the main Zoho window.

3. **Choose one of the following options:**

   - *Reply All:* To reply to the sender as well as to everyone copied on the original e-mail, click the Reply All button.

   - *Reply:* To reply to the just the sender, click the Reply button.

   The Reply dialog box opens, as shown in Figure 7-6.

4. **If you want to add additional recipients, enter those addresses in the To, Cc, and Bcc fields.**

   See the earlier section, "Composing Your Zoho E-Mails" for more on these fields.

5. **(Optional) Edit the Subject line.**

Figure 7-6:
Replying to
an e-mail in
Zoho Mail.

6. **Type your reply in the body of the e-mail.**

   The original text of the e-mail is included in the reply and is noted with a vertical bar on the left, setting it off from any text you add.

7. **Click the Send link to send your e-mail and close the Reply dialog box. A small reply icon will appear in the Inbox at the right next to the e-mail you replied to.**

Forwarding an e-mail

The other option besides replying to an e-mail is forwarding it. Forwarding e-mail lets you pass along e-mail.

It's easy to forward an e-mail — just follow these steps:

1. **In the Folders section of the left pane, click the folder containing the e-mail you want to forward.**

2. **Click the subject of the e-mail you wish to forward, opening that e-mail in the main Zoho window.**

3. **Click the Forward button above the e-mail's body.**

   The Forward dialog box opens, as shown in Figure 7-7.

   Forwarding an e-mail works just like replying to an e-mail (as described in the preceding section), with three exceptions:

   • The To box is blank, so you have to fill in the e-mail address of the person (or e-mail addresses of the people) you want to forward the e-mail to.

   • Zoho Mail prefaces the subject with Fwd: so you know it's forwarded e-mail.

   • Zoho Mail adds a message at the beginning of the e-mail's body, indicating that this is a forwarded message.

Figure 7-7:
Forwarding
an e-mail in
Zoho Mail.

4. **In the To, Cc, and Bcc fields, enter the addresses of the people you want to forward the message to.**

   See the earlier section, "Composing Your Zoho E-Mails" for more on these fields.

5. **(Optional) Edit the Subject line.**

6. **(Optional) Add additional text to the body of the e-mail.**

7. **Click the Send link at left to send your e-mail and close the Forward dialog box.**

   When you send a forwarded e-mail, that e-mail goes to your recipient(s), of course — and it also shows up in your Sent mail folder.

Setting a vacation reply

Sometimes, you might want to set up an automatic reply to e-mails: for example, configuring your e-mail program to reply automatically to all incoming e-mails with a vacation message something like:

> I'm in Hawaii, and you're not. I'll be back on August 12th and will catch up with my e-mail then. If you have an emergency, please refer it to my assistant, Tyler Smith. Aloha!

You can set up Zoho Mail to send vacation replies (and, needless to say, vacation replies need not just be used for vacations). If you're out of the office for whatever reason — at a meeting, for example — you might want Zoho to handle your e-mail for you, telling everyone when you'll be back.

Here's how to create and activate a vacation reply:

1. **Click the Settings link.**

2. **Click the Personalize tab.**

3. **Click the Vacation Reply tab, shown in Figure 7-8.**

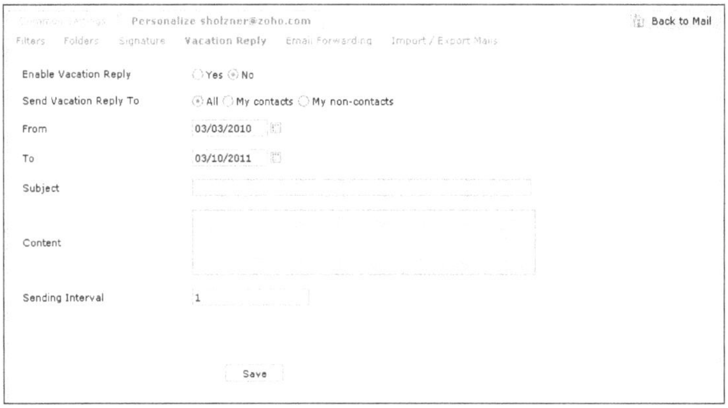

Figure 7-8:
The
Vacation
Reply tab in
Zoho Mail.

4. **Fill in the following fields, as desired:**

- *Enable Vacation Reply:* Select the Yes radio button to activate your vacation reply.

- *Send Vacation Reply To:* Select the radio button that corresponds to who you want the vacation reply sent to. (I cover Zoho Mail contacts in a few pages.) Your three options are All, My Contacts, and My Non-Contacts.

- *From:* Click the calendar icon to the right of the From date box, opening a calendar control. Click the date you want to start sending your vacation reply in response to e-mails.

- *To:* Click the calendar icon to the right of the To date box, opening a calendar control. Click the date you want to stop sending your vacation reply in response to e-mails.

- *Subject:* Enter the subject you want to give to your vacation reply e-mail.

- *Content:* Enter the body of your vacation reply e-mail (plain text only).

- *Sending Interval:* Enter the amount of time in days that Zoho Mail waits to send another vacation reply to any given e-mail address.

5. **Click Save.**

   When you're done with the Personalize tab, click the Back to Mail button at right, closing the Settings tab.

Vacation replies are very useful, and they can augment your professional image. Just remember to turn them off (by selecting the No radio button in the Enable Vacation Reply section of the Vacation Reply tab) when you get back to the office.

Managing Your Inbox

There are several ways to manage your e-mail, such as deleting unwanted e-mails, moving e-mails to other folders, and marking e-mail.

It's outta here: Deleting e-mail

In time, your e-mail is going to accumulate (let's hope you don't fall into the clutches of spammers, which would mean your e-mail would pile up very quickly), and you're probably not going to want to keep all that e-mail.

Here are the two ways to delete e-mails from your Inbox — or any Zoho Mail folder. Here's what you do:

1. **In the Folders section of the left pane, click the folder that contains the e-mail you want to delete.**

2. **Select the e-mail you want to delete:**

   - *To select a single message to delete:* Click the subject of the e-mail, which gives that entry a yellow background in the Inbox.

   - *To mark multiple e-mails for deletion:* Select the check box at the beginning of each entry that you want to delete.

3. **Click the Delete button (above the list of entries) to delete the e-mail or e-mails you selected.**

Unlike other deletion operations in Zoho, no confirmation dialog box appears (Do you wish to delete?) when you click the Delete button in Zoho Mail. The e-mail you delete is moved to the Trash folder instead. To delete it permanently, you must open the Trash folder (click the Trash folder in the Folders section of the left pane), select the e-mail, and then click Delete. Otherwise, Zoho Mail routinely deletes mail in the Trash folder by itself when the e-mail becomes 30 days old.

Organizing your e-mail with folders

When you're going through your mail, Zoho Mail offers you the ability to transfer e-mail to the Inbox, Spam, or Trash folder. (Bear in mind that if you transfer e-mail to the Trash folder, you'll have to open the Trash folder at some point and delete it, or rely on Zoho Mail's 30-day limit.)

Here's how to transfer e-mail between folders:

1. **Click a folder in the Folders section in the left pane of Zoho Mail.**

2. **Select the e-mail you want to move:**

   • *To select a single message to move:* Click the subject of the e-mail, which gives that entry a yellow background in the Inbox.

   • *To mark multiple e-mails to move:* Select the check box at the beginning of each entry.

3. **Click the down arrow next to the Move button on the toolbar and then select which of the following folders you want to transfer the selected e-mails to:**

   • Inbox

   • Spam

   • Trash

   That gives you more organizing power.

Zoho gives you a set of standards folders to start with, but you also have the option of creating additional folders to organize your e-mail. If you want to create a new folder, follow these steps:

1. **In the Folders pane, click the plus button to the right of the word Folders.**

   The New Folder dialog box appears.

2. **Enter the name of the new folder in the text box.**

3. **(Optional) If you want the new folder to be a subfolder of an existing folder, select the parent folder.**

4. **Click OK.**

   Your new folder appears in the Folders pane. If you created a subfolder, you may have to click the plus button to the left of the parent folder to display it.

A word about spam

E-mail spam (unwanted mass e-mail, usually commercial) — everyone hates it, but some people fall for it and buy things advertised with spam, unfortunately — otherwise it would disappear. What can you do about not getting spam in Zoho Mail?

First, Zoho Mail has one of the best spam filters around. Because spam is based on mass-mailing, Zoho Mail can detect what it suspects is spam by watching where it's sent. It reads and takes into consideration the body of the e-mail, whether the return address is genuine, and whether links or return e-mail headers and so on are faked before marking e-mail as spam.

E-mail that Zoho Mail sends you that it considers spam shows up in your Spam folder. This folder is a lot like the Trash folder: In fact, e-mails in the Spam folder are automatically deleted after approximately 30 days.

You can also report e-mail as spam yourself, and with just the single click of a button. Just click the Report Spam button in the e-mail's entry in the Inbox. This button is directly to the left of the red X that deletes the e-mail.

Marking e-mail with flags and bolding

Another way you can take charge of your Inbox (as well as other folders) is by marking your e-mail with flags and bolding. For example, if you mark an e-mail as important, a red flag appears in its entry in the Inbox. If you mark it as unread, its entry in the Inbox is in bold, and so on.

To manage mail markers, such as flags or bolding, follow these steps:

1. **Select the folder that holds the e-mail you want to mark.**

2. **To select the message(s) you want to mark, choose one of the following options:**
   - *To mark a single message:* Click the subject of the e-mail, which gives that entry a yellow background in the Inbox.
   - *To mark multiple e-mails:* Select the check box at the beginning of each entry.

3. **Click the down arrow next to the Mark As button in the toolbar and select one of the following options:**

- *Read:* Mark the e-mail as read.

- *Unread:* Mark the e-mail as unread.

- *Spam:* Mark the e-mail as spam.

- *Archive:* Mark the e-mail as an archived e-mail.

- *Info:* Mark the e-mail as an informational e-mail.

- *Important:* Default e-mails have a small black-and-white flag in their folder entries. This flag appears just before the e-mail address of the person who sent the e-mail. When you mark e-mail as important, that flag turns to red although it's not the easiest to see.

- *Follow Up:* When you mark an e-mail for follow-up, a small flag appears in the title bar of the e-mail when you open that e-mail. Again, however, it's not easy to see.

- *Clear Flag:* Clears any flags.

Handling Attachments in Zoho E-Mail

What would e-mail be without attachments? Whether you're sending a report to your boss or family pictures to Aunt Ida, being able to e-mail files is important. In this section, I take a look at how to work with attachments — both sending and getting them.

Adding attachments to your e-mail

You can add an attachment to your e-mail in two ways — either add a file from your computer, or add a file from another Zoho application.

To add an attachment from your computer, follow these steps:

1. **Click the Attach link in the Compose dialog box.**

   The File Upload dialog box appears.

2. **Browse to the document you want to attach.**

3. **Select the document to upload by clicking it; then click Open.**

   The attachment appears by name in the Attachments box in the Compose dialog box at right, as shown in Figure 7-9.

Figure 7-9:
The Attach-
ments box.

Attachment

To attach a Zoho document, follow these steps:

1. Click Attach from Docs in the Compose dialog box.

The Attach from Zoho Docs dialog box appears, as shown in Figure 7-10.

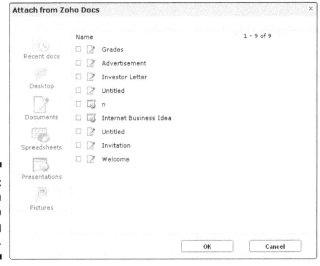

Figure 7-10:
The Attach
from Zoho
Docs dialog
box.

2. Select the check box in front of all the documents you want to attach.

3. Click OK to close the dialog box.

The attachment appears by name in the Attachments box (upper right) of the Compose dialog box.

After you attach your file(s), continue writing your e-mail as normal, and then click Send to send it and close the Compose dialog box.

If you discover that you attached the wrong document, you can delete it by clicking the red X to its right in the Attachments box.

Opening e-mail attachments

When you receive an e-mail with an attachment, you see a small paper clip icon in the e-mail's entry in the Inbox, as shown in Figure 7-11.

You can open an attachment through the Attachments dialog box or by clicking the attachment within the message itself.

Attachments icon

Figure 7-11:
A new
e-mail
showing an
attachment.

Follow these steps to open a document or download multiple documents in the Attachments dialog box:

1. Click the paper clip icon in the e-mail's Inbox entry.

The Attachments dialog box opens, displaying a list of your attachments by name.

2. Choose one of the following options:

- *To open an attachment:* Click the attachment you want to open, which causes your browser to download and open the attachment.

- *To download multiple attachments:* Select the check box in front of the attachments you want to open and then click the Download as ZIP button. Zoho Mail puts the selected attachments into a Zip file, and your browser downloads the file.

If you want to open the attachment within the message itself, follow these steps:

1. **Open the e-mail by clicking its subject in its Inbox entry.**

   The attachment(s) are displayed by name in the open e-mail (refer to Figure 7-11).

2. **Click the attachment in the box in the open e-mail.**

   Your browser downloads and opens the attachment.

Searching Your E-Mail

Zoho Mail lets you search your e-mail, and that's good for serious e-mail users. Some people use their e-mail practically as virtual filing cabinets, keeping track of contacts and projects with their Inbox. For example, if you're the head of a corporate project management team, you might get a lot of e-mail reports on the progress of various projects. By making your e-mail searchable, you can keep tabs on past progress and organize that e-mail.

Searching all messages

To search all the e-mail in your folders, simply enter the search term into the Search box (shown in Figure 7-12) and then click the Search button.

All e-mails that contain your search term are displayed in the search results. For example, you can see the search results for the search term *attachment* (that is, the search is for the word "attachment" in Figure 7-12). Zoho Mail found two e-mails — one in the Sent folder, and one in the Inbox folder. Note that Zoho Mail opens the search results in a new tab, which is labeled with the search term (*attachment* here), as shown in Figure 7-12.

Click to narrow your search

Search box

Figure 7-12:
Search
results in
Zoho Mail.

To open an e-mail, just click its subject, which causes Zoho Mail to open and display the e-mail at the bottom of the window. When you're done with the search results, click the X button in the tab to close the tab.

Zoho Mail can search only attached Zoho documents, plain text documents, and zipped combinations of those documents. So don't attach documents in non-Zoho format and expect Zoho Mail to be able to search them.

Restricting searches

By default, Mail searches search everything in an e-mail — subject, To fields, the mail body, and so on. Better yet, you can select only the parts of e-mails you want to search.

To restrict a search to only specific parts of e-mails, such as the subject lines, click the button just to the left of the search box, opening a menu with these items:

- ✔ Subject
- ✔ Sender
- ✔ Subject or Sender Contains
- ✔ To: or Cc:
- ✔ Attachment name
- ✔ Attachment contents
- ✔ Mail Contents
- ✔ Search in All Folders
- ✔ Search in Folder

Select the item you want to add to the search, such as the Sender field. Zoho Mail places a check mark in front of all the items you select, and your search will search only those items of your e-mails.

That's useful, for example, if you want to exclude a field from a search. For example, you and your recipient may have kept the same subject line even as your e-mails started straying far from the original topic. By omitting the subject line from the search, you can target only the e-mails that have to do directly with what you're looking for.

Searching specific folders

By default, Zoho Mail searches through all mail folders when it conducts a search, but you can restrict it to search through just a specific folder. Here's how to do that:

1. **Click the folder you want to search in the Folders section of the left pane.**

2. **Click the button just to the left of the Search box (refer to Figure 7-12), opening the drop-down menu.**

3. **Select the Search in Folder menu item.**

   This sets the current folder as the folder that Zoho Mail searches.

4. **Enter the search term in the Search box.**

5. **Click the Search button.**

This feature is useful to know if you're searching for a common term and don't want to see search results from all folders at the same time, which can clutter up the search results considerably.

Saving E-Mail on Your Computer and Printing E-Mail

You can leave e-mail on Zoho Mail indefinitely (except in the Spam and Trash folders, where e-mail is deleted after 30 days), but you can also easily save e-mail to your computer.

To save an e-mail to your computer (HTML e-mail is saved as an HTML document, plain text e-mails as TXT documents), follow these steps:

1. **In the Folders section of the left pane, select the folder that contains the e-mail you want to save.**

2. **Click the subject of the e-mail you want to save, opening that e-mail at the bottom of the main Zoho window.**

3. **Click the down arrow next to the More Options button that appears above the e-mail's text, opening a drop-down menu.**

4. **Choose Save from the drop-down menu.**

   Your browser opens a dialog box asking whether you want to download the e-mail as a document.

5. **Select a name and location for the e-mail.**

6. **Click OK to save the document.**

Working with Your Address Book Contacts

When you send an e-mail, Zoho Mail automatically adds the recipient(s) to your *address book* — a collection of e-mail addresses — and you can save yourself some time when composing e-mail by getting e-mail addresses from your address book.

You can open your address book when you compose an e-mail. Here's how to do that:

1. **Click the Compose button.**

   The Compose dialog box opens in a new window.

2. **Click the Address Book link at the top of the Compose dialog box.**

   Your address book opens on the left side of the window, as shown in Figure 7-13.

Figure 7-13:
Using the address book in Zoho Mail.

   3. **To select an e-mail address, mark the check box to the left of the address. Then click the To, Cc, or Bcc button at the bottom of the panel, depending on whether you want the address to appear in the To, Cc, or Bcc field, respectively.**

   4. **Close the address book by clicking the X button at the upper right in the address book.**

   5. **Finish composing your e-mail.**

Using your address book is a handy timesaver, and also makes sure that you don't have to worry about spelling e-mail addresses correctly.

Your address book can get full pretty quickly because Zoho Mail automatically adds your recipients' e-mail addresses to the address book. As of this writing, there's no way to manage the addresses in your address book — no way to delete e-mail addresses, for example.

Organizing Your E-Mail with Labels and Folders

Zoho Mail also lets you organize e-mail by using labels and by creating your own mail folders.

A *label* is a small mark that has a name and a color, and you can apply labels to individual e-mails. You can also search for all e-mails with a particular label, such as "urgent" or "New project." Zoho Mail doesn't come with any built-in labels; you create and name them yourself.

You can also organize your e-mail by creating new folders in Zoho Mail. As I discuss earlier in this chapter, Zoho Mail comes with built-in folders, such as Inbox, Outbox, Trash, and Sent. But there isn't a folder named Mail From Freddie — surely that was an oversight on Zoho's part? It turns out that you can add and name your own folders in Zoho Mail, and you find out how to do that in this section.

Creating and using labels

You can create new labels easily in Zoho Mail, and then apply your new labels to various e-mails. One of the main selling points of labels is their flex-ibility. You can create a label and apply it to many different e-mails; you're not tied to a single e-mail.

Creating a label

Here's how to create a label:

1. **Click the down arrow next to the Labels button on the toolbar (not the Labels bar in the left-hand pane) and then choose New Label from the drop-down menu that opens.**

   The New Label dialog box opens, as shown in Figure 7-14.

Figure 7-14:
Create a
new label.

2. **Enter the name of the new label in the dialog box.**

3. **Click the down arrow next to the color box to reveal a drop-down menu of eight color names, and then select a color for your new label.**

4. **Click OK, closing the New Label dialog box.**

   You created a new label. Zoho Mail adds the new label name to the Labels drop-down menu, making that label accessible to you.

All the labels you create in Zoho Mail also appear in the Labels section in the left pane of Zoho Mail. I created the Urgent label shown in Figure 7-15.

Applying a label to an e-mail

You can assign the labels you've created to e-mails with a simple click of the mouse. Just follow these steps:

1. **Click the folder where the e-mail you want to label is contained in the Folders section of the left-hand pane.**

2. **Select the e-mail to label in the folder, or select the check boxes in front of all e-mails you want to label.**

3. **Click the Labels button on the toolbar.**

   A drop-down menu opens, listing all the available labels (as well as the New Label option).

4. **Select the label you want to apply to the selected e-mail(s).**

   Zoho adds the label to the e-mail(s) you selected. That label (a small colored box) appears in the labeled e-mails' entry in the folder (right in front of the subject), as well as at the top of the e-mail when you open it for reading, as shown in Figure 7-15.

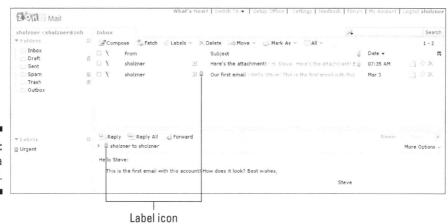

Figure 7-15:
Using a
new label.

Label icon

When you click a label in the Labels section, Zoho displays all the e-mails
that are labeled with that label, making it easy to use labels to organize your
e-mails.

Creating new folders

Say that you decided that having a label named Urgent isn't enough for your
purposes. You need a whole new folder named Urgent to contain urgent
e-mails.

Can you create such a folder in Zoho Mail? Yes. Just follow these steps:

1. **Click the plus icon to the right of the word Folders in the Folders bar
   in the left pane.**

   The New Folder dialog box opens, as shown in Figure 7-16.

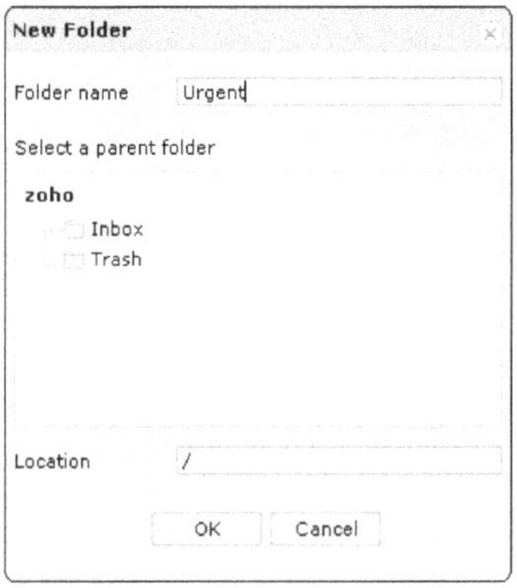

Figure 7-16:
The New
Folder
dialog box.

2. **Enter the name of the new folder in the Folder Name text box.**

   By default, the new folder is a *parent folder,* meaning that it's not a sub-folder of another folder.

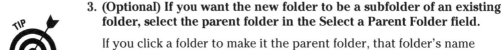

3. **(Optional) If you want the new folder to be a subfolder of an existing folder, select the parent folder in the Select a Parent Folder field.**

   If you click a folder to make it the parent folder, that folder's name appears in the Location box in the New Folder dialog box.

4. **Click OK to create the new folder and close the New Folder dialog box.**

   The new folder — Urgent, for example — appears in the Folders section of the left-hand pane in Zoho Mail, as shown in Figure 7-17.

Figure 7-17:
A new
folder.

New folder

You can open the new folder — although there will be no e-mail in it yet — by clicking it in the Folders section in the left-hand pane of Zoho Mail.

To move e-mail to and from the new folder, look for the new folder you just created in the menu when you click the down arrow next to the Move button. To move e-mail to the new folder, just select that e-mail and then select that folder's name from the Move button's drop-down menu.

Reading Your E-Mail Offline

E-mail applications on your laptop or desktop let you read your e-mail (just not get new e-mail or send e-mail) when you're offline. Zoho Mail can do the same with help from Gears by Google. Find you how to install Gears at the end of Chapter 3.

To configure Zoho Mail for offline e-mail reading, make sure that Gears is installed and then follow these steps:

1. **Click the Setup Offline link at the top of Zoho Mail.**

   The Offline Settings dialog box opens, as shown in Figure 7-18.

Figure 7-18: Setting up offline e-mail reading.

```
Zoho Mail - Offline Settings                                          x

Download options:
Number of mails to download initially, to setup offline mode: Recent  50  ∨  mails
Number of Sent mails to be available offline:                 Recent  25  ∨  mails
☐  Download Images and Attachments in mail

Other options:
☑  Create Desktop Icon

              Setup Offline    Cancel
```

2. **Set the following options for offline e-mail reading:**

   • *Number of Mails to Download Initially, to Setup Offline Mode:* From the drop-down box, select a value for the number of e-mails you want to download from the online version of Zoho Mail.

   • *Number of Sent Mails to Be Available Offline:* From the drop-down box, select the value for the number of sent e-mails you want to have available offline.

   • *Download Images and Attachments:* Select this check box if you want to make images and attachments available offline.

   • *Create Desktop Icon:* Select this check box if you want Gears to create an icon for Zoho Mail on your desktop.

3. **Click the Setup Offline button to close the dialog box.**

The next time you're offline, you can navigate your browser to `mail.zoho.com`, and Zoho Mail appears. You can read your e-mail; you just can't receive new e-mail or send e-mail while you're offline, of course.

Part III
Managing Data

The 5th Wave   By Rich Tennant

"Unless there's a corrupt cell in our spreadsheet analysis concerning the importance of trunk space, this should be a big seller next year."

In this part . . .

The data workhorses of the Zoho suite are in this part: Sheet and Reports.

Zoho Sheet is the Zoho spreadsheet application. It's as powerful as any spreadsheet application costing hundreds of dollars, and gives you everything you'd expect, from entering data to working with functions and formulas.

Zoho Reports is the Zoho database application, which you use to create relational databases that connect data from table to table. You get a guided tour to this application in this part.

Chapter 8

Zoho Sheet: All Your Data Cell by Cell

In This Chapter

▷ Creating a new spreadsheet and entering data

▷ Saving and deleting a spreadsheet

▷ Adding and deleting rows and columns

▷ Formatting a spreadsheet

▷ Sorting data

▷ Creating charts

▷ Using formulas and functions

▷ Collaborating and sharing a spreadsheet

▷ Exporting a spreadsheet

▷ Creating pivot tables

*Z*oho Sheet — one of the standard Zoho applications — is a very powerful spreadsheet tool. For data you need to keep track of and view in table form, give Sheet a try. Whether you're simply tracking inventory, or you're a real estate investor running a what-if scenario to see whether an investment is worth the risk, Sheet is the perfect app because you can use it to make your spreadsheets come alive by using formulas to work with the data entered into a spreadsheet.

If you're familiar with Microsoft Excel or Calc from OpenOffice.org, you're going to find a great deal of similarity here: You're already a leg up. Sheet is very similar to Excel and Calc, with a few additions, such as sharing your spreadsheets with others.

In this chapter, you find out how to create a new spreadsheet, how to enter data, edit that data, organize your data, add and delete columns and rows, create charts, and more.

Getting Started with Zoho Sheet

To start using Sheet, navigate your browser to `http://sheet.zoho.com`, enter your Zoho username and password, and then click the Sign In button. (See Chapter 1 for more on this process.) When Sheet appears, you'll already have a default spreadsheet set up for you, as shown in Figure 8-1.

The two toolbars you use are the

- ✔ **Action toolbar:** Use the tools here to perform actions such importing, exporting, and sharing spreadsheets.

- ✔ **Formatting toolbar:** Use these tools to format the data that appears in each cell. For example, apply bold, italic, and underline.

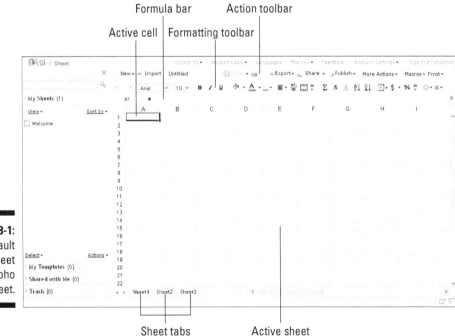

Formula bar   Action toolbar

Active cell   Formatting toolbar

Figure 8-1:
A default
spreadsheet
in Zoho
Sheet.

Sheet tabs   Active sheet

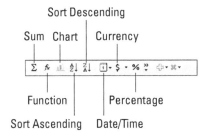

Sort Descending

Sum   Chart   Currency

Function   Percentage

Sort Ascending   Date/Time

Underneath the two toolbars is the Formula bar, where you enter the formulas you can use in Sheet to work with your data. Read all about formulas later in this chapter.

In the left-hand pane is the My Sheets section, which presents an overview of your spreadsheets. It also has other sections, such as a Trash section for when you delete a spreadsheet.

The real meat of Sheet takes place in the actual spreadsheet that you see in Figure 8-1, which is the grid of cells that takes up most of the window. Just like in other spreadsheet apps, rows are labeled with numbers, and columns with letters. The top-left cell in a sheet — the first cell — is cell A1. The cell to the right of it is cell B1, the cell just underneath A1 is A2, and so on. That's how you address each cell in a sheet, with a letter and a number: A1, B4, and so on.

Each spreadsheet can be made up of multiple sheets. In fact, the default spreadsheet that Zoho Sheet creates for you when you first open Sheet contains three sheets. You can move between those sheets by clicking the tabs at the bottom of the window, labeled Sheet1, Sheet2, and Sheet3.

To add a new sheet to an existing spreadsheet, right-click one of the tabs at the bottom of the spreadsheet window and choose Insert. To open an existing spreadsheet, click the link to that spreadsheet that appears in the left-hand pane of Sheet.

Entering Data

Entering data into a Sheet spreadsheet works in much the same way as it does in Excel or Calc, so no need to spend too much time on the basics. Entering data into a spreadsheet is simple: You just click the cell and type or paste your data. You don't have to start entering your data with cell A1.

When you click a cell, the cell appears with a bold black outline, indicating that it's the *active cell* — the target of anything you type — and your keystrokes appear there. When you're entering data, pressing the Tab key moves the active cell to the next cell to the right. And the arrow keys work to move the active cell where you want.

To edit the contents of a cell, double-click that cell, which makes the text insertion cursor appear. To delete the contents of the active cell, just press the Delete key.

Zoho Sheet comes with many keyboard shortcuts; you can see them in Table 8-1.

Table 8-1	Sheet Keyboard Shortcuts
Action	*Shortcut*
Save file	Ctrl+S
Insert a new worksheet	Shift+F11
Add/edit cell comment	Shift+F2
Insert the current date in cell	Ctrl+;
Insert the current time in cell	Ctrl+Shift+;
Start a formula	Equal sign
Navigate	
Move to next cell in row	Tab
Move to previous cell in row	Shift+Tab
Up one screen	Page Up
Down one screen	Page Down
Go to cell command	Ctrl+G
Toggle expand and collapse of Formula bar	Ctrl+Shift+U
Edit	
Edit active cell	F2
Cancel cell entry	Escape key
Delete selected cell / cell range	Delete
Delete one character to right while typing in a cell	Delete
Delete one character to left while typing in a cell	Backspace

Action	*Shortcut*
Select	
Select whole spreadsheet	Ctrl+A
Select column	Ctrl+Space
Select row	Shift+Space

You can also work with ranges of cells in Sheet. You can select whole ranges of cells and work with them all at once, formatting their contents the same way, copying them, pasting data into a range, or cutting a whole range of cells. (Just use the standard keyboard shortcuts you're used to: Ctrl+C, V, and X, respectively.) To create a range of cells, drag the mouse from the upper-left cell in the range to the lower-right cell in the range. You can also click a column or row header to select all the corresponding columns or rows.

When you select a range of cells, a bold outline appears around the range, and a hollow plus sign appears at the range's lower-right corner. Sheet treats ranges of cells the same way as it would treat a single cell. For example, when you paste a multirow and multicolumn range, the cells in all the range's rows and columns are pasted at once.

To save your spreadsheet, click the Save button (the one that displays a diskette icon) on the Action toolbar. If you haven't already given your spread-sheet a name, Sheet asks for a name, as shown in Figure 8-2. Give it a name and then click OK.

Figure 8-2:
Saving a spread-sheet.

After you save a spreadsheet, the new name for the spreadsheet appears in the My Sheets section of the left-hand pane, as shown in Figure 8-3.

To delete a spreadsheet, go to its line in the left-hand pane, click the down-pointing arrow at the extreme right, and select the Send to Trash item. Then click the Trash bar in the left-hand pane, opening the Trash section. Click the check box next to the item you want to delete, click the down arrow next to the Actions item at lower right in the Trash section, and select Delete Item.

Spreadsheet name

Figure 8-3:
A saved
spread-
sheet.

Adding and Deleting Rows and Columns

One of the most fundamental manipulations you can make with spreadsheets is to add or delete new rows or columns.

Adding a new column

Say you need to modify a spreadsheet by adding a column between two existing columns. Just follow these steps:

1. **Right-click any cell in the column to the right of where you want to insert a new column.**

2. **From the menu that appears, choose Insert⇨Column Before.**

   If you clicked the column to the left of where you want to insert a new column, choose Column After.

   The new column appears. In Figure 8-4, the new column becomes column D. The old column D, which held employee titles, becomes column E.

Now you're free to enter new data — say, employees' IDs, as shown in Figure 8-5.

Figure 8-4:
Add a
column.

New column

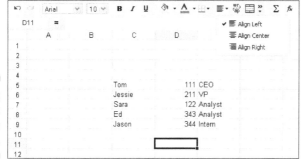

Figure 8-5:
Enter data
into a new
column.

In the figure, the text in the new column aligns to the right. If you want to align it to the left, select the text in the new column and click the Alignment button (opening the Alignment menu, as shown in Figure 8-5), and then choose Align Left.

Adding a new row

Similarly, you can also add new rows to a spreadsheet:

1. **Right-click the row below where you want to insert a new row.**

2. **From the menu that spears, choose Insert⇨Row Above.**

   If you clicked the row above where you want to insert a new column, choose Row Below.

   The new row appears, as shown in Figure 8-6.

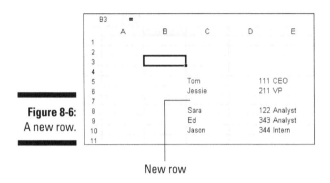

Figure 8-6:
A new row.

New row

Adding Comments and Data Formats

Data is just that: data. Sometimes you need a little behind-the-scenes commentary. For that, use the comment feature in Sheet. And when it comes to numbers, Sheet is a whiz. There are all kinds of built-in formats, such as Currency, Date/Time, and Percentage formats. Using these formats makes your data appear in the correct format (for example, with a $ sign in front of it), and helps Sheet know how to treat your data.

Adding a comment

Sometimes, just raw data in a cell doesn't say enough. For example, you have a currency amount in a cell, but you want to note that it's questionable, or perhaps that it's last year's data. Adding a comment to the contents of a cell can be very helpful. Follow these steps:

1. **Right-click the cell to which you want to add a comment.**

2. **From the menu that appears, choose Insert Comment.**

3. **Enter your comment in the Insert Comment dialog box that opens, as shown in Figure 8-7.**

Figure 8-7:
Add a comment here.

4. Click OK.

A red triangle appears in the upper left of the cell you added a comment to, as shown in Figure 8-8.

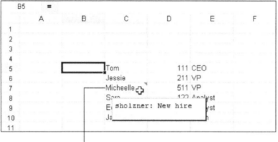

Figure 8-8:
This cell
holds a
comment.

This cell has a comment.

To read the comment, hover the mouse over the cell with the comment. A pop-up appears, showing the comment and its author, as shown in Figure 8-8.

You can also edit and delete comments:

✔ **To edit a comment:** Right-click the cell with the comment, and then choose Edit Comment. In the menu that opens, edit the comment text in the Edit Comment dialog box.

✔ **To delete a comment:** Right-click the cell with the comment and choose Remove Comment. The comment and red triangle both disappear.

Using date, currency, and percentage formats

Wouldn't it be nice if that column of dollar amounts actually displayed a $ sign in front of every amount? Or that column of percentages displayed a % sign after each item? You can format each item using $ signs, % signs, and more. Using formatting is way better than typing a $ character yourself in front of an item, which makes Sheet treat the item as text, not as a number. This is a big deal because Sheet can't, for example, add such items to display their sum.

To format an item in a cell as a dollar amount — so that a dollar sign appears in front of it — do the following:

1. Select the cell (click it).

2. Click the down arrow next to the Currency button on the Formatting toolbar to open the drop-down menu shown in Figure 8-9.

Figure 8-9:
Currency
format
options.

3. **Choose the currency type you want to use.**

   The data in the cell is formatted using the currency type you choose, and the appropriate currency symbol appears in the cell before the amount.

Formatting data in date/time format works much the same:

1. **Select the cell you want to format.**

2. **Click the down arrow next to the Date/Time button (to the left of the Currency button) on the Formatting toolbar.**

3. **Choose a date/time format.**

   You see choices like 15 Aug 06, 15 August 2006, and so on.

To format numbers as percentages, use the Percentage button (to the right of the Currency button).

Organizing Your Data by Sorting

Columns of words or numbers are nice, but you might get a little tired scanning up and down them for the entry you want. Sheet allows you to sort your data into orderly columns. That's good if you have a set of names, for example, and want to alphabetize them. Or if you have a set of numbers and want to order them from lowest to highest or highest to lowest.

Performing a standard sort

Sheet offers you a quick way of sorting your data into ascending or descending rows. For example, say you have data on fruits in a spreadsheet named Produce, and you want to sort this data, row by row, alphabetically.

To sort data like this, you want to perform a *standard sort:*

1. **Select the data you want to sort.**

   Be sure to select all the columns you want, or Sheet sorts only the columns you do select, which might leave data in some rows unsorted. Sheet won't sort data row by row automatically. See Figure 8-10.

Figure 8-10:
Running a
standard
sort.

2. **Choose your sort type:**

   • *Sort Ascending (as shown in Figure 8-10):* Orders your data from 0–10 and a–z.

   • *Sort Descending (to the right of the Sort Ascending button):* Sorts your data from 10–0 and z–a.

Performing a custom sort

Maybe you want a more sophisticated type of sort: say, by quantity of each item and not by the item's name. That seems to be a problem because you have to select all the columns you want to sort at the same time. So how can you tell Sheet which column's data to sort by, if you don't want to use the first selected column of data to sort on?

You can do a *custom sort:*

1. **Select the data you want to sort (select all columns).**

   Be sure to select all the columns you want, or Sheet sorts only the columns you do select, which might leave data in some rows unsorted. Sheet won't sort data row by row automatically.

2. **Right-click the selected area.**

3. **From the menu that appears, choose Sort➪Custom Sort.**

   The Sort dialog box opens, shown in Figure 8-11. You can sort on up to three criteria with this dialog box.

Figure 8-11:
Custom
sorting data
in Zoho
Sheet.

4. **From the top drop-down list, select the first column you want to sort (your *primary sort*).**

5. **Select the Ascending or Descending radio button to indicate which type of sort.**

6. **Repeat Steps 5 and 6 for up to two more columns to sort on, using the middle and bottom drop-down lists (respectively) for your second- and third-level sorts.**

7. **Select list options (both optional):**

   - *Contains Header check box:* If you want your sort to include the column header (the button at the top of the header with the column's letter in it)

   - *Case Sensitive check box:* If you want your sort to be case sensitive (alphanumeric sorts only)

8. **Choose a sort orientation radio button:**

   - *Sort Top to Bottom* (the default)

   - *Sort Left to Right*

9. **Click OK to execute the sort.**

A Picture Is Worth a Thousand Words: Creating Charts

Presenting your data in rows and columns is just one way of looking at it. As a visual option, you can chart your data instead — say, create a pie chart or a graph of your data. To chart your data visually, just follow these steps:

1. Select the data you want to sort (select all columns).

2. Click the Chart button, opening the Add Chart dialog box shown in Figure 8-12.

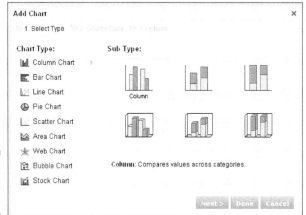

Figure 8-12:
Add a chart
here.

3. From the Chart Type list, click the type of chart you want.

4. From the Sub Type area on the right, click the specific chart you want.

5. Click the Next button, opening the second page (Source Data) of the Add Chart dialog box.

   From this page, you can select the range of cells for your chart in range format: for example, D6:E11. Because you already selected the data (in Step 1) to display in your chart before opening the Add Chart dialog box, you're all set and don't need to enter a range here. (Your range should already be displayed in the dialog box.)

6. Click the Next button, opening the third page (Options) of the Add Chart dialog box, as shown in Figure 8-13.

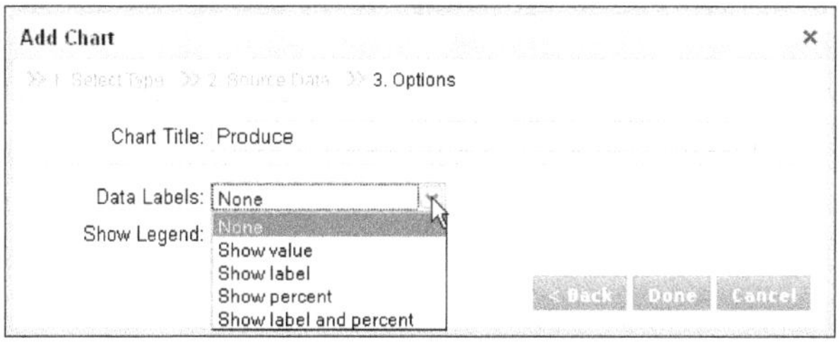

Figure 8-13:
Enter chart
options
here.

7. **Set your chart options:**

- *Enter a title for your chart.*

- *Use the Data Labels drop-down list to set how you want your data labeled in the chart (shown in Figure 8-13).*

  This item lets you label the sections of your pie or the bars in your charts with data values.

- *Leave the Show Legend check box selected (it is, by default) to have a legend appear showing which color bars or slices stand for which data items.*

8. **Click the Done button to dismiss the Add Chart dialog box and create your chart.**

   See an example chart in Figure 8-14.

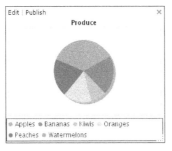

Figure 8-14:
A new chart in Zoho Sheet.

Serious Data Crunching: Using Formulas and Functions

Spreadsheets can do more than just look pretty: They can crunch your data as well. You can use formulas to read the data in your cells, crunch it, and display the result in a new cell. For example, you might want to take the average of a column of numbers. Or you might have a long column of numbers to add, and a formula can do that. In fact, adding columns of numbers is such a common thing to do that Sheet includes a dedicated button to sum a column of numbers for you — no formula needed.

I start with a look at the Sum button first because summing is probably the most common use of numerical operations in Sheet, and then I show you how to use formulas in general.

Using the Sum button

The easiest way to add a column of numbers is to use the Sum button. All you have to do is select the numbers you want to add and then click the Sum button on the Formatting toolbar.

When you do, Sheet adds the numbers automatically and inserts their sum into the cell right under the column of numbers. See Figure 8-15 for an example.

Figure 8-15:
Sum a
column of
numbers.

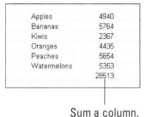

Apples	4940
Bananas	5764
Kiwis	2367
Oranges	4435
Peaches	5654
Watermelons	5353
	28513

Sum a column.

Creating a formula

You can also use math operators to create your own formula to crunch data in Sheet. Here are the math operators you can use:

Operator	Function
+	Addition
–	Subtraction
*	Multiplication
/	Division

Although I don't want to get ahead of myself here, you aren't limited to using only +, –, *, and /. Read more in the upcoming section, "Using functions in Sheet."

In Sheet, formulas are connected with a particular cell. That is, the formula for a cell tells Sheet what data (usually from other cells) to crunch so that the results appear in the cell. You can refer to other cells with the column/row convention in Sheet, such as D5 or F99.

Taking the data presented in Figure 8-15, say you wanted to add all the numbers of fruit explicitly. To do that with a formula, just follow these steps.

1. Click the cell that will contain the formula, making it the active cell.

The cell address (in this example, E12) appears in the first text box in the Formula bar. If any formula already exists for that cell, that formula is displayed in the second text box in the Formula bar.

2. Enter the formula in the second, larger text box in the Formula bar.

While you enter the formula, it appears in the active cell as well as in the Formula bar.

For this example, address the numbers to add by cell, E6 through E11. Start your formula with an equal sign so that Sheet knows you want the result to appear in the active cell. The formula to use to add the column of numbers in Figure 8-16 is

$=(E6 + E7 + E8 + E9 + E10 + E11)$

The parentheses are optional.

Besides cell addresses, you can also use numbers in formulas, as well as functions, which are coming up next.

Formula

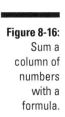

Figure 8-16:
Sum a
column of
numbers
with a
formula.

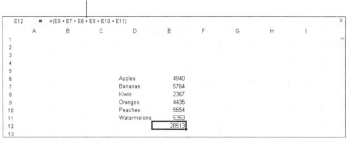

3. Press Enter.

Doing so makes the active cell move to the cell directly beneath the cell you're entering the formula to. It also makes Sheet evaluate your formula and display the result in the cell in which you placed the formula.

To edit the formula for a cell, just click that cell. The formula for that cell appears in the larger text box in the Formula bar, and you can make your changes there.

Using functions in Sheet

If you don't want to write all the cell addresses that you're adding in formula [like =(E6 + E7 + E8 + E9 + E10 + E11) in the preceding example], you can use a shortcut: the SUM function. The SUM function is one of the built-in functions in Sheet, and there are dozens of them. In this case, all you have to do is to pass the range of cells you want to add to the SUM function.

In Sheet, you create a range of cells like this:

cell address 1:cell address 2

where cell address 1 is the first cell in the range, and cell address 2 is the last cell in the range.

For example, to add the numbers from cells E6 through E11, use the range E6:E11, and append the SUM function like this:

SUM(E6:E11)

To make this into a formula, add the required = sign in front, like this:

=SUM(E6:E11)

Instead of summing E6 through E11, say you want the average number of each item. In that case, use the AVERAGE function like this:

=AVERAGE(E6:E11)

And to count the number of cells in the range E6:E11, use the COUNT function:

=COUNT(E6:E11)

Sometimes, a function can be used for a single cell value. For example, say you wanted the hyperbolic cosine of the value in cell D6. You could use the COSH function:

=COSH(D6)

Dozens of functions come built in to Sheet. You can get an idea of the highlights in Table 8-2.

Table 8-2	Selected Sheet Built-in Functions
Function	*Action*
AVERAGE	Returns the average of its arguments.
CEILING	Rounds a number to the nearest integer.
COLUMN	Returns the column number of a cell.
CONCATENATE	Combines multiple text strings into one string.
COUNT	Returns how many numbers are in the list of arguments.
DAY	Returns the day of a date value.
DEGREES	Converts radians to degrees.
EXP	Returns e raised to the power of a value.
FIND	Finds a string of text within another string.
FV	Returns the future value of an investment.
INT	Rounds a number down to the nearest integer.
MAX	Returns the maximum value from a list of values.
MEDIAN	Returns the median of a set of values.
NOW	Returns the computer system's date and time.
PMT	Returns the periodic payment for an annuity.
PV	Returns the present value of an investment.
RAND	Returns a random number (between 0 and 1).
REPLACE	Replaces part of a string with another string.
SEARCH	Returns the position of a string within a string.
STDEV	Estimates the standard deviation.
SUM	Adds all the numbers in a range of cells.
VALUE	Converts a text string into a number.
WEEKDAY	Returns the day of the week for a date value.

You can find the complete list of Zoho Sheet functions at `http://sheet.zoho.com/functions.do`. Many functions are available I didn't have room for here, such as AMORDEGRC, which calculates the amount of depreciation for a settlement period as degressive amortization.

Sharing Spreadsheets

Like with other Zoho applications, you can share Sheet spreadsheets or individual sheets. This is one of the great advantages of Sheet — you can share your data with others easily; no e-mail attachments needed!

Inviting others to share a spreadsheet

To share a spreadsheet or individual sheets, follow these steps:

1. **In an open spreadsheet, click the down arrow next to the Share button.**

2. **From the menu that appears, choose Invite.**

   The Share This Document dialog box opens to the Invite tab, as shown in Figure 8-17.

3. **Decide how to share the spreadsheet:**

   - *The whole spreadsheet:* Select the Whole Document radio button.

   - *Only specific sheets:* Select the Specific Sheets radio button.

     Zoho opens a drop-down list of sharing options (read-only, read, write, or hide) for each sheet, and you can set the permissions for each sheet.

   - *Read only:* To assign read-only individual viewers of the spreadsheet, enter their e-mail addresses in the Individuals text box in the Read Only Members section of the dialog box.

     To invite a group or groups as read-only members, enter the group name, or group names, in the Groups box; or, click the Add Groups link to select groups to add.

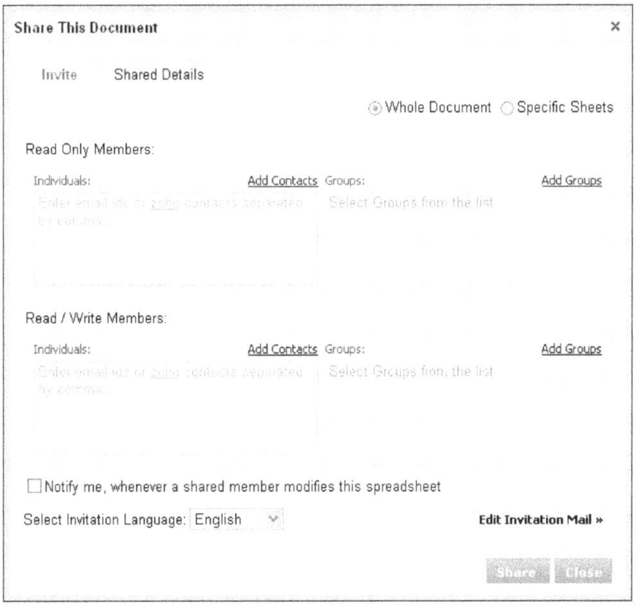

Figure 8-17: Set up sharing here.

To see how to create groups, see Chapter 3 on Zoho Writer.

• *Read/write:* To assign read/write viewers of the spreadsheet, enter their e-mail addresses in the Individuals text box in the Read/Write Members section of the dialog box.

To invite a group or groups as read/write members, enter the group name, or group names, in the Groups box; or, click the Add Groups link to select groups to add.

4. (Optional) Select the Notify Me, Whenever a Shared Member Modifies This Spreadsheet check box if you want to be notified when a read/write member modifies the spreadsheet.

Zoho will send you an e-mail if your spreadsheet is modified.

There's no other way to know whether a read/write member modifies your spreadsheet besides getting notification e-mails unless you happen to be watching as the edited cells flash yellow while they're actually being edited.

5. Select the language for the invitation.

The default is English.

6. Click the Share button.

The Share This Document dialog box displays the Shared Details tab, as shown in Figure 8-18, showing who is allowed to share your spreadsheet, and what permission those people have.

Figure 8-18: Review sharing details.	Share This Document ✕ Invite Shared Details View sharing for: Whole Document ▾ This document is shared to following members: **Shared Members** **Permission** **Action** nlconner Read / Write Change Permission | Remove ☑ Notify me, whenever a shared member modifies this spreadsheet

7. Click the X button at the upper right to close the dialog box.

The people you invite get an e-mail like this:

Hi nlconner,

sholzner has shared a spreadsheet with you on Zoho Sheet named 'Produce'. It is available under the 'Shared with Me' list in your Zoho Sheet Account.

Visit `http://sheet.zoho.com/open.` `do?docid=504651000000006003` **to access this document.**

Thanks,

The Zoho Sheet Team

Invitees can click the link in the e-mail to open your spreadsheet, or they can open Sheet and click the name of your spreadsheet in the Shared with Me section of Sheet's left-hand pane.

To change someone's status (from read-only to read/write, for example), click the down arrow next to the Share button and select the Edit Shared Details item.

When others share your spreadsheet

When someone shares your spreadsheet and starts viewing it, you're notified. The text at the lower right in Sheet changes from 0 Viewing to 1 Viewing, as shown in the lower right of Figure 8-19.

And clicking the 1 Viewing message opens the Sharing pane in Sheet.

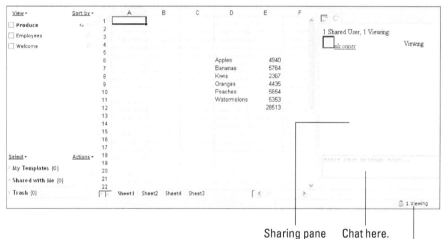

Figure 8-19:
The Sharing pane.

Sharing pane   Chat here.

Click to open the Sharing pane.

You can chat with others who are sharing your spreadsheet by entering your message in the chat box at the bottom of the Sharing pane and then pressing Enter. People sharing your spreadsheet can send you messages as well, as shown in Figure 8-20.

Handling changes made by others

When someone with read/write permission for your spreadsheet makes a change to that spreadsheet, the only warning you get that someone is making changes to your spreadsheet is that the changes appear in the cell that's being edited, and the cell's background flashes yellow briefly.

If you selected to be notified whenever a shared member modifies your document (see the earlier section, "Inviting others to share a spreadsheet"), you get an e-mail like this when someone makes a change to your spreadsheet:

> Hi sholzner,
>
> nlconner has made changes to your spreadsheet named 'Produce'.
>
> Visit `http://sheet.zoho.com/open.do?docid=504651000000006003` to access this document.
>
> Thanks,
>
> The Zoho Sheet Team

Figure 8-20: Chat with someone sharing a spread-sheet.

Publishing on the Web

You can also share your spreadsheets by publishing them on the Web. Here's how:

1. **In an open spreadsheet, click the down arrow next to the Publish button.**

2. **Choose Embed in Website/Blog.**

   Zoho displays a dialog box asking whether you want to rename your spreadsheet before making it public.

3. **(Optional) Rename the spreadsheet if you like.**

4. **Click OK.**

   The Embed to Website Blog dialog box opens, as shown in Figure 8-21.

Figure 8-21:
Publish spread-sheets from here.

5. **Click the Continue button.**

   As shown in Figure 8-22, the Embed to Website/Blog dialog box displays a code snippet that you can place in a Web page or blog to embed the spreadsheet there.

   The Embed to Website Blog dialog box also displays a URL for the spreadsheet, which is hosted at `http://zoho.com` for you. Navigating to the spreadsheet's URL displays that spreadsheet.

You can use either the code snippet or the URL to share your spreadsheet on the Web.

Embed To Website Blog ✕

To embed this in your web page, copy and paste the following HTML snippet:

```
<iframe width="500" height="400" frameborder="0"
scrolling="no" src="http://sheet.zoho.com/publish
/sholzner/untitled-1"> </iframe>
```

Select Snippet

Embed Options

☐ Show in Zoho public documents

☑ Allow to export

☐ Hide the formulas used

Figure 8-22:
Embedding
information.

This document is shared publicly and can be viewed in following URL:

http://sheet.zoho.com/public/sholzner/untitled-1

Normal View   HTML View   Printable Version

The Cool Stuff: Creating Pivot Tables

Even more functionality is built into Sheet, such as *pivot tables,* which you can use to compare your data and create summaries in different ways. For example, say you have the data on the salespeople shown in Figure 8-23.

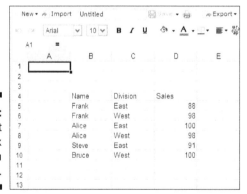

Figure 8-23:
Use a pivot
table to look
at data in
new ways.

Note that some salespeople sell in both the East and West divisions, giving them more than one row. It would be easier to redo this table and create a sum for each column.

That's what pivot tables let you do: reorganize and summarize your data. They can break out a column of data (such as the Division column in Figure 8-23) into different columns: say, one column per data item in the original column.

In this example, note that the original Division column has two items in it — East and West — which will become columns in a pivot table in the following step list.

Here's how to create a pivot table:

1. **Open a worksheet from which you want to create a pivot table, such as the data in Figure 8-23.**

2. **Click the Pivot button on the Action toolbar.**

3. **From the drop-down menu that appears, choose Create Pivot Table.**

   The Create Pivot Report dialog box opens, as shown in Figure 8-24.

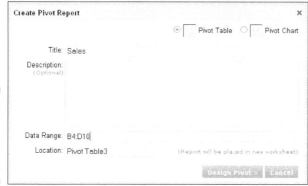

Create Pivot Report   ✕

                 ⊙ ☐ Pivot Table   ○ ☐ Pivot Chart

       Title: Sales

Description:
(Optional)

Data Range: B4:D10|

Location: Pivot Table3   (Report will be placed in new worksheet)

Design Pivot >   Cancel

Figure 8-24: Name the pivot table and set its data range.

4. **Enter the name of the pivot table.**

5. **(Optional) Enter a description for the pivot table.**

6. **Enter the range of data in the spreadsheet you want to include in your pivot table.**

   In the data range you specify, be sure to include any text you placed at the head of any columns to label those columns. The pivot table will label its columns using the same column headers.

7. **Click the Design Pivot button, opening the Design Pivot dialog box you see in Figure 8-25.**

8. **Drag the original column (from where it appears at the left in the dialog box) whose values you want to become the new columns in the pivot table to the Columns box.**

   That's the Division column in this example because I want its two items (East and West) to become new columns in the pivot table.

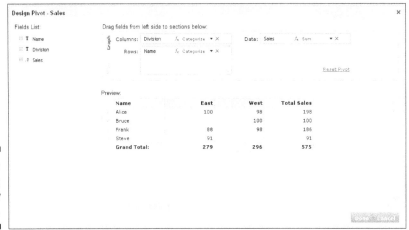

Figure 8-25:
Designing
the new
pivot table.

9. **Drag the original column(s) (from where they appear at the left in the dialog box) you want to make into rows to the Rows box.**

   That's the Names column in this example because I want to give one row to each of the salespeople in the pivot table.

10. **Drag the original column (from where it appears at the left in the dialog box) whose values you want to treat as the primary data for the pivot table to the Data box at the right.**

    That's the Sales column in this example because I want to compute and display the total sales.

11. **Click the Done button to close the Design Pivot dialog box and to add the pivot table to the spreadsheet.**

While you're designing your pivot table, you can get a preview of what it'll look like at any time by clicking the Click Here to Generate Pivot link in the Design Pivot dialog box.

The new pivot table, with a name like Pivot Table1, is given a tab in your spreadsheet. To take a look at the pivot table, click its tab. For instance, you can see the new pivot table for this example in Figure 8-26.

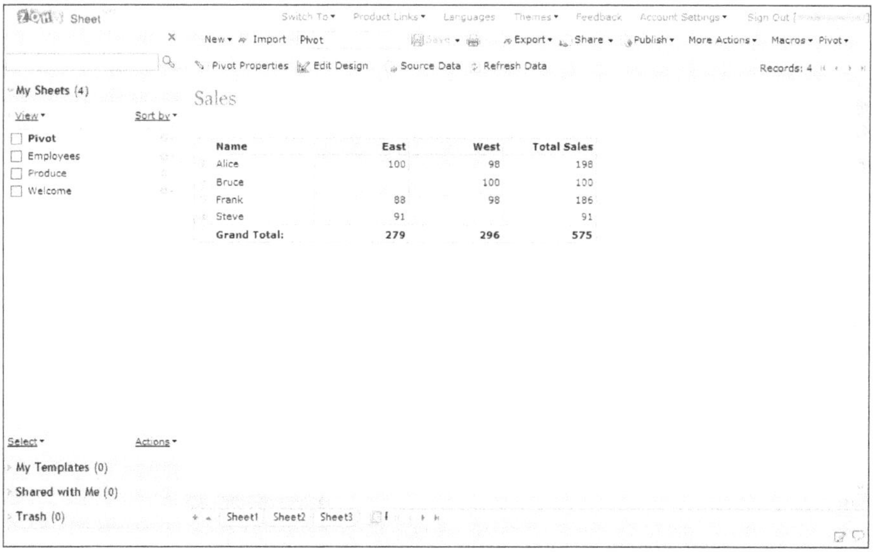

Figure 8-26: The new pivot table.

Chapter 9

Zoho Reports: Creating
Online Databases

In This Chapter

▷ Creating a new database

▷ Entering records and saving your data

▷ Working with tables

▷ Sorting and filtering data

▷ Viewing your data

▷ Sharing your data

Z oho lets you create your own databases with the Zoho Reports application. Databases typically organize your data into tables, and a table looks
something like a spreadsheet.

These table columns are *fields* in database terminology. The rows contain the
actual data for the table: *records.*

You can use Zoho Reports to view the data in your tables in different ways,
or use a database language like SQL (Structured Query Language) to extract
data from tables. For example, you might want only the phone numbers of
those people whose last (or first) name starts with *Jam,* and by using SQL,
you could get those records easily.

In this chapter, you take a look at creating new databases, entering data into
them, and extracting data in various ways. It's as powerful as any desktop
database application — and it's free and online.

Getting Started: Creating a Database

You can find Zoho Reports at `http://reports.zoho.com`, which is shown
in Figure 9-1. You can log in with your Zoho username and password (see
Chapter 1 for more details).

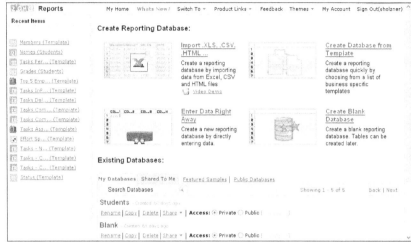

Figure 9-1:
The main
page of
Zoho
Reports.

Before working with the data in a database, you have to create that database, and Reports gives you four options (these are available on the home page — click the My Home link):

✔ Import .XLS, .CSV, .HTML

✔ Create Database from Template

✔ Enter Data Right Away

✔ Create Blank Database

If you use Reports for any length of time, you'll probably use all these options at one time or another. I discuss each option in the sections that follow.

Importing a database

The simplest option for creating a database in Zoho Reports is to have an existing database you want to import. You can import databases in three formats:

✔ **XLS format (Microsoft Excel):** You can import Microsoft Excel spreadsheets and convert them into Reports tables. Interestingly, you can't import Microsoft Access databases.

✔ **CSV format (comma-separated values):** Data is held in a plain text field, with the extension .csv. Data in it is separated by commas.

✔ **HTML format:** This format contains tables as HTML tables.

Here's an example that imports a Phones database table. To convert this table into HTML format, you place the name you want for the table columns at the head of the HTML table, and Reports names the various fields in the table using those names.

Name	*Phone*
Richard	555.4943
Sue	555.5934
Tina	555.6543
Dan	555.4432
Jessica	555.5684

Here's what the HTML table looks like containing the phone data:

```
<table>
  <tr>
    <td>Name</td>
    <td>Phone</td>
  </tr>
  <tr>
    <td>Richard</td>
    <td>555.4943</td>
  </tr>
  <tr>
    <td>Sue</td>
    <td>555.5934</td>
  </tr>
  <tr>
    <td>Tina</td>
    <td>555.6543</td>
  </tr>
  <tr>
    <td>Dan</td>
    <td>555.4432</td>
  </tr>
  <tr>
    <td>Jessica</td>
    <td>555.5684</td>
  </tr>
</table>
```

To convert this HTML document into a database table in Reports, just follow these steps:

1. **Sign in to Zoho Reports using your Zoho username and password.**

2. **Click the Import .XLS, .CSV, .HTML link, opening the Step 1 of 3: Create Database (Import) dialog box you see in Figure 9-2.**

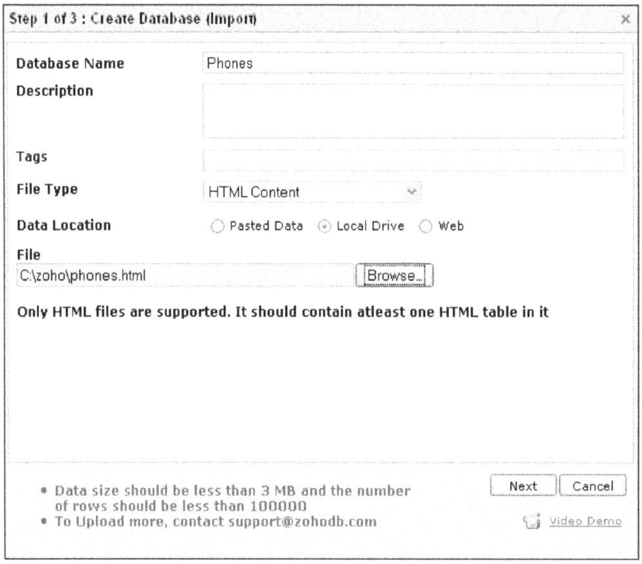

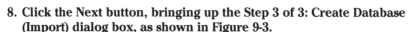

Step 1 of 3 : Create Database (Import)

Database Name   Phones

Description

Tags

File Type   HTML Content

Data Location   ○ Pasted Data ⊙ Local Drive ○ Web

File
C:\zoho\phones.html   [Browse...]

Only HTML files are supported. It should contain atleast one HTML table in it

• Data size should be less than 3 MB and the number of rows should be less than 100000
• To Upload more, contact support@zohodb.com

[Next] [Cancel]

Video Demo

Figure 9-2:
Begin the
import.

3. **Enter a name for the new database in the Database Name text box.**

4. **From the File Type drop-down list, select the data format of the data you're importing: CSV, XLS, or HTML.**

5. **Click the Browse button and browse to the document you want to import from your computer.**

6. **Click Open in the File Upload dialog box.**

7. **Click the Next button, bringing up the second page of the dialog box.**

   The second page of the dialog box shows an overview of your data in a table. If you're importing from a multiple-sheet spreadsheet, it first asks you to select the sheets you want to import; do that, then click Next.

   Don't worry if not all the rows of your data are visible; Reports shows only the first few rows here.

8. **Click the Next button, bringing up the Step 3 of 3: Create Database (Import) dialog box, as shown in Figure 9-3.**

9. **Enter a name for your new table in the Table Name text box.**

10. **Make sure the data format of the fields is correct in the table itself. If it's not, select the correct data format at the head of each column from the drop-down list boxes.**

    The available formats for fields are

Auto Number	*Currency*
Date	Decimal Number
Decision Box	E-mail
Multi Line Text	Number
Percent	Plain Text
Positive Number	

11. **Click the Create button.**

    Zoho Reports displays a summary of your database in a dialog box.

12. **Click the Close button to create your new database.**

    Zoho Reports displays a dialog box offering to create a new report (summary) of your database.

13. **Click No.**

    Zoho Reports opens your new database table for editing, as shown in Figure 9-4.

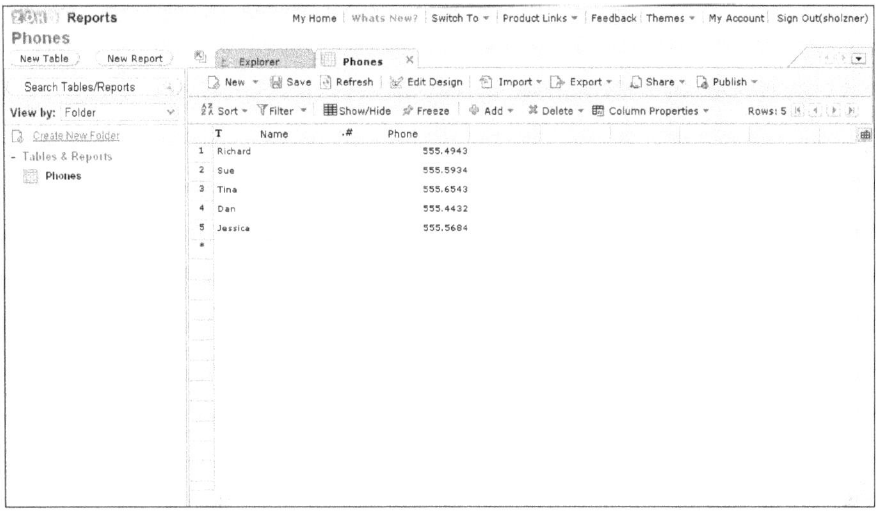

Figure 9-4:
A new data-
base table.

Congratulations! You created your first Zoho Reports database table. Keep reading to see how to enter and edit new data in the table.

To open the database you just created, click the My Home link to open the home page, and a list of your databases by name appears in the left-hand pane. Click the name of the database you want to open.

Creating a database from a template

The second easiest way to create a new database is to use an existing *template* — that is, a pre-existing database with built-in tables and fields. Zoho Reports offers three built-in templates.

- ✔ **Project Manager:** Manage your projects and track the tasks in it with detailed reporting.

- ✔ **Issue Manager:** Collect, assign, and track issues/bugs in your development projects with detailed reporting.

- ✔ **Google Adword Campaign Performance Analysis:** Lets you analyze Google Adword campaign performance.

Here's how to create a new database from one of these templates:

1. **On the Zoho Reports home page (which you can access by clicking the My Home link), click the Create Database from Template link (refer to Figure 9-1), opening the Create Database from Template dialog box shown in Figure 9-5.**

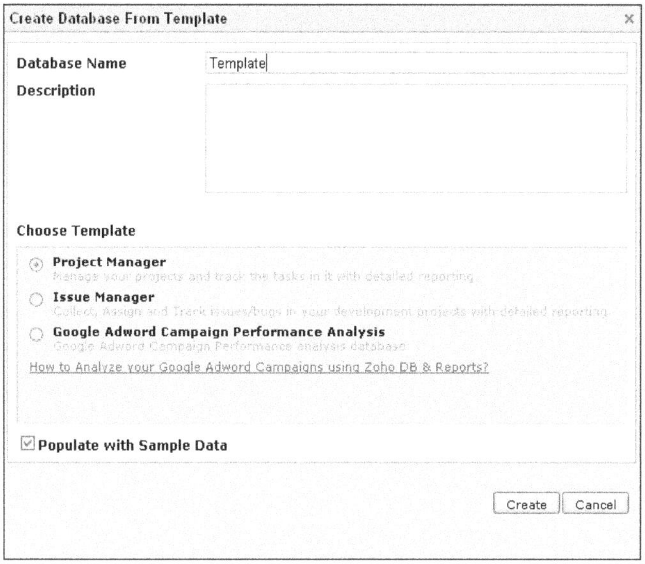

Figure 9-5:
Begin to
create a
database
from a
template.

2. **Enter a name for the new database in the Database Name text box.**

3. **(Optional) Enter a description for the new database in the Description box.**

4. **Select a template, using one of the three radio buttons, in the Choose Template box.**

5. **(Optional) If you want the database to be populated with sample data, select the Populate with Sample Data check box.**

    You might want to play around with the database to see if it fits your needs before continuing to Step 6.

6. **Click the Create button.**

    Zoho Reports opens the new database and displays the available tables, as shown in Figure 9-6.

To look at one of the tables in the new database, just click it to open it. For example, clicking the Members table opens that table for editing, as shown in Figure 9-7.

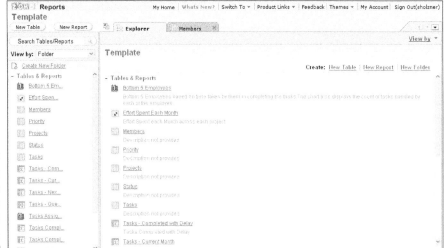

Figure 9-6:
A new database based on a template.

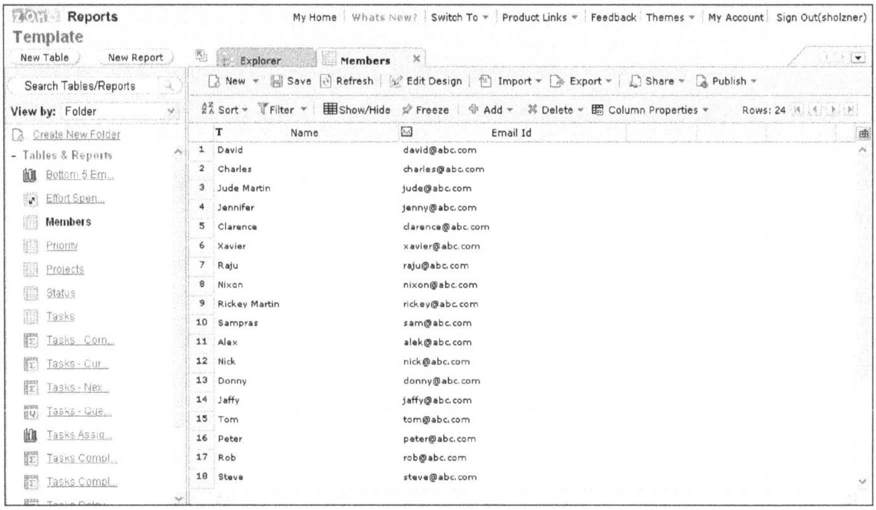

Figure 9-7:
A new database table.

Creating a database right away

If you can't wait to start entering your data, the Enter Data Right Away option for creating a database is for you. Using this option, you're presented with a blank table almost immediately. You can type your data into the table. Then, when you save the table, Reports asks you for a name for the table. Follow these steps to create a database right away:

1. **In Zoho Reports (click the My Home link to get you to the home page if needed first), click the Enter Data Right Away link (refer to Figure 9-1), opening the Enter Data Right Away dialog box.**

2. **Enter a name for the new database in the Database Name text box.**

3. **(Optional) Enter a description for the new database in the Description box.**

4. **Click the Create button.**

   Zoho Reports opens your new database table, as shown in Figure 9-8.

Figure 9-8:
A new
empty data-
base table.

This new database table is entirely empty and unnamed. When you save the table, Zoho Reports asks you for a name.

To name the columns in the new table, double-click the column headers. They turn into text boxes, into which you can enter new column names.

Creating a blank database

The most flexible — and also probably the most commonly used option for creating a new database — is the Create Blank Database option. This option allows you to create a database and customize the fields in each record (that is, the columns) before you enter data. That's the usual procedure for creating a database table: You design it first, before entering any data.

Here are the steps for creating a blank database:

1. **In Zoho Reports (click the My Home link to get you to the home page first if needed), click the Create Blank Database link, opening the Create Blank Database dialog box.**

2. **Enter a name for the new database in the Database Name text box.**

3. **(Optional) Enter a description for the new database in the Description box.**

4. **Click the Create button.**

   Zoho Reports creates your new database and also opens the Create New Table page, as shown in Figure 9-9.

Figure 9-9:
Table-
creation
options.

The four table-creation options available for blank databases are

- Import from .XLS, .CSV, .HTML Files

- Using Design View

- Enter Data Right Away

- Query Table

The most common way of designing a table is with the Design view, which I show you in the next section.

Giving Your Data a Home: Creating Database Tables

You created a new database, so now it's time to add a new table to your database (unless you already did). The most common way to do this in Zoho Reports is to create a blank database and use the table Design view to create and customize a new table.

Database tables are where your data goes. As I mention earlier, each *row* is a record, and each *column* is a field. A data type is associated with each field, so you should set that data type (such as plain text, or decimal) when you design your table.

Here's an example. Say that you're teaching a class on Zoho Reports, and you want to keep track of your students' names and grades in a database table, with one column named Name and one column named Grade. In this case, determining the data types of both columns is easy. They'll be plain text because names are text, and the students' grades will be letters.

After you design your table and create it, you can stock your table with data.

As I mention earlier, the usual way to design your own table is when you create a blank database in Zoho Reports. When you import a database, the tables already exist; when you create a table from a template, Zoho Reports creates the tables for you; and when you want to start entering data immediately, Zoho Reports creates a generic table for you, but you still have to customize it.

So, for discussion purposes, I show you how to design a table the usual way: by starting with a blank database. To create a blank database, follow the steps listed in the earlier section, "Creating a blank database." Those steps leave you at the Create New Table page (refer to Figure 9-9), ready to create your new table.

Here's how to design and create your new table:

1. **Click the Using Design View link in the Create New Table page (refer to Figure 9-9), opening the Design view as shown in Figure 9-10.**

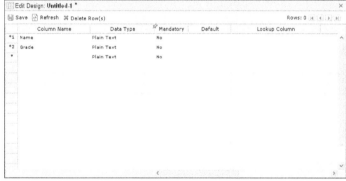

Figure 9-10:
Design a
new table.

2. **Enter the name of the new column in the Column Name column.**

   In Figure 9-10, I use Name to indicate the student's name.

3. **Select a data type for the new column in the Data Type column of the first row.**

   By default, Zoho Reports gives every new column the data type Plain Text, which is the most common data type.

To select a different data type, double-click the Data Type item for the column you're creating, and then select the new data type from the drop-down list that appears. Here are the possible items in this list:

Auto Number	***Currency***
Date	Decimal Number
Decision Box	E-mail
Multi Line Text	Number
Percent	Plain Text
Positive Number	

You might think you can just click the Data Type row to make the drop-down list of data types appear, as is standard with other applications. In Zoho Reports, you have to double-click it, despite the fact that clicking it gives the item a yellow border as it's selected.

4. **Specify whether the column is mandatory — that is, must contain data.**

   The two choices in the Mandatory column are Yes and No (the default is No), and you can switch between them by double-clicking the item in the Mandatory column and selecting Yes or No from the drop-down list. (Again, single-clicking the item only selects it and gives it a yellow border, not allowing you to change the setting.)

5. **(Optional) Enter a default value for the new field in the Default column.**

   Zoho Reports allows you to give the fields in your new database table default values. For example, you could set the default value of a number field named Count to 0 or some other value.

6. **(Optional) Enter a lookup column in the Lookup Column column.**

   Lookup columns are how Zoho Reports supports *relational databases.* In a relational database, you can tie fields together between tables. For example, a column named ID in one table can be a lookup into another table with an ID column. To tie tables, double-click the Lookup Column column, opening a drop-down list box that lists your other tables and the columns in those tables.

7. **(Optional) Scroll the Design view to the left, displaying two new columns: Formula and Description. You can enter data in these fields as follows:**

   • *Formula:* If you want to enter a formula tying the current field to the contents of other fields, double-click the Formula column and enter your formula.

   • *Description:* You can also add a description of the current field in the Description column for the new column.

8. **To add another new column to your table, click the next cell down in the Column Name column and follow Steps 2–7 to create the new column.**

9. **When you're done designing the rows in your table, click the Save icon (the diskette icon at the upper left in Design view).**

   If you haven't given the new table a name yet, the Save As dialog box opens.

10. **If warranted, enter a name for your new table in the Save As dialog box, as shown in Figure 9-11.**

   In this example, I'm calling the new table Grades.

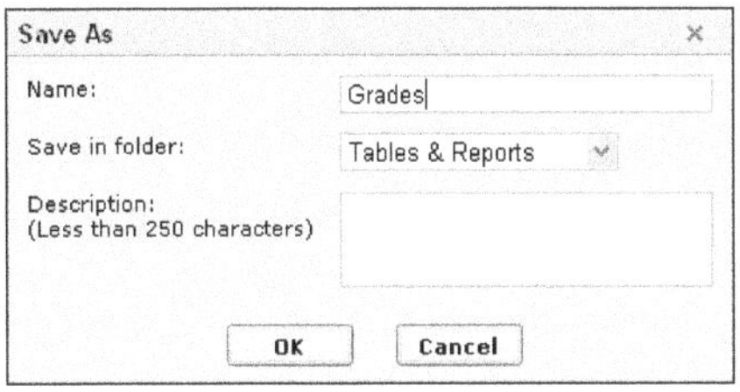

Figure 9-11:
Saving a
new table.

11. **Click OK to close the Save As dialog box.**

12. **Click the X button at the upper right to close the Zoho Reports Design view window.**

   Zoho Reports opens the new table to allow you to enter data.

Entering Data into a Database Table

After you create a table in a database, you're ready to enter data into the new table. You can create a standard or a related table:

- **Standard:** A stand-alone table
- **Related:** A table the connects to another table

Creating a standard table

To create a standard table, just follow these steps:

1. **Double-click the cell where you want to enter data.**

2. **When the text cursor appears, enter your data.**

3. **To move to the next lower row, press the down arrow. To move to the next column, double-click the cell you want to enter data in.**

4. **Continue Steps 1–3 until all your data is entered, as shown in Figure 9-12.**

Figure 9-12:
Entering
data into a
new table.

5. **When you finish adding new data to your table, click Save.**

After you save your new table, it's added to your database.

If you sign out of Zoho Reports and come back later, you can open your database by clicking it in the left-hand pane of Zoho Reports. Doing so opens the database, as shown in Figure 9-13.

Figure 9-13:
An open
database.

The tables in the database are listed when you open a database. The Grades database table is listed in Figure 9-13.

Clicking a table name in the database opens that table for editing, and you can double-click a cell to make a text cursor appear in the cell.

Creating related tables

A lookup column allows you to connect one table with another, creating a *relational database,* where tables are related to each other.

Zoho Reports supports relational databases. Here's an example, and how to implement it. Say that you're tracking building projects in an aircraft assembly plant. You want to keep track of the project name, the ID of the project's leader, and the first name and last name of the project leader in a table:

Project	*Leader's ID*	*Leader's First Name*	*Leader's Last Name*
Wings	111	Ed	Lane
Engines	122	Jenna	Carson
Wheels	111	Ed	Lane
Windows	122	Jenna	Carson

This table actually duplicates a lot of data: Ed Lane's ID, first name, and last name appear twice, as do Jenna Carson's. Wouldn't it be better if you could just refer to the leader of each project simply by ID?

Project	*Leader's ID*
Wings	111
Engines	122
Wheels	111
Windows	122

Okay, that means you don't have to enter the leaders' first and last names, which is easier. But what about when you actually need to find their names? You could have a second table, which gives the names of each leader by ID like this:

Leader's ID	*Leader's First Name*	*Leader's Last Name*
111	Ed	Lane
122	Jenna	Carson

Great. Now the Leader's ID column ties these two tables together.

In Zoho Reports, you would tie these tables together in this way. Say you had the second table already built. When you're designing the first table and adding the Leader's ID column, double-click the Lookup Column field. A list of the other tables in the database appears, with the fields in those tables listed under the table names, as shown in Figure 9-14.

Select the lookup column you want, which would be the ID table in the second table in this example.

After you create a lookup column, you can just double-click it when editing the table, and Zoho Reports reads the possible values for that column from the related table and displays them in a drop-down list. Just select the value you want.

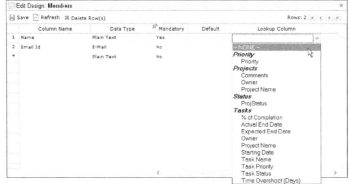

Figure 9-14:
Selecting
a lookup
column.

Making Changes to a Table

Databases aren't typically static, and you might want to make changes to a table's setup — say, insert new columns or rename a column.

You can make changes to a table when you're editing the table. First, take a look at making changes to the columns in a table, and then the rows.

If you have large-scale changes to make to a table, you might want to open it in the Design view again. To do that when you're editing a table, click the Edit Design button.

Making changes to the columns

When you're editing a table and want to make changes to the columns of the table, right-click a column header to open a drop-down menu. Here are the items in the menu that you can select from:

- **Sort:** A submenu with three items appears: Sort Ascending, Sort Descending, and Remove Sorting. When you add sorting to a column, all the records in your table are sorted using the values in that column.

- **Hide Column:** Hides the column from view while you're editing it but doesn't remove it from the table.

✔ **Freeze Column:** Locks the column from further editing until you unfreeze it by selecting this item again. Good to use to avoid inadvertent changes to your data.

✔ **Add Column:** Adds a new column to the far right in your table. When you select this item, Zoho Reports asks you for the new column's name and data type.

✔ **Add Formula Column:** Allows you to add a new formula column to a database table.

✔ **Format Column:** Allows you to format how the column appears when you're editing the table. In particular, a dialog box opens where you can choose the alignment of the data in the column when you're editing the table: left, right, or center.

✔ **Rename Column:** Allows you to rename a column. Zoho Reports asks you for the new name for the column. Enter the new name and then click OK. You can also (optionally) add a description for the column in the Description box before clicking OK.

✔ **Change Datatype:** Allows you to change the data type of a column. Clicking this item opens a dialog box with a drop-down list of data types. After you make your choice, click OK.

Be careful when you change a column's data type. When you change from one data type to an incompatible type — for example, from Email Addresses to Currency — you might lose some data.

✔ **Delete Column:** Deletes the column whose header you're right-clicking.

Making changes to the rows

Besides working with the columns in a table, you can also work with the rows in a table. However, the options when you're editing a table to make changes to the rows in the table are limited compared with what you can do with columns.

To make changes to the rows in a table when you're editing that table, right-click the row header (which shows a number) and select from one of these menu items:

✔ **Add Row:** Add a new row to the end of your database table.

✔ **Delete Row(s):** Delete a row or rows.

✔ **Delete All Rows:** Delete all the rows in your table.

When editing a table, you can also add or delete rows in a table using the Add or Delete button on the toolbar.

Sorting and Filtering the Data in a Database Table

You can handle your data by sorting and filtering it in Zoho Reports. *Sorting* a table does just what it sounds like: You sort records based on the value in a particular field. For example, if you have a table of people's names and want to sort on their last name, Zoho Reports can do it for you.

Comparatively, *filtering* data allows you to apply a specific criterion with which you extract matching records in a database.

From A to Z: Sorting data

Sorting data in a table is particularly useful when you have a lot of data in long columns in a table. If your columns are 2,482 entries long, it can help to sort them based on, for example, customer name.

Say you have a table of projects, and one column contains project names. To sort your table based on those names, follow these steps:

1. **In Zoho Reports, open the database you want (click it in the left-hand pane).**

2. **Open the table you want to sort (click it in the left-hand pane).**

3. **Right-click the column header of the column you want to sort on, as shown in Figure 9-15.**

   You could also click the Sort button (upper left, above the table).

4. **Choose an option from the drop-down menu:**

   • Sort Ascending

   • Sort Descending

   • Cancel Sorting

After you make your selection, the table is sorted on the values in your column.

Getting selective: Filtering your data

You can also shorten tables considerably by filtering out just the data you want. Say you have a table with a number of different projects: The

DB project, the Show project, the People project, and so on — and there are many rows in the table.

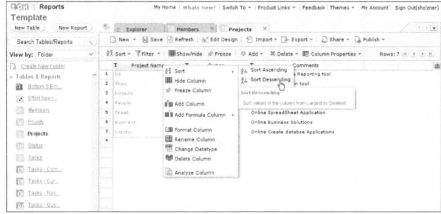

Then say that you get interested in only one project: the DB project. Here's how you can filter the table so that only records whose Project Name column contains DB are displayed:

1. **In Zoho Reports, open the database you want.**

2. **Open the table you want to sort.**

3. **Click the Filter button (above and to the left of the table).**

4. **Choose Create New Filter from the drop-down menu that appears.**

   A new drop-down box appears at the top of every column, as well as these buttons:

   • Hide

   • Apply

   • Clear

   • Close

   • Save (New)

5. **Click the down arrow next to the drop-down list box whose column you want to filter, opening this list of items (see Figure 9-16):**

   • Contains

   • Does Not Contain

   • Is

- Is Not
- In
- Not In
- Starts With
- Ends With
- Is Empty
- Is Not Empty

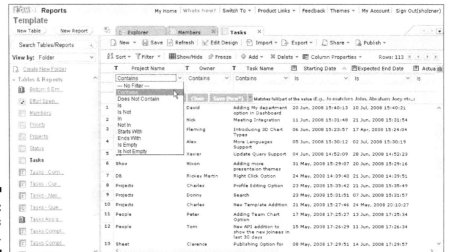

Figure 9-16:
Set a filter's
criterion.

6. **Select the criterion you want to filter on.**

7. **Enter the data to filter on (such as the word you want the field to contain) in the text box below the drop-down list.**

8. **Click the Apply button.**

   Zoho Reports filters the table.

You can see how the table in Figure 9-17 was filtered to show only records whose Project Name field contains DB.

Filtering a table doesn't actually make any changes to the table until you save that table.

To save your filter, click the Save (New*) button and give it a name.

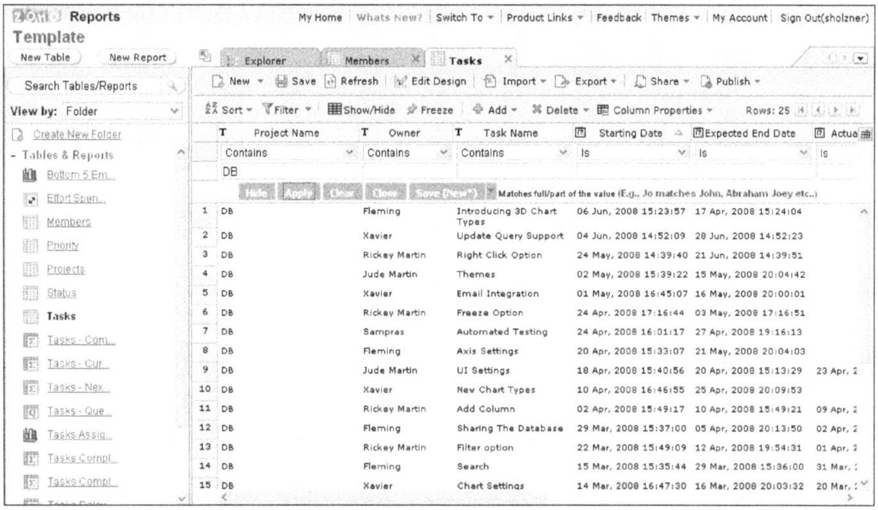

Figure 9-17:
A filtered
table.

Querying the Data in a Database Table with SQL

Sorting and filtering tables can be very useful, but databases can get more powerful still with SQL (Structured Query Language). Using SQL, you can set your own search criteria, such as phone numbers starting with a certain area code, or friends whose last names begin with "M." That is, SQL allows you to customize the way you extract data from a database.

SQL is the database language that lets you do just about everything that you can do with databases. You can search for records with fields that contain a dollar amount greater than a specific value, for example, or search for books that include the word "Germany" in their titles.

Say you have a Grades table, which holds the names and grades of students. You want to create a new table, based on the Grades table, that contains only the students' names. To do that, you could use an SQL statement. To create a new table from an old one and copy specific columns into the new table, you execute an SQL statement — a *query* — like this:

```
SELECT "column1", "column2", "column3", "column4" FROM "table"
```

The SELECT statement creates a new table and copies only column1, column2, column3, and column4 (the names of the columns you want to add to the new table) from the table named table.

In this example, you want to rctain only the Names column, which makes the SQL look like this:

```
SELECT "Name" FROM "Grades"
```

To create a new table in Reports based on an SQL query, follow these steps:

1. **In Zoho Reports, open the database you want.**

2. **Click the New Table button.**

3. **Click the Query Table item.**

   The [New Query Table]* tab opens, as shown in Figure 9-18.

Figure 9-18:
Creating an
SQL query.

4. **Enter your SQL query to create a new table, as shown in Figure 9-18 (where the query is SELECT "Name" FROM "Grades").**

5. **Click the Execute Query button.**

   Zoho Reports executes your query and shows the result in a preview table, as shown in Figure 9-19.

6. **If your query worked, click the Save button to save the query.**

7. **Enter a name for the query in the Name text box of the Save As dialog box that appears.**

8. **(Optional) Select a folder in which to save the query (in the Save to Folder box in the Save As dialog box).**

9. **(Optional) Enter a description of the query (in the Description box in the Save As dialog box).**

10. **Click OK to save the query and close the Save As dialog box.**

    The new query-based table appears as an entry in the list of tables in the left-hand pane of Zoho Reports, just like the other tables in the database. This way, you can easily execute the query on tables again.

Figure 9-19:
A new query
table.

A Window into Your Tables: Viewing Your Data

There are different ways to view your tables: in table form, yes, but also in other forms, such as charts. Charts are particularly useful — as they say, a picture is worth a thousand words. To access these alternate views, click the New button right above the table to open these choices:

- ✔ New Tabular View
- ✔ New Chart View
- ✔ New Pivot View
- ✔ New Summary View

The standard: Tabular view

Tabular view — the one you're already familiar with — is great if you want to take a look at your data all spelled out in rows and columns. If you have a table whose default form is, say, Chart view, you can also see its data in table form by selecting the New Tabular View menu item.

Graphics at work: Chart view

If a table contains numerical data, you can also view it as a chart. This is helpful when just looking at lists of numbers isn't enough; for example, it might be better to view your data in a pie chart.

As I mention earlier, to view data as a chart, open your table and click the New button and then choose New Chart View.

Zoho Reports opens a window that asks the color scheme you want, the labels for the axes, and other details. When you're done, click the Click Here to Generate Chart link.

Figure 9-20 shows a sample chart with employee data.

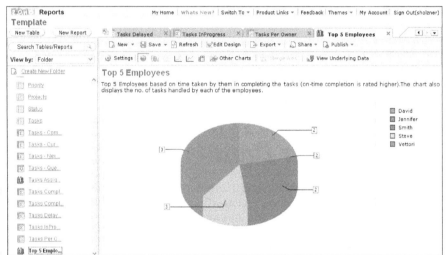

Figure 9-20:
A table in
Chart view.

Reorganize data with Pivot view

Pivot views are much like the pivot tables in Zoho Sheet, which you can read about in Chapter 8. As I discuss there, pivot tables enable you to reorganize your data. For example, say you have a table with 200 rows but only four different items in one of the columns. That's a little awkward. When using a pivot table, you can "pivot" how you view the data by giving each of the four items their own column, which reduces a lot of redundancy in the table.

To create a pivot table, open the table you want to reorganize, click the New button, and choose New Pivot View.

Zoho Reports opens a page that allows you to create a Pivot view by dragging columns and rows just like you create pivot tables with Zoho Sheet. For more details, take a look at Chapter 8.

Summarizing with Summary view

Summary views are another good way to view your data. As you can tell from the name, use this tool to summarize your data. That works by allowing you to group data together and then create summaries by group.

For example, say you have a table of sales data, with separate data for four sales regions: east, west, north, and south. Using Summary view, you can group the four sales regions together and take a look at, for example, total sales by age group, gender, price, and so on.

Here's how to create a Summary view for a table:

1. **In Zoho Reports, open the database you want.**

2. **Open the table you want a summary of.**

3. **Click the New button.**

4. **Choose New Summary View from the drop-down menu that appears.**

   This opens the page you see in Figure 9-21, which allows you to create a Summary view.

Figure 9-21:
A new summary table.

5. **Drag the columns you want to group by from the left into the Group By box.**

6. **Drag the column whose data you want to summarize into the Summarize box.**

   Zoho Reports displays the new summary table, as shown in Figure 9-21.

Sharing a Database

Like other Zoho applications, you can share your Report databases with others.

Unlike other applications, however, there's actually very little indication that someone is sharing your database: no notification pop-up, no e-mails when someone else edits your database, and no yellow background on cells that are being edited. Perhaps this lack of notification will change.

To share a database, or just a view, with someone else, follow these steps:

1. **In Zoho Reports, open the database you want.**

2. **Click the Share button.**

3. **Choose Share This View to share the current view, or choose Share This Database to share the current database.**

   The invitation dialog box opens.

4. **Enter the e-mail addresses of the people you want to share with in the Step 1 box.**

   If you want to share with a group, select the Share with Group check box.

5. **Select the radio button for the permission you wish to grant: Read Only or Read Write.**

6. **(Optional) Edit the invitation e-mail.**

7. **Click the Share button.**

The people you've shared with get an e-mail like this:

Hi,

Check out my "Grades" Sheet in the link below:

http://reports.zoho.com/ZDBDataSheetView.cc?OBJID=97322
000000004012&STANDALONE=true

Thank you and have a nice day,

sholzner

The people you invited can click the link in the e-mail to open your view or database, or they can sign in to Zoho Reports and find your view or database on their Shared to Me tab on the Zoho Reports home page (the page that shows the four ways to create a database).

And, the people you invited can now share your view or database and also make changes. However, as I mention earlier, you won't get any notification of those changes. For example, a student could change her grade!

Part IV
Using Zoho for Your Business

The 5th Wave   By Rich Tennant

©RICHTENNANT.

F. MUTT

"Ms. Lamont, how long have you been sending out bills listing charges for 'Freight,' 'Handling,' and 'Sales Tax,' as 'This,' 'That,' and 'The Other Thing?'"

In this part . . .

Zoho specializes in business applications, and this part takes a look at some very useful apps.

Zoho Projects helps you schedule your team's projects, keeping track of everyone's progress. You can share everything with your team members: timelines, calendars, milestones, scheduled tasks, and more.

Use Zoho Invoice to create, track, print, and send (via e-mail) your company's invoices, which you can customize with your company's logo.

Zoho CRM is the suite's customer relationship management system: It's huge! Use this app to track everything from potential customers to sales orders when you close the deal.

Chapter 10

Zoho Projects: Managing Your Team's Timeline

In This Chapter

▶ Creating a new project

▶ Adding users and tasks

▶ Assigning tasks and roles

▶ Creating project milestones

▶ Managing users

▶ Scheduling meetings

▶ Tracking time

▶ Using forums

▶ Generating reports

▶ Working with documents

*P*roject management isn't an easy task. If you're a project manager, you assign people their tasks, set up meetings, make sure that everyone stays on schedule, and track your team's progress. If you're a team member, you have to keep checking the schedule to make sure you stay on top of things, find out when and where the meetings are, and so on.

Zoho Projects gives you a great project management tool. Using this online application, you can set up and manage a project, add team members, schedule meetings and tasks, and (hopefully) keep everyone on track.

You take a look at Zoho Projects in this chapter. From scheduling tasks to scheduling meetings, all the project management power you need is right here. Projects gives you all that any desktop project manager would give you — plus the chance to keep your team coordinated by collaborating online.

It All Begins Here: Getting Started With Zoho Projects

To start with Zoho Projects, navigate your browser to `http://projects.zoho.com`, as shown in Figure 10-1. Note that you'll need a Zoho username and password to get started (see Chapter 1).

Figure 10-1:
Zoho
Projects.

The first thing Zoho Projects does is ask you to set up a *project portal* — a URL that is easily accessible by the members of your team. Use this form:

```
http://yourchosenname.projects.zoho.com
```

where *yourchosenname* is the name you choose for your portal.

Zoho Projects will let you know whether the name you chose is already taken.

After you enter the name for your project portal, click the Create New Project button. Zoho Projects sends you an e-mail like this:

> Welcome to Zoho Projects - Project Management Service
>
> Your account in Zoho Projects has been successfully created.
>
> Your Login: *xxxxxxxxxxxxxxxxxxxxxx*
>
> Your Portal: http://sholzner.projects.zoho.com

Please save this e-mail for future reference because it contains important login information. If you encounter difficulties logging in, please contact support@zohoprojects.com.

Zoho Projects

Your browser takes you to your login page, as shown in Figure 10-2.

Purchase a plan here.

Click to customize.

Your Projects home page

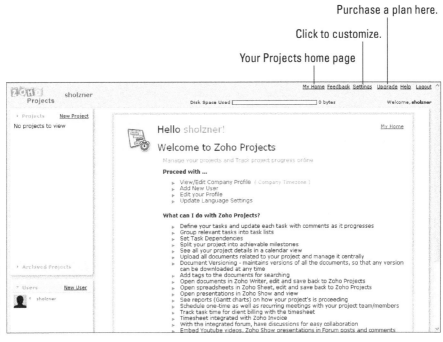

Figure 10-2:
The Zoho
Projects
login page.

The login page gives you an overview of Zoho Projects and links to these common tasks:

- ✔ View/Edit Company Profile
- ✔ Add New User
- ✔ Edit Your Profile
- ✔ Update Language Settings

Note the Upgrade link at the upper right of the login page. Zoho Projects lets you create one project for free, but that's it. Although a single free project is enough to give you a test drive of Zoho Projects, you might want to continue with the application, and that costs money. The current monthly fees for the five supported plans appear in Table 10-1.

Table 10-1	Zoho Projects Plan Prices				
	Free	*Standard*	*Express*	*Premium*	*Enterprise*
Monthly charge	$0	$12	$20	$35	$80
Number of projects	1	10	20	50	Unlimited
Number of users	Unlimited	Unlimited	Unlimited	Unlimited	Unlimited
Number of templates	0	4	8	10	20
Storage	100MB	2GB	3GB	5GB	25GB
Gantt charts	Yes	Yes	Yes	Yes	Yes
Time tracking	Yes	Yes	Yes	Yes	Yes
RSS	Yes	Yes	Yes	Yes	Yes
Calendar	Yes	Yes	Yes	Yes	Yes

If you have yet to sign up for a monthly paid plan, Zoho Projects displays a red ribbon at the top of every page you go to, explaining that you can create only one project. Click the Hide This link to hide this reminder.

Note the My Home link, also at the upper right in Figure 10-2. That's a link to your Zoho Projects home page, which lists your tasks, meetings, and milestones for all your projects.

You and your team members get a Zoho Projects home page, where you can see where you are with all your projects. If you haven't yet created any projects, there's nothing available on your home page. In fact, your home page isn't available yet, either.

Customizing Zoho Projects the Way You Like It

The first step in using Zoho Projects is to customize the application's settings before creating any projects. Click the Settings link at the upper right of any Zoho Projects page, which opens the Settings page to the General Settings tab, as you see in Figure 10-3.

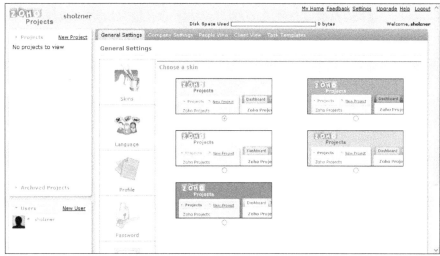

Using the General Settings tab

The General Settings tab includes a number of icons corresponding to the settings categories at the left. Clicking those icons displays the available setting options at the right.

Here are the General Settings categories you can use to customize Zoho Projects. To open one of these categories, just click its icon:

- ✔ **Skins:** A *skin* is a color scheme, and you can customize the look of Zoho Projects with the five possible skins you see in Figure 10-3.

- ✔ **Language:** You can customize Zoho Projects to display in any of 15 languages. When you click the Language icon, a drop-down box appears listing the possibilities. Select the language you want and then click the Update Language Settings button.

- ✔ **Profile:** This section lists your public information, accessible by other Zoho Projects users. Here, customize your name (login, full, nickname), job title, and phone number (office, residence, and mobile).

    When you start with Zoho Projects, it uses your username (sholzner, in my case). You might want to change that before giving all your team members access to a project.

- ✔ **Password:** Use to reset your password.

- ✔ **Photo:** Use to upload an optional photo of yourself.

Using the Company Settings tab

On the Company Settings tab (see Figure 10-4), you can set information about your company.

Figure 10-4:
The
Company
Settings tab.

The categories are

- ✔ **Profile:** Set your company's profile, as you can see in Figure 10-4. Settings here include your company name, Web address, street, city, state, country, zip code, time zone, e-mail, and the project portal URL.

- ✔ **Date Format Settings:** Use this setting to select 12- or 24-hour time settings as well as the date format (for example, European or US) setting.

- ✔ **Logo:** Upload a company logo.

- ✔ **Powered by Logo:** Upload a logo that Zoho Projects displays as "powering" your pages.

Creating a New Zoho Projects Project

Creating a new project is simple; just follow these steps:

1. **Click the New Project link (upper left of the login page), which opens the Add Project dialog box you see in Figure 10-5.**

2. **Enter the name for the new project.**

   In this example, I use the name Midland.

Figure 10-5: The Add Project page.

3. **(Optional) Enter a description for the new project.**

4. **Click the Add Project button.**

The project window you see in Figure 10-6 opens.

Figure 10-6: The new project's dashboard.

The tabs available on this page are Dashboard; Tasks & Milestones; Calendar; Meetings; Documents; Timesheet; Reports; Forums; and Users.

The first tab — Dashboard — is selected by default, and it gives you an overview of the current state of your project.

Welcome to the Project dashboard

You can control all aspects of a project from its *dashboard,* which summarizes your project at a glance, giving you an overview of what's happening with a project. You can see these sections of the dashboard in Figure 10-6:

✔ **Week Ahead:** A day-by-day calendar of upcoming items

✔ **Recent Documents:** Recently used documents

> ✔ **Recent Forum Posts:** A summary of what's been going on in the project forum
>
> ✔ **Recent Forum Comments:** A summary of forum comments
>
> ✔ **Latest Project Activity:** A summary of the activity on the project

Adding users

The first step in building a project is to set up the users in your project. When you create a task, Zoho Projects asks you to list the participants.

To add users to your project, click the Users tab, opening the tab shown in Figure 10-7. Then follow these steps:

Figure 10-7: Add users here.

1. **Click the Add User button, opening the Add New User box, as shown in Figure 10-8.**

2. **Fill in the new user's e-mail address.**

3. **Select the new member's role from the drop-down list box (contractor, manager, or employee).**

   Manager has the most privileges.

4. **Click the Add User button.**

Figure 10-8: Add a new user here.

After you add your new users, you can see them from the Users tab, as shown in Figure 10-9. The R, O, and M labels hold Residence, Office, and Mobile phone numbers, respectively.

Figure 10-9:
View users
here.

You can also add client users to a project. In the preceding steps, just click the Add Client User button instead of Add User. *Client users* are your business clients who might also have a vested interest in how your project is coming along. They're not usually part of your company. For example, a client user might be a vendor of some kind.

Getting busy: Adding tasks to a project

After you add a few users and let Zoho Projects know about them, you can put them to work with a new task. Tasks are the fundamental building blocks of Zoho Projects. You create tasks, assign people to them, add them to task lists, and keep track of milestones using tasks.

For example, say you have a task named Create Plan that comes at the beginning of a project. To create such a task and let Zoho Projects know about it, follow these steps:

1. **From your Zoho Projects home page, click the Tasks & Milestones tab.**

2. **Click the New Task button.**

   This opens the page you see in Figure 10-10.

3. **Enter the new task's name.**

4. **If you have a task list set up (I discuss these shortly) to which you want to add the current task, select the task list from the Task List drop-down list.**

   Task lists allow you to group individual tasks into collections.

Figure 10-10:
Create a
new task
here.

5. **To indicate the project owner, select that person's entry from the Project Members list box and then click the right-arrow button next to the list.**

   The user you selected is moved to the Owner box, indicating that that person is the project's owner.

6. **(Optional) Select the Send Mail Notification check box if you want each team member to be notified of the new task.**

   This check box is selected by default.

7. **Click the Advanced Options link, opening the bottom half of the page shown in Figure 10-10.**

   Because most tasks have a start date and end date, and/or a priority, opening the Advanced Options section is a good idea.

8. **Enter the project's start date.**

9. **Set the project's duration and end date by doing one of the following:**

   • Enter the project's duration in the Duration field.

   • Enter the project's end date in the End Date field.

10. **Select a priority for the task from the drop-down Priority list.**

    • Normal

    • Low

    • Medium

    • High

    • None

11. If the task is already partially completed, select the amount already complete from the % Completed drop-down list box.

The % Completed drop-down list box lists amounts in 10 percent increments from 10% to 100%.

12. Click the Add Task button.

Projects creates a new task, adds it to the project, and then opens the new task box shown in Figure 10-11. Note that the new task, Create Plan, has been added to the task summary here.

Task name

Figure 10-11:
A new task.

Each project member will get a notification e-mail like this:

Company: sholzner

Project: Midland

———

Following task assigned to you by sholzner

Task List - General

Task Title - Create Plan

Start Date - 03-18-2009

End Date - 03-30-2009

Duration - 13 days

Priority - None

% completed - 0 %

———————————

To view the task list, login to

https://sholzner.projects.zoho.com

Your new task will be added to the calendar if you gave it a starting date, and you can see the new task in the Week Ahead section of your home page, as shown in Figure 10-12.

Figure 10-12:
View tasks here.

View tasks in the calendar.

To edit or delete a task, click the Tasks & Milestones tab on the Zoho Projects home page and then hover the mouse over the name of the task you want to delete or edit. A pencil icon and a red X icon appear to the left of the task name:

✔ **To edit a task:** Click the pencil icon.

For example, you could add a task to a new task list.

✔ **To delete a task:** Click the red X icon.

On the day the task is scheduled for, you see the task in a section named Today's Tasks on your home page. You can mark a task as completed by selecting the check box to the right of the task.

Creating a task list

When you create a new task, you get the option of adding it to a task list. A *task list* is just what it sounds like: a way of assembling related tasks together. In real life, tasks often come in groups, and that's what task lists are all about.

Using a task list, you can also indicate that tasks are related. For example, you might have a task list named Stage 1, which comprises the tasks Create Plan, Get Approval, and Launch Stage II.

Here's how to create a task list:

1. **From your Zoho Projects home page, click the Tasks & Milestones tab.**
2. **Click the New Task List link.**

   This opens the page you see in Figure 10-13.

Figure 10-13: Create a new task list here.

3. **Enter the name of the new task list.**
4. **(Optional) If you have milestones related to the task list, select them from the Related Milestone drop-down list box.**

   I talk about milestones shortly.
5. **Click the Add Task List button.**

   The new task list is added to the list of tasks on the Tasks & Milestones tab of your home page.

To add an existing task to a new task list, edit the task to add it to a task list (see the preceding section for details), or click the Add Task link that appears under the task list on the Tasks & Milestones tab.

A sense of progress: Creating project milestones

If you've ever worked on a project in a business or academic environment, you know that milestones are very important. A *milestone* is like a marker, marking the end of a phase of a project.

You can keep track of where you are in a project and set deadlines with milestones. Milestones get added to a project's calendar, and the help to keep your team on track. You can name milestones, and you can set start and end dates for them in Zoho Projects. To add a milestone, follow these steps.

1. **From your Zoho Projects home page, click the Tasks & Milestones tab.**

2. **Click the New Milestone link.**

   This opens the page you see in Figure 10-14.

Figure 10-14:
Create a
new mile-
stone here.

3. **Enter the name of the new milestone.**

4. **Enter the start date of the milestone, if there is one.**

5. **Enter the end date of the milestone.**

6. **Select the owner of the milestone from the drop-down list of project members.**

7. **Select Internal (that is, internal to your company) or External from the Milestone Flag drop-down list box.**

   The default is Internal.

8. **Click the Add Milestone button.**

   The new milestone is added to the Tasks & Milestones tab of your home page — not under the default General tab (which lists general tasks), but under the Upcoming Milestones tab, as you can see in Figure 10-15.

In addition, you can see the new milestone in the calendar at the right in the page, as shown in Figure 10-15. Hovering your mouse over the milestone gives its details, as you can see in Figure 10-15.

In addition, the new milestone appears in the Week Ahead calendar of your home page.

To edit or delete a milestone, click the Tasks & Milestones tab on the Zoho Projects home page, click the Upcoming Milestones tab, and hover your mouse over the name of the milestone you want to edit or delete. A pencil icon and a red X icon will appear to the left of the milestone name. To edit the milestone, click the pencil icon. To delete the milestone, click the red X.

Figure 10-15
A new
milestone.

Using Your People Skills: Managing Your Users

There are all kinds of considerations when it comes to managing people. Fortunately, though, managing people in Zoho Projects is pretty easy.

For example, you can change their roles (contractor, employee, or manager), add new users, delete users (that is, delete them from the project, not delete them in real life, no matter how much we might want to sometimes), and e-mail users.

Changing roles

As I mention earlier, the Zoho Project roles you can assign are contractor, employee, and manager. (Read about this in the earlier section, "Adding users.") Although people don't often jump between roles like those in real life, if that happens, you can easily make the change in Zoho Projects.

Interestingly, this is the only change you can make to users in a project besides deleting them (and, of course, adding or removing them from tasks). As you'd expect, you can't edit other people's profiles although you can edit your own.

To change a user's role, follow these steps:

1. **Click the Users tab on your project's home page.**

2. **Find the user you want.**

3. **Click the pencil icon at the upper right in their box.**

4. **From the drop-down list box appears, select the new role.**

5. **Click the Update button that appears.**

If you click the pencil icon in your own box, your profile will open, and you can make edits there, rather than in the drop-down Role box that appears.

Adding a new user

I discuss how to add a user in the earlier section, "Adding users."

Deleting a user

Life changes, and your team might change as well. Members are called to work on other projects, or perhaps they quit. You can remove users from the project with a simple click.

Removing a user from a project is similar to adding a user. On the Users tab (on the Zoho Projects home page), click the red X in the box belonging to the user you want to remove from the project. When Zoho Projects prompts you, confirm the removal by clicking OK in the dialog box that opens.

E-mailing a project's users

Keeping in touch with your team members is essential to any project, and you can do that with Zoho Projects, which allows you to e-mail one or all of your project's team members.

To send e-mail to team members, follow these steps:

1. **From your Zoho Projects home page, click the Users tab.**

2. **Click the Send Message link.**

3. **Enter the e-mail's subject in the Subject field that appears, and then enter the e-mail's body in the Message field.**

4. **Select the members to e-mail from the To list.**

To select multiple members, hold the Ctrl key while you click their user IDs in the To field. To select a range of members to e-mail, click the first member in the range, move the mouse to the last member in the range, press Shift, and then click the last member.

5. **Click the Send Message button to send the e-mail.**

Some Face Time: Setting Up Meetings with Zoho Projects

As any team member knows, meetings are a necessity for any project. You can schedule meetings among your project members easily with Zoho Projects. Here's how:

1. **From your Zoho Projects home page, click the Meetings tab.**

2. **Click the New Meeting link to open the page shown in Figure 10-16.**

Figure 10-16: Creating a new meeting.

3. **Enter the meeting name and then the meeting date and time.**

4. **Click the Advanced Options link to enter the meeting location and duration.**

5. **Select a reminder time for your meeting participants from the Remind All list.**

    The default reminder time is On Time, but you can select times from 15 minutes to one day before the meeting.

6. **(Optional) If you want to repeat the meeting, select a repetition frequency from the Repeat drop-down list.**

    If you select a repeat time, you can also select a number of times to repeat the meeting from the End After drop-down list.

7. **Select the project members you want to attend the meeting from the Project Members list. Click the right-arrow button to move the selected members to the Meeting Participants list.**

8. **Click the Schedule Meeting button.**

   The new meeting appears in the Meetings tab's Upcoming Meetings tab, and it also appears in the Week Ahead calendar on your project's home page, as shown in Figure 10-17.

Figure 10-17:
Meetings
show on the
calendar.

Meeting

Each meeting participant will get an immediate e-mail like this:

   Dear Participants,

   Team meeting notification

   Meeting Title - Strategy Meeting

   Meeting Scheduled On - 03-18-2009 11:00 AM

   Meeting Scheduled/Organized By - sholzner

And, if you selected a reminder time, the meeting participants also get an e-mail at that time as well.

Getting a Long-Term Overview with the Built-in Calendar

Zoho Projects is good at giving you reminders of today's events, and even giving you a picture of the week ahead on your home page. But what if you need a longer view?

A longer time frame is often necessary to plan your project successfully. You might not be able to execute a task on the day it's scheduled, or you may need some time to prepare, for example. How about getting a bird's-eye view of the tasks, milestones, and meetings in your project?

You can do that with the project calendar, which you reach by clicking the Calendar tab on the project's home page. The calendar appears, as shown in Figure 10-18.

New meeting

New Task   Filter by user.   Filter by event.

Figure 10-18:
The Zoho
Projects
calendar.

New Milestone

The days of the month that have already elapsed are shaded in light yellow, and tasks, meetings, and milestones are all marked on the calendar. The calendar is the tab to check to keep track of your project in the longer term.

To view last month's calendar, or next month's, just click the arrows that appear on either side of the name of the month, at the top of the calendar. (Other months are available too, of course — just keep clicking the arrow.)

You can also click any item, milestone, task, or meeting to open that item.

Filtering the Calendar view

If you're in charge of a big project, there might be more meetings, milestones, and tasks than you can handle in the calendar. To simplify things, you can filter your calendar by user and by event.

Filtering by user

You can filter the calendar so that only items connected with a specific user appear. This gives you a snapshot of how your project appears to a particular team member, which is a valuable way of looking at things in management terms as well as simplifying what you see in the calendar.

To see the calendar for a single user only, start on the Calendar tab of the Zoho Projects home page. Then follow these steps:

1. **Click the drop-down list box that appears to the right of the month name at the top of the calendar (refer to Figure 10-18).**

   The drop-down list displays the names of all the project members.

2. **Select the project member that you want to filter the calendar on.**

   The calendar displays only the tasks, meetings, and milestones for that member.

Filtering by event type

When it first appears, the calendar shows all meetings, tasks, and milestones. Because that might well be too much information to absorb at one time, you can filter the calendar by type of event.

To filter the calendar to show just meetings, tasks, or milestones, click the link you want at the top of the calendar (refer to Figure 10-18). You can display all meetings, tasks, and milestones; or only one type of event.

Creating events from the calendar

When you're looking at the overview you get from the calendar, you might see that a certain day is perfect for a meeting. Or that a particular task should be scheduled on a given day.

Zoho Projects makes your job easier because you can add tasks, milestones, and meetings directly from the calendar. Being able to add new events directly from the calendar is a very powerful asset of Zoho Projects because you can fit events into your calendar while getting an idea of where they fit into the whole overview.

From the Calendar tab, hover the mouse over the day to which you want to add a task, milestone, or meeting. Click any of the three buttons that appear in the day's box in the calendar (refer to Figure 10-18):

✓ New Task

✓ New Milestone

✓ New Meeting

A new page opens to schedule the corresponding event (with the day already filled in).

Keeping Track of Time

Setting up tasks, milestones, and meetings is all very well, but if you're a project manager, you also have to keep track of where team members' time is going. For example, say you have a budget and you enlisted contractors to help you get your project done. If you've used up nearly your whole budget but are less than halfway through the project, you're in trouble. Thus, you need to keep track of how much time the members of your team are using. After you get an idea where the time is going, you can readjust your team's goals and emphasis to match your resources.

You keep track of time in Zoho Projects with the Timesheet. The Timesheet is a shared resource. All project members have access to it, and they can all log their time in it. Access the Timesheet from your project's home page (the Timesheet tab).

Project members can keep track of their time with the Timesheet by manually logging time spent or by letting Project do it for them.

Logging time with the Timesheet

Project members can log their time manually — recording it on the Timesheet — with a few simple clicks.

To log time for a particular day, follow these steps. Start on the Timesheet tab, which you access from the Zoho Projects home page:

1. **Click the Log Time button, opening the dialog box you see in Figure 10-19.**

2. **Enter the date of the time you want to log.**

3. **Select the task you're logging time for.**

4. **Enter the number of hours you wish to log.**

5. **(Optional) Enter any notes to explain your log entry.**

6. **Select Billable or Non-billable from the Billing Status drop-down list.**

7. **Click the Add to Timesheet button.**

   Log Time closes, and the newly logged time is added to the Timesheet.

Hover the mouse over a day in the Timesheet, and a button appears at the upper left. Click that button (which has a clock on it) to open Log Time, with the current date selected.

Figure 10-19:
Log time
on the
Timesheet.

Logging time with the Projects timer

Zoho Projects also has a built-in timer that lets you click a clock icon to start and stop logging time when you work on a task.

To log time using the clock icon, follow these steps:

1. **From your Zoho Projects home page, click the Tasks & Milestones tab.**

2. **Hover the mouse over the task you want to start working on.**

   A green clock icon appears to the left of the task name.

3. **Click the green clock icon to start logging time.**

   The green clock icon turns red.

4. **Click the red clock icon to stop logging time on the task.**

   The red clock icon turns green.

Having Your Say Using Zoho Projects Forums

Keeping in touch with your project's members is essential to the success of projects, and Zoho Projects is up to the task. For example, your schedule may have changed, and you need to bring everyone up to date. Or you might want to share the results of a task with project members.

Zoho Projects supports a project forum that allows you put up posts, to which people can comment.

Creating a forum post

Creating a new post on the Zoho Projects forum is simple. Just follow these steps:

1. **From your Zoho Projects home page, click the Forums tab.**

2. **Click the New Forum Post button.**

   A post dialog box opens, as shown in Figure 10-20.

Figure 10-20:
Create a
new forum
post here.

3. **Enter the title of your post.**

4. **Enter the text (content) of your new post.**

5. **Select a category for your post.**

6. **Click the Attach link to add an attachment to your post.**

7. **(Optional) If you want to notify project members of the new post, select their usernames from the Notify This Post To list.**

8. **Click the Submit button to post your message.**

   Your new post appears on the Forums tab, as shown in Figure 10-21.

Figure 10-21:
A new
forum post.

Adding a comment to a post

In addition to posting, project members can add comments to posts as well. Just as you do when creating a post, start on the Forums tab of the Zoho Projects home page.

1. **Click the Add a Comment link under the post to which you want to add a comment.**

   This opens the comment dialog box you see in Figure 10-22.

2. **Enter your comment.**

3. **(Optional) If you want to attach a document, click the Attach link and navigate to the document in the dialog box that appears.**

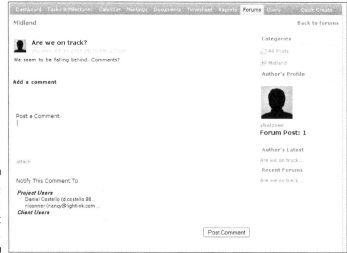

Figure 10-22: Add a comment to a post.

4. **(Optional) Send notification of the new comment to any project members.**

5. **Click the Post Comment button.**

Generating Reports

Zoho Projects has a built-in way of keeping track of the overall progress of your project, task by task, with reports. Reports are generated as *Gantt charts* that show various events as horizontal bars on a timeline. (A Gantt chart displays a bar chart of a project's schedule.) You can chart tasks or milestones.

Zoho Projects creates reports automatically. To see the reports it prepared for your project, follow these steps:

1. **From your Zoho Projects home page, click the Reports tab.**
2. **To see various reports for your project, click one of the links:**
   - *Task - Graph View:* Shows a Gantt chart for the tasks in your project
   - *Task - List View:* Shows a table of charts and times for the tasks your project
   - *Milestone Report:* Shows a Gantt chart for your milestones

Working with Documents

Sharing documents with the members of your project can be useful. You might have a memo from your boss that the other members of your team need to see, for example. You can post any documents that you can upload with your browser.

To post a new document to Zoho Projects where the project members can get at it, follow these steps:

1. **From your Zoho Projects home page, click the Documents tab.**
2. **Click the Upload New File link.**

   This opens the dialog box you see in Figure 10-23.
3. **Select the file you want to upload: Click the Browse button, navigate to the file, select it, and click Open.**
4. **(Optional) Add a comment about the file.**
5. **Add any tags you want to associate with the file.**

   Tags let you associate keywords with an item, in this case, a file. Tags make it easier to search for items by keyword.

6. **Select the folder to upload the new file from the Select Folder drop-down list.**

   By default, the current project's folder is selected.
7. **(Optional) If you want to notify any project members of the new upload, select them from the Notify This Document To list.**

Figure 10-23:
Upload
a project
document to
share.

8. Click the Upload File button.

Zoho Projects uploads your file and displays a link to it on the Documents tab, as you see in Figure 10-24.

You can also create new Zoho Writer or Sheet documents by clicking the New Document or New Spreadsheet button on the Documents tab.

Figure 10-24:
Find shared
project
documents
here.

Chapter 11

Zoho Invoice: Billing Your Customers

In This Chapter

▸ Configuring Zoho Invoice

▸ Setting your company profile

▸ Setting your currency type, time zone, and tax information

▸ Adding and deleting customers and contacts

▸ Managing and adding inventory

▸ Selecting a payment gateway

▸ Creating and sending invoices

*I*f you have a small business and have to bill your customers, Zoho Invoice is for you because you can use it to manage setting up and billing customers. You can use Invoice to track what's due and what's been received. You can follow the whole invoice lifecycle, from creating invoices to sending them to getting paid. You can even automate recurring invoices.

Of course, getting paid is one of the most satisfying parts of any business, and Zoho Invoice is there to make the process easier. If you need to invoice your customers, you can easily lose track unless you have a clear-cut plan. Zoho Invoice gives you that plan. Zoho CRM (discussed in the next chapter) handles all customer relations needs, from tracking down leads to setting up ad campaigns — and it also lets you create invoices. But if all you want to do is invoice your customers, Zoho Invoice is far simpler.

So read on for all this and more, including how to customize Zoho Invoice.

Getting Started with Zoho Invoice

To start with Zoho Invoice, navigate your browser to `http://invoice.zoho.com` and sign in with your Zoho username and password. (To find out how to get a Zoho username and password, see Chapter 1.) When you do, you get a confirmation e-mail from a Zoho customer service rep.

When you sign in for the first time, Invoice displays a Quick Setup page that asks you for your time zone, currency type, company name, and, optionally, your company's address. Enter that information and click the Start Invoice button.

Next, the Zoho Invoice Welcome page appears, as shown in Figure 11-1.

Click to edit a profile.

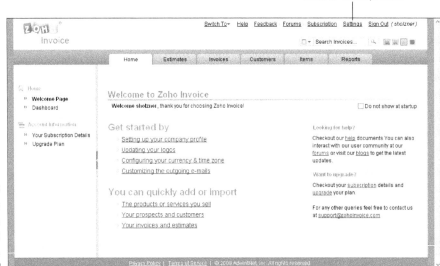

Figure 11-1:
Start here
in Zoho
Invoice.

The Welcome page tells you the steps you need to get started with Zoho Invoice. Here, you can do basic tasks, such as setting up your company profile, configuring your currency and time zone, and customizing outgoing e-mails. You can also quickly add or import products or services you sell, your prospects and customers, and invoices and estimates.

After you use Zoho Invoice for a while, you probably won't want to see the Welcome page anymore. Just select the Do Not Show at Startup check box.

Although you can use Zoho Invoice gratis, you must pony up monthly for more advanced packages, as detailed in Table 11-1. In a nutshell, the difference between the pricing plans is how many invoices/estimates per month you are allowed. Other than this, the only difference is that the free version doesn't offer unbranded e-mails (e-mails without the Zoho logo). The other Invoice features — such as number of customers, template availability, multicurrency support, customer support, and SSL encryption — are standard between packages.

Table 11-1	Zoho Invoice Pricing Plans	
Package	*Monthly Fee*	*Invoices/Estimates per Month*
Elite	$35	1,500
Premium	$25	500
Standard	$15	150
Basic	$8	25
Free	Um, free	5

Setting up your company profile

A good thing to do when setting up Zoho Invoice is to customize your company profile. Your company profile contains information about your company; that information will appear, well formatted, on your invoices.

To customize your company's profile, click the Setting Up Your Company Profile link on the Welcome page. (Refer to Figure 11-1.) Doing so opens the Company Profile page you see in Figure 11-2.

Then follow these steps:

1. **Enter your company name and industry.**

2. **Enter when your fiscal year starts.**

3. **Enter your mailing information, including street address, city, state or province, zip or postal code, and country.**

4. **Enter information about the contact person for your company, including that person's Zoho ID, phone and fax numbers, e-mail address, and Web site URL.**

5. **(Optional) If you have additional information you want to record about your company, scroll down to the Custom Fields section.**

   For example, you might have a VAT ID you want to record that must appear on your invoices, or a government tracking number.

   a. *Enter the label of each additional piece of information (for example, VAT ID) in a Label box.*

   b. *Enter the value of each additional piece of information in a Value box.*

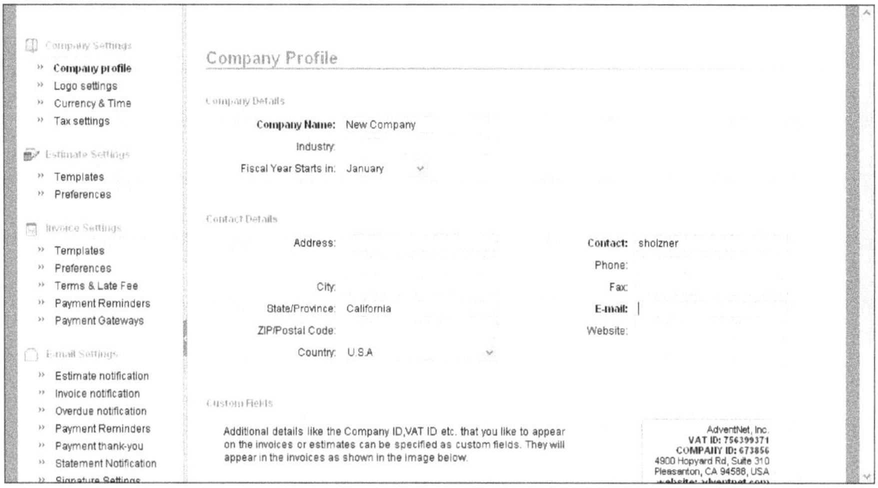

Company Profile

Company Details

Company Name: New Company
Industry:
Fiscal Year Starts in: January

Contact Details

Address: Contact: sholzner
                                Phone:
City: Fax:
State/Province: California   E-mail:
ZIP/Postal Code: Website:
Country: U.S.A

Custom Fields

Additional details like the Company ID,VAT ID etc. that you like to appear on the invoices or estimates can be specified as custom fields. They will appear in the invoices as shown in the image below.

AdventNet, Inc.
VAT ID: 756399371
COMPANY ID: 673856
4900 Hopyard Rd, Suite 310
Pleasanton, CA 94588, USA

Figure 11-2:
Set your
company
profile here.

6. **Click Save to save your company's profile, or click the Save & Next button to open the Logo Settings page, which I discuss in the following section.**

Your company profile is saved. The new profile appears, with all the fields filled in.

You can edit your company's profile at any time. Just click the Setting Up Your Company Profile link again from the Welcome page, or click the Settings link (upper right) on any Zoho Invoice page.

Adding your company logo

Another way to customize an invoice is to add your company logo to Zoho Invoice. There are actually two logos that you need to set: the system logo and the invoice logo.

- **System logo:** This logo appears at the upper left on all Zoho Invoice pages. It's an entirely online thing. Zoho Invoice prefers a file size of 140px (pixels) x 60px at 72 dpi. The maximum file size is 1MB.

- **Invoice logo:** This logo appears at the upper left in all your actual invoices. It's what the customer sees. Zoho Invoice prefers a file size of 580px x 250px at 300 dpi. The maximum file size is 1MB.

You can provide logo files in JPG, GIF, PNG, or BMP format. Zoho Invoice will size the image to fit.

To set your company's logos, follow these steps. (Remember that you need to upload two logos.)

1. **From the Welcome page, click the Updating Your Logos link to open the Logo Settings page you see in Figure 11-3.**

   Alternatively, click the Settings link on any Zoho Invoice page. Then click the Currency & Time link in the left-hand pane.

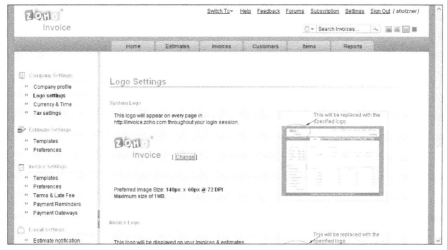

Figure 11-3: Add logos here.

2. **Click the Change link in the System Logo area.**

   A text box and a Browse button appear.

3. **Click the Browse button, opening the File Upload dialog box.**

4. **Navigate to the image file you want to upload, select it, and then click the Open button.**

   The File Upload dialog box closes, and your filename and path appear in the text box.

5. **Repeat Steps 2–4 but click the Change link in the Invoice Logo area.**

6. **Click the Next button to finish adding your logos.**

   Zoho takes you to the Currency and Time Zone page, which is discussed in the following section.

Setting your currency and time zone

Invoices are all about money, so it shouldn't come as a surprise that Zoho Invoice wants to know what currency you're using in your invoices. And as far as dates and times on your invoices go, Zoho Invoice wants to know what your time zone is.

Those items are easy to set. Just follow these steps:

1. **From the Welcome page, click the Configuring Your Currency & Time Zone link to open the Currency and Time Zone page you see in Figure 11-4.**

   Alternatively, click the Settings link on any Zoho Invoice page. Then click the Currency & Time link in the left-hand pane.

Figure 11-4: The Currency and Time Zone page.

2. **Select your currency from the Currency Code drop-down list.**

3. **Confirm that the currency symbol is correct for your currency.**

4. **If you don't like the currency format that Zoho Invoice selected, select a different one.**

5. **Select your time zone.**

6. **Select the date format that you prefer.**

7. **Click Save to save your settings or click the Save & Next button to move to the Tax Settings page.**

Specifying tax information

No one likes paying taxes, but they're a fact of life. It's important to include sales taxes on your invoices, if they apply.

To set up sales tax on the Tax Settings page, follow these steps:

1. **Click the Settings link on any Zoho Invoice page. Then click the Tax Settings link in the left-hand pane.**

   The Tax Settings page appears, as shown in Figure 11-5.

Figure 11-5:
The Tax
Settings
page.

2. **Specify your tax ID.**

3. **Specify a tax percentage.**

4. **Specify what the tax should be applied to: the billing amount (ItemAmount) or the billing amount plus the tax (ItemAmount + 1).**

5. **Repeat Steps 2–4 for up to three taxes (for example, federal, state, and local).**

6. **Click Save to save the tax information, or click the Save & Next button to save the tax information and go on to the templates for the estimates.**

Telling Zoho Invoice About Your Customers

Before you can send invoices to your customers, you have to give Zoho Invoice the details about those customers. Start by adding all your customers to Zoho Invoice, which keeps track of them and helps you create invoices with ease.

Zoho Invoice makes a distinction between *customers* and *clients:*

✔ **Customer:** A business that buys from you

✔ **Contact:** A person in a company that you can actually talk to

Manually adding customers

To add a customer to Invoice, follow these steps:

1. **Click the Customers tab on any Zoho Invoice page, which opens the Active Customers page that you see in Figure 11-6.**

Figure 11-6: The Active Customers page.

2. **Click the New Customer button, opening the Add New Customer page you see in Figure 11-7.**

3. **Enter the customer name.**

4. **Select the payment terms.**

   Payment terms are the number of days before the invoice payment is due. The options are

   - Net 15 (days)
   - Net 30 (days)
   - Net 45 (days)
   - Net 60 (days)
   - Due on receipt

5. **Select the customer's currency code.**

Figure 11-7:
The Add
New
Customer
page.

Add New Customer

Customer Name |

Payments Terms   Net15   ∨

Currency Code   USD - US Dollar   ∨

Contact Details [Add New Contact]

	First Name	Last Name	E-mail	Office Phone	Mobile
None ∨					
None ∨					
None ∨					

Address (Billing)   Address (Shipping)   ☑ Same as billing address.

6. **Enter the Contact Details for your contact at the company.**

   The options are

   - *Salutation:* Dr, Mr, Mrs, Miss, and Ms
   - *First name*
   - *Surname*
   - *E-mail address*
   - *Office phone number*
   - *Mobile phone number*

7. **Repeat Step 6 for up to three contacts at the customer's company.**

8. **Enter the customer's billing information:**

   - Address
   - City
   - State/province
   - Zip/postal code
   - Country
   - Fax

9. **Enter the customer's shipping information:**

   - Address
   - City
   - State/province
   - Zip/postal code
   - Country
   - Fax

If all the shipping information is the same as billing information, select the Same as Billing Address check box.

10. **(Optional) If you have any customer information that you want to appear on estimates and invoices, such as VAT IDs, add a label for the custom field in the Label field.**

11. **(Optional) If you have a value for a custom field, enter it in the Value field.**

12. **Repeat Steps 10 and 11 for up to three custom fields.**

13. **(Optional) Add any notes you want to associate with this customer in the Notes box.**

14. **Click the Save Customer button.**

    Zoho Invoice displays a Customer Details page for the new customer, as you can see in Figure 11-8.

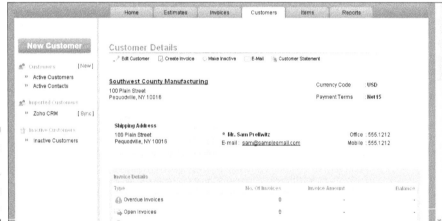

Figure 11-8:
The Customer Details page.

If you click the link to that customer, the Customer Details page opens for that customer (refer to Figure 11-8).

The next time you click the Customers tab, you see an overview of the new, active customer, as shown in Figure 11-9.

Importing customers

You don't need to go through the rigmarole of adding new customers manually. If you have your customers' details in a spreadsheet or table, you can import those details directly.

Import customers from here.

Figure 11-9:
The new
customer
on the
Customers
tab.

Your spreadsheet has to be formatted so that each cell has the label that Zoho Invoice expects for that field (matching what you see in the Add New Customer page), like this:

Customer Name	*Southwest County Manufacturing*
Payments Terms	Net12
Currency Code	USD - US Dollar
First Name	Sam
Last Name	Prellwitz
E-mail	sam@sampleemail.com
Office Phone	555-1212
Mobile	555-1212
Address	100 Plain Street

You can import your data in two formats:

- ✔ **CSV:** Comma-separated values
- ✔ **TSV:** Tab-separated values

To import customers in either format, simply follow these steps:

1. **Save your customer information spreadsheet in CSV or TSV format.**
2. **Click the Customers tab on any Zoho Invoice page.**
3. **Click the Import Customers link. (Refer to Figure 11-9.)**

4. **On the Import Customers page, click the Import link next to either the CSV or the TSV entry, as appropriate.**

5. **Click the Browse button.**

6. **Navigate to your CSV or TSV file using the Upload File dialog box that appears.**

7. **Select the file to upload and then click Open.**

   The File Upload dialog box closes, and Zoho Invoice automatically imports the file you selected.

You can also import customers from Zoho CRM (Customer Relationship Management; see Chapter 12). To do that, follow these steps:

1. **Click the Customers tab on any Zoho Invoice page.**

2. **Click the Import Customers link.**

3. **On the Import Customers page, click the Import from Zoho CRM link.**

4. **Enter your Zoho CRM username.**

5. **Enter your Zoho CTM API key.**

   To get your API Key, sign in to Zoho CRM with administrative privileges, choose Setup⇨Request API Key, and follow the instructions there.

6. **Click the Save & Import button.**

Importing contacts

Just like you can import customers, you can import contacts as well. For example, if a contact sends you an e-mail with a vCard attachment, you can import that card directly into your contacts.

You can import contacts in four formats:

- ✔ **CSV (Comma Separated Value):** CSV format
- ✔ **TSV (Tab Separated Value):** TSV format
- ✔ **vCard:** VCF format
- ✔ **Outlook Express CSV:** CSV format

To import a contact, follow these steps:

1. **Click the Customers tab on any Zoho Invoice page.**

2. **Click the Active Contacts link in the left-hand pane.**

3. **Click the Import Contacts link.**

   You can also access the Import Contacts link from the Customer Details page; click the Edit Customers link and then click the Import Contacts link.

4. **On the Import Contacts page (see Figure 11-10), click the Import link next to the format of the data you want to import.**

5. **Click the Browse button that appears.**

6. **In the File Upload dialog box that opens, browse to the file you want to upload, select it, and click Open.**

   The File Upload dialog box closes, and Zoho Invoice uploads your file and imports the contacts immediately.

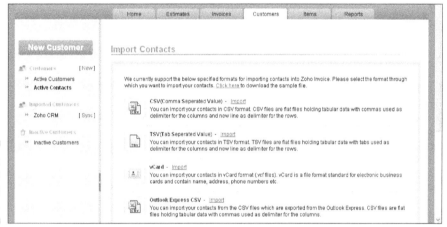

Figure 11-10: The Import Contacts page.

You can also export your contacts (for example, suppose that someone in the shipping department needs them). Just click the Export Contacts link at the top of the Edit Customers page.

Editing customers and contacts

Things change, and so do customers and contacts.

For example, a customer might move to a new address. Or your contact might move to a new department. In either case, you need to edit the customer's details.

Editing a customer's details is a snap; just follow these steps:

1. **Click the Customers tab on any Zoho Invoice page.**

2. **On the Active Customers page that opens, click the name of the customer whose details you want to edit.**

3. **On the Customer Details page that opens (refer to Figure 11-8), click the Edit Customer link at the upper left.**

   You can also click the pencil icon in the customer's entry that appears on the Active Customers page that opens when you first click the Customers tab.

4. **Make the edits you want to the customer's details.**

5. **Click the Save Customer button.**

Deactivating and reactivating customers

At some point, you might lose a customer. Perhaps the company goes out of business. In that case, you might have to make that customer's record inactive in Invoice.

It's simple to deactivate customers. When you make a customer inactive, they are moved to the Inactive Customers folder.

To deactivate a customer, start on the Active Customers page. There, select the check box(es) next to the customer(s) you want to make inactive and then click the Make Inactive button.

Zoho Invoice moves the customer(s) to the Inactive Customers folder. To make an inactive customer active again, select the check box to the left of the inactive customer in the Inactive Customers folder and then click the Make Active button.

Deleting contacts

You can also delete contacts. Just follow these steps:

1. **Click the Customers tab on any Zoho Invoice page.**

2. **On the Active Customers page that opens, click the Active Contacts link in the left-hand pane.**

3. **On the Active Contacts page that appears, click the pencil icon in the entry of the contact you want to edit.**

4. **On the Customer Details page that opens, click the red X icon to the left of the contact you want to delete.**

Zoho Invoice deletes the contact immediately.

When you delete a contact, Invoice doesn't display a dialog box asking for confirmation: It just deletes the contact immediately.

5. **Click the Save Customer button.**

Creating Your Inventory

Before you can send out estimates or invoices, you have to tell Invoice about the items you sell. Those items can be either goods or services — it makes no difference to Invoice.

Setting up new items in your inventory isn't hard. Just follow these steps:

1. **In Zoho Invoice, click the Items tab.**

2. **Click the New Item button.**

3. **On the Add New Item page that opens (as shown in Figure 11-11), enter a name for the item.**

Figure 11-11: The Add New Item page.

4. **(Optional) Enter a description for the item.**

5. **Enter a rate (price per item) for the item in the currency you already selected when you first signed in to Zoho Invoice.**

6. **Select up to two taxes that apply to the item.**

7. **Click the Save Item button.**

The form is cleared in preparation for more new items.

8. **After you finish entering new items, click the Close button.**

The new item is displayed on the Items tab, as shown in Figure 11-12.

Figure 11-12:
A new item
on the
Items tab.

Getting Paid: Selecting a Payment Gateway

After you set up your inventory, you can also set up your *payment gateway* — that is, the folks who will handle your payments, such as PayPal.

Zoho Invoice can include a link in any estimates or invoices you mail to customers. If you include such a link, your customers can pay online simply by clicking the link.

Currently, Invoice lets you insert an online payment link for these payment services:

✔ PayPal (www.paypal.com)

✔ Google Checkout (http://checkout.google.com)

✔ Authorize.Net (www.authorize.net)

To have Invoice add an online payment link to any of these services, just follow these steps:

1. **In Zoho Invoice, click the Settings link (at the upper right).**

2. **In the left-hand pane, click the Payment Gateways link.**

   This opens the Online Payment Settings page you see in Figure 11-13.

3. **Enter the appropriate information for any payment gateways that apply:**

- *For PayPal:* PayPal E-mail ID and (optionally) Page Style
- *For Google Checkout:* Merchant ID and Merchant Key
- *For Authorize.Net:* API LoginID and Transaction Key

4. **Click Save.**

Zoho Invoice inserts an online payment link in your e-mails.

Customizing Your E-mail Notifications

Zoho Invoice sends out e-mail notifications of your new estimates and invoices, and you can customize the e-mails it sends. Invoice also lets you send out other types of e-mail, such as reminders and general messages.

Invoice provides you with a template for its e-mail notifications. In the template, the fields that will be filled when the e-mail is sent are surrounded by percent signs (%), such as %LastName% for a contact's last name.

Here's what the e-mail notification template looks like for an estimate:

Hi %FirstName% %LastName%,

Thanks for your interest in our services. We are pleased to attach our price quote with this e-mail.

Feel free to give us a call at %CompanyPhone% or e-mail <a href=" mailto:%CompanyEmail% ">%CompanyEmail% </a> for any clarification.

Assuring you of our best services at all times.

And here's what the e-mail notification template looks like for invoices:

Hi %FirstName% %LastName%,

Thanks for using our services. Attached is the invoice for the P.O.# %P.O.Number%. Please forward it to the relevant person to process the payment.

To make a payment online, click on the following link - %PayPalLink%.

Feel free to give us a call at %CompanyPhone% or e-mail <a href=" mailto:%CompanyEmail% ">%CompanyEmail% </a> for any clarification.

Assuring you of our best services at all times.

You can also send a payment-received notice. Read how in the upcoming section, "Happy Days Are Here Again: Marking an Invoice as Paid."

Editing these templates is easy. Just follow these steps:

1. **In Zoho Invoice, click the Settings link.**

2. **In the left-hand pane, click the Estimate Notification link or the Invoice Notification link, depending on which e-mail template you want to customize.**

   This opens the Estimate Notification page or the Invoice Notification page, respectively.

3. **Edit the e-mail or invoice template.**

4. **Click Save.**

Getting New Business: Creating and Sending Estimates

After you set up your customers and your inventory, it's time to send some estimates.

To get new business, send out estimates that outline what the customer will pay for your products or services.

To create and send a new estimate, here's all you do:

1. **In Zoho Invoice, click the Estimates tab.**

2. **Click the New Estimate button.**

   This opens the Add New Estimate page, shown in Figure 11-14.

Figure 11-14:
The Add
New
Estimate
page.

3. Select the customer.

See the round plus button in Figure 11-14? Click it to add a new customer if you want.

4. Select a template.

- *Service Templates:* Classic, Modern, Plain, Professional
- *Product Templates:* Classic, Modern, Plain, Professional
- *Fixed Price Templates:* Classic, Modern, Plain, Professional

5. (Optional) Select a currency and an exchange rate.

6. Enter a unique estimate number for the estimate.

The auto-generate option creates an estimate number for you.

7. (Optional) Enter a reference number for the estimate.

The *reference number* might be your internal tracking number for the customer or account, for example.

8. (Optional) Change the estimate date from today's date to a more correct value.

For example, you might be creating an estimate for anticipated future prices and want to date the estimate in the future to distinguish it from other estimates.

9. Select an item from your inventory.

10. Select the quantity of the item.

11. Change the rate if you don't want to use the rate stored with the item in your inventory.

12. (Optional) Enter a discount for the item.

13. (Optional) Select up to two taxes to apply to the item.

14. **If you want to add another item, click the Add New Item link and repeat Steps 9–13.**

15. **(Optional) Enter notes in the Customer Notes section.**

16. **(Optional) Enter terms and conditions in the Terms & Conditions box.**

17. **Save the estimate (click Save), send it (click Send), or print it (click Print).**

Zoho Invoice displays an Estimate Details page, as you see in Figure 11-15, with a summary of your estimate.

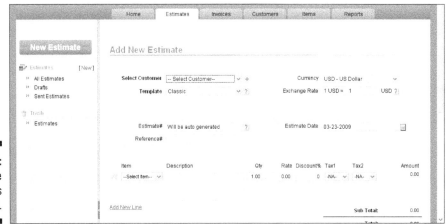

Figure 11-15: An Estimate Details page.

When you send your estimate, it's sent (as an attached PDF file) to the customer's contact that you added when you created the customer's record.

You can see what the PDF file looks like in Figure 11-16.

Figure 11-16: A new estimate.

The Payoff: Creating and Sending Invoices

At last, it's time to send your invoice. You sold your goods or services to the customer, and it's time to bill them.

To create and send a new invoice, just follow these steps:

1. **In Zoho Invoice, click the Invoices tab.**

2. **Click the New Invoice button.**

3. **On the Add New Invoice page, select the customer.**

4. **Select a template:**
   - *Service Templates:* Classic, Modern, Plain, Professional
   - *Product Templates:* Classic, Modern, Plain, Professional
   - *Fixed Price Templates:* Classic, Modern, Plain, Professional

5. **(Optional) Select a currency and exchange rate.**

6. **Select an invoice date.**

7. **Select the invoice terms (such as due on receipt).**

8. **Enter the due date of the invoice.**

9. **Enter a unique invoice number for the invoice.**

10. **(Optional) Enter a PO (purchase order) number.**

11. **(Optional) Select a late fee.**

12. **Select an item from your inventory.**

13. **Select the quantity of the item.**

14. **Change the rate if you don't want to use the rate stored with the item in your inventory.**

15. **(Optional) Enter a discount for the item.**

16. **(Optional) Select up to two taxes to apply to the item.**

17. **If you want to add another item, click the Add New Item link and repeat Steps 12–16.**

18. **(Optional) Enter notes in the Customer Notes section.**

19. **(Optional) Enter terms and conditions in the Terms & Conditions box.**

20. **Save the invoice, send it, or print it.**

    Zoho Invoice displays an Invoice Details page.

    When you send your invoice, it's sent to the customer's contact that you added when you created the customer's record as an attached PDF file.

You can see what the PDF file looks like in Figure 11-17.

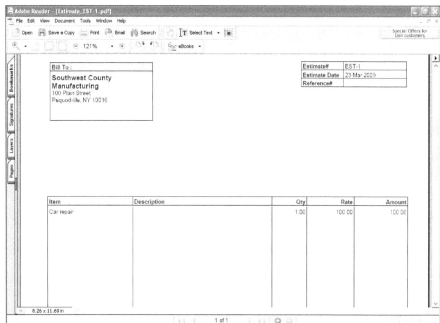

Figure 11-17:
A new
invoice.

Happy Days Are Here Again: Marking an Invoice as Paid

The final step in handling an invoice is to mark it as paid.

You can mark an invoice as paid in Zoho Invoice by following these steps:

1. **On the Invoices tab of Zoho Invoice, click the Add Payment for This Invoice icon.**

    This icon is at the right in the entry for the invoice.

    This opens the Add Payment page, as you can see in Figure 11-18.

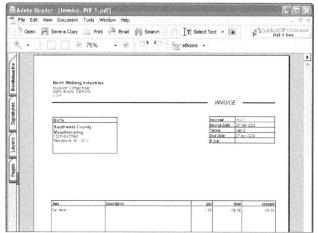

Figure 11-18:
The Add
Payment
page.

2. **Enter the date the payment was received.**

3. **Enter the amount received.**

4. **Select the payment method in the Mode box.**

5. **(Optional) Add a description for the payment.**

6. **(Optional) If you want to acknowledge payment, select the Send Payment Acknowledgement E-mail check box.**

7. **Click the Save Payment button.**

If you decide to send an e-mail acknowledgment of the payment, your contact(s) at the customer's company will receive an e-mail something like this one:

> Hi Sam Prellwitz,
>
> We have received your payment of $100.00 against our invoice INV-1 dated 23 Mar 2009.
>
> Thanks
>
> Invoice Team
>
> North Midland Industries
>
> Email: sholzner@zoho.com

If you have an overdue invoice, click the Overdue Invoices link at the left in Zoho Invoice (on the Invoices tab) and then click the invoice you're concerned about from the list that appears. Zoho Invoice lets you send a reminder with the Send button.

Chapter 12

Zoho CRM: Managing Your Customers

In This Chapter

▷ Selecting the plan right for you

▷ Setting up and customizing Zoho CRM

▷ Adding and managing users

▷ Creating profiles

▷ Working with Zoho CRM modules

▷ Creating, editing, and deleting records

▷ Creating custom views

*W*hen you're involved in business, keeping your customers happy is critical to your success. And that's what Zoho CRM (Customer Relationship Management) is all about. With Zoho CRM, you can automate the whole sales process from getting leads to closing the sale. It's a complete sales and marketing tool.

Using Zoho CRM gives you these advantages:

✔ **Sales and marketing:** Coordinate sales and marketing by connecting sales with ad campaigns, lead monitoring, sales forecasts, and more.

✔ **Customer support:** Zoho CRM supports handling of cases and solutions to help you handle customer service with ease.

✔ **Inventory management:** Monitor your products with a complete inventory management system.

✔ **Role-based security:** Control access to data by user roles.

✔ **Reports:** Track sales and marketing trends with built-in reports and interactive dashboards.

Choosing the Right CRM Edition

Zoho CRM is record-oriented, allowing you to enter sales leads, track customers, as well as track inventory. Three plans are available for Zoho CRM, giving you different levels of customer relationship–management power. Here are the three editions, each of which offers different levels of tools (see the Zoho CRM page for more details):

- ✔ **Free Edition:** You get salesforce and marketing automation, inventory management, a calendar, reports, a dashboard, batch importing of up to 1,500 records, and up to 100MB of disk space. This edition is free for three users.

- ✔ **Professional Edition:** Includes all the features that the Free Edition contains, plus disk space of 250MB, batch importing of up to 10,000 records, e-mail marketing, Web forms to handle data, and more. Cost is $12 per user per month.

- ✔ **Enterprise Edition:** This edition offers all that the Professional Edition gives you, plus 500MB of disk space, batch importing of up to 20,000 records, and additional tools. Cost is $25 per user per month.

You can see a comparison of the three plans at `www.zoho.com/crm/zohocrm-pricing.html`.

No matter what plan you select, the first three users are free. After that, you'll pay per user.

Creating Your Zoho CRM Account

To get started with Zoho CRM, create a new account. You can start with your Zoho account, but Zoho will create a new account especially for Zoho CRM. (For more information about creating a Zoho account, see Chapter 1 — and note that you'll also have to create a Zoho CRM account to use CRM.)

To start with Zoho CRM, follow these steps:

1. **Navigate your browser to `http://crm.zoho.com`, and enter your Zoho username and password.**

2. **Click the Sign In button.**

   Zoho CRM displays a warning message (see Figure 12-1) stating that if you already have a Zoho CRM account, you should click the Cancel button and log in with your existing user ID.

3. **To create a New Zoho CRM account, click the Continue button.**

Figure 12-1:
Signing in to
Zoho CRM.

4. **Choose which Zoho CRM plan you want.**

   Read about your three edition choices in the preceding section.

5. **Respond to the Zoho CRM query for the CRM Requirements field.**

   This step is required. You must enter some text indicating what you want in a CRM application. Zoho presumably uses this information to improve Zoho CRM.

6. **Click Continue.**

   Zoho CRM opens. See Figure 12-2.

Click to see more tabs.

Links to create new items

More links

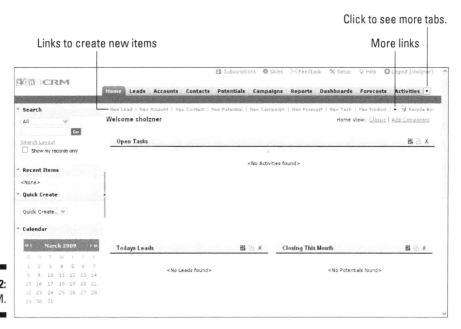

Figure 12-2:
Zoho CRM.

Getting a Look at the Zoho CRM Interface

The first thing you notice about Zoho CRM is the number of tabs at the top, including Home, Leads, Contacts, Campaigns, and the like — all items you need to professionally manage your customer relations.

As if that weren't enough, nine more tabs are available from a drop-down menu that opens when you click the down arrow at extreme right of the last tab (the Activities tab). These tabs include Products, Vendors, Sales Orders, Invoices, and more. If this seems like tab overload, I show you how to customize them in the upcoming section, "Hiding tabs."

Directly underneath the tabs are links you use to create new items. These items are the components you use to create new projects in CRM, such as new leads, accounts, and even advertising campaigns. And more new item–creation links appear when you click the down arrow to the right of the links bar, including New Case, New Quote, New Sales Order, and others.

Zoho CRM keeps track of what's going on in terms of tasks. A *task* can be creating a new sales lead, creating a purchase order, and so on. You can see that the biggest section in the main window of Zoho CRM is Open Tasks. That's where you keep track of what's going on.

Underneath the Open Tasks section are the Todays Leads section (for hot customer leads you're tracking down) and the Closing This Month section (to keep track of deals that need your attention).

In the left pane of Zoho CRM are four sections:

- ✔ **Search:** Searches through all your records
- ✔ **Recent Items:** Keeps track of the most recent items you've been working on, with links to each item
- ✔ **Quick Create:** Gives you a drop-down list box from which you can create the same items that you can from the new items links discussed earlier
- ✔ **Calendar:** Shows what's coming up in your CRM efforts

Customizing Zoho CRM

Zoho CRM has hundreds of items you can customize when you start setting up customer accounts. One of the quickest things to customize first are the tabs that appear in CRM, which you can hide, rearrange, and rename. You can even add new *components,* which are mini-applications you can add to your CRM home page.

Hiding tabs

You're probably not going to need all 19 tabs. Here's how to hide the tabs you don't need (note that you can't hide the Home tab):

1. **Click the Setup link at the top of any Zoho CRM page.**

2. **Click the Organize Tabs link.**

   The Organize Tabs page appears, as shown in Figure 12-3, where you can hide tabs.

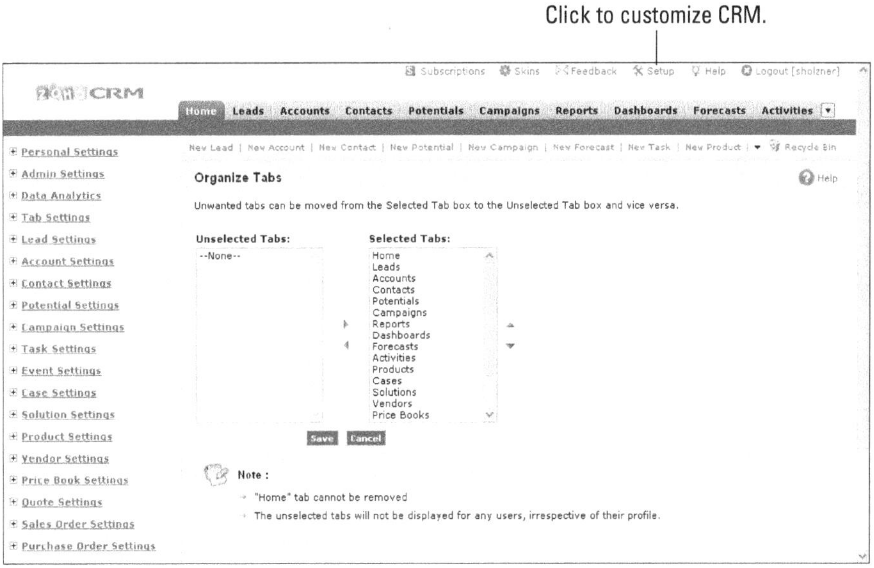

Click to customize CRM.

Figure 12-3: Hide tabs here.

3. **To hide a tab, follow these steps:**

   a. From the Selected Tabs list, select the tab(s) you want to hide.

   b. Click the left-pointing arrow.

   c. Click Save to close the Organize Tabs page.

   To restore a hidden tab, revert the process. Select it from the Unselected Tabs list and then click the right-pointing arrow.

4. **Click the Home tab to get back to the home page.**

Rearranging and renaming tabs

You can also rearrange and rename tabs from the Organize Tabs page. Like deleting a tab, first select the tab from the Selected Tabs list (as described in the preceding section). Then do the following to rearrange a tab:

1. **To reorder the tabs, click the up arrow next to the Selected Tabs list to move a tab higher in the list; click the down arrow to move a tab lower in the list.**

2. **Click Save.**

You can also rename tabs. Click Rename Tabs from the Setup page, and then click the Edit link next to the tab you want to rename. Enter the new name and click the Save button. Note that you cannot rename the Home tab.

Adding and deleting components

Zoho CRM is a big application, and not everything can fit on the home page at once. Each item on the home page is a *component* — such as Open Tasks and Todays Leads — but you can customize Zoho CRM by adding more components. The advantage to adding a new component is that you can watch some aspect of Zoho CRM, such as the campaigns you have running or the products you're offering.

Here's how to add a new component:

1. **In Zoho CRM, click the Add Component link at the top right of the home page.**

   This opens the Add Component dialog box you see in Figure 12-4.

Figure 12-4:
Add a
component
here.

2. **Select the new component from the Module drop-down list in the Add Component dialog box. The choices include Leads, Accounts, Campaigns, Forecasts, and others.**

   The Add Component dialog box expands to show the Select Custom View section, as shown in Figure 12-5.

Figure 12-5:
Choose a
custom view
for the new
component.

3. **Enter the name you want to give to the component.**

   This name will appear in the component's title bar.

4. **Select how many columns you want the component to display.**

5. **Select the custom view you want the component to display.**

   All components have multiple views, displaying different data, and the drop-down list box will be populated with the view choices available for the component you selected. For example, the Leads view lets you see current leads.

6. **Click Save to add the component.**

There's no Cancel button in the Add Component dialog box. If you want to cancel the operation and not complete the process of adding a component, click the X button in the upper right of the dialog box to close it.

Dozens of components and views are available in Zoho CRM. To get an idea of which ones might be useful for you, experiment with the Add Component link.

To remove a component from the home page, click the X button at the upper right in the component.

Getting People Involved: Managing Users

CRM users are the people you work with: folks in sales, marketing, inventory, and so on. To let them work with Zoho CRM, you have to let CRM know about them.

First, you add users. Then, you let Zoho CRM know what the users do in your organization — that is, you set (specify) their *role.* You can specify a user's role in your company when you add new users. After that, you can set a user's *profile,* which indicates the user's access to certain information, such as modules, records, and so on.

Adding new users

To add new Zoho CRM users, follow these steps:

1. **Click the Setup link at the top of any Zoho CRM page.**

2. **Click the Users link (in the Admin Settings section).**

   This opens the Users page, which shows the current users in Zoho CRM. Out of the gate, that's just you.

3. **Click the Add User button.**

   This opens the page you see in Figure 12-6.

   Up to now, your account has been a personal account. Now that you're adding new users, though, Zoho CRM upgrades your account to a company account automatically.

4. **To begin the upgrade of your account, enter your company name.**

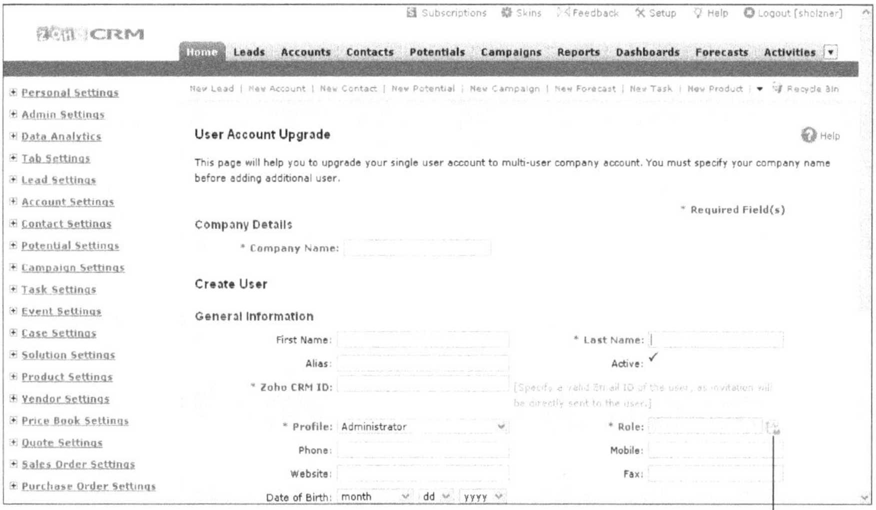

Figure 12-6:
Adding new
Zoho CRM
users here.

Click to select a user role.

5. **For each new user, enter the required fields for General Information (in the Create User section): Last Name, Zoho CRM ID, Profile, and Role.**

   • *Zoho CRM ID:* This can be a valid e-mail of the new user.

   • *Profile:* You have two options: Administrator and Standard. Read more about profiles in the upcoming section, "Creating a profile."

   • *Role:* Click the button next to the Role box and select a role from the dialog box that opens. Zoho CRM comes with two roles built in: CEO and Manager. In the Free Edition, you're limited to those two roles. In the Professional Edition, you can have up to three roles. In the Enterprise Edition, you can have up to 250 roles.

6. **(Optional) Enter the nonrequired General Information fields for the new user, including Alias, Date of Birth, Web site, and various phone numbers.**

   An alias can be a nickname.

7. **(Optional) Enter the street address, city, state, zip code, and country of the new user.**

8. **Enter the remaining required fields to complete setting up a new user: Language, Country Locale, and Time Zone.**

   The defaults for these fields are US English, United States, and Greenwich Mean Time (GMT), respectively.

9. **Click the Create New User button.**

   This creates the new user; the Zoho CRM ID is the new user's e-mail address.

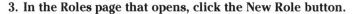
Creating new roles

After you create a new user, you can create a new *role* (which specifies the user's role in your company). To create a new role, follow these steps:

1. **Click the Setup link at the top of any Zoho CRM page.**

2. **Under Admin Settings, click the Roles link.**

   If you don't see the Roles link, you haven't added at least one new user to Zoho CRM. See the preceding section.

3. **In the Roles page that opens, click the New Role button.**

   If you're using the Free Edition, you'll get an error message saying you can't create new roles and inviting you to upgrade.

4. **In the New Role page that opens, enter the name of the new role.**

5. **Select the role immediately above the role you're creating.**

   CRM uses this information to set up a hierarchy.

6. **Choose whether users in this role can share data with others in this role.**

7. **(Optional) Enter a description of the role.**

8. **Click Save.**

Assigning a role to a user

After you create a role, you can assign it to users. Just follow these steps:

1. **Click the Setup link at the top of any Zoho CRM page.**

2. **Under Admin Settings, click the Users link.**

3. **On the Users page that opens, click the name of the user whose role you want to change.**

4. **On the User Details page that opens, click the Edit button (at the bottom).**

   This opens the Edit User Details page, as shown in Figure 12-7.

5. **Click the button next to the Role field.**

   A window opens, displaying the available roles.

6. **Click the role you want to assign to the user.**

   The window displaying the roles closes.

7. **Click Save.**

Figure 12-7:
The Edit
User Details
page.

Creating a profile

Profiles specify the access levels of your users. Using a profile, you can control which records — and even which fields in a record — users have access to. Zoho CRM comes with two built-in profiles:

- ✔ **Administrator:** Users with an Administrator profile have full data access privileges in Zoho CRM. They can manage users, roles, profiles, and data sharing with no restrictions.

- ✔ **Standard:** Users with a Standard profile have no privileges with regards to users, roles, profiles, and data sharing.

The Free Edition can have only 3 profiles, the Professional Edition can have 10, and the Enterprise Edition can have 25.

To create a new profile, follow these steps:

1. **Click Setup, and then, under Admin Settings, click Profiles.**

   The Profiles page opens, showing the profiles you already have.

2. **Click the New Profile button.**

   This opens the New Profile page, as shown in Figure 12-8.

3. **Enter the name of the new profile.**

4. **Select a profile to "clone."**

   When you create a new profile, you start by cloning an existing profile. Then you modify its access settings.

Figure 12-8:
The New
Profile page.

5. (Optional) Enter a description for the profile.

6. Click Save.

This opens the Profile Details page you see in Figure 12-9.

Figure 12-9:
The Profile
Details
page.

7. Click the Edit button.

This displays all permissions as check boxes, as you see in Figure 12-10.

8. Make the edits you want to the profile's permissions. You set permissions for items such as Leads, Accounts, Contacts, and so on.

You can set each of these items to specify whether a tab will be visible for users with the new profile; whether users can view the item; and whether users can create, edit, and delete new instances of the item.

9. Click Save.

10. Click Close.

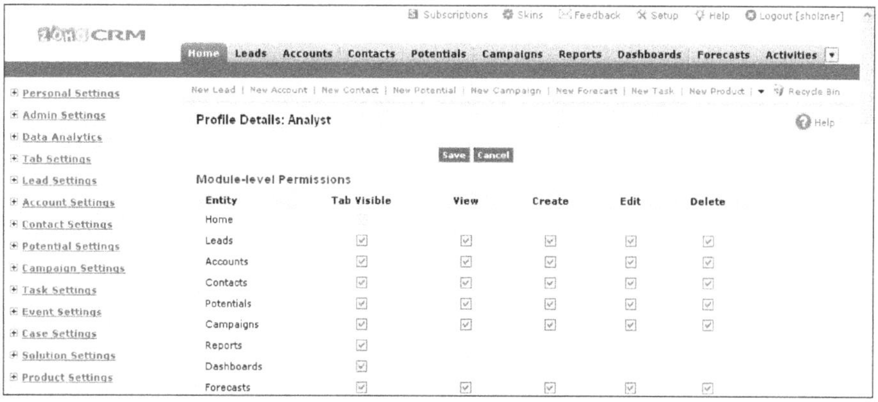

Figure 12-10:
Editing
the Profile
Details
page.

All about Zoho CRM Modules

After you add new users and assign them new roles, it's time to start creating your own campaigns in Zoho CRM. That starts with an understanding of Zoho CRM *modules,* which are like mini-applications you can use in Zoho CRM.

The various sections of Zoho CRM — marketing, sales, inventory, and so on — are all supported by modules. There's one tab per module. For example, when you create a new marketing campaign, you use the Campaigns module. You name the new campaign and then create records in the campaign corresponding to the tasks in the campaign.

Zoho CRM has about two dozen modules, from Campaigns to Vendors, from Leads to Accounts. Fortunately, you work with all the modules in more or less the same way: You create a new campaign, for example, and add new records to it, just like you do with the other types of modules.

To get a clearer picture of how Zoho CRM works, this section gives you an overview of the Zoho CRM modules. Then you find out how to work with a specific module in the section "Putting a Zoho CRM Module to Work," later in this chapter.

Welcome to the Marketing modules

You use the CRM Marketing modules to create new marketing campaigns, new events, and so on. Here are the modules in this group and what they do (to access one of these modules, just click its tab):

✔ **Campaigns:** This is a big one! A new marketing campaign lets you specify marketing objectives, mark whether they've been reached, track costs, and compare costs with other campaigns.

✔ **Events:** Events are like tasks: They're used in sales, marketing, and other modules. Events keep track of a promotion of some kind, recording the location, date, time, and so on. Like tasks, they appear in the activities tab. Create new events from the Campaigns tab.

✔ **Tasks:** You add tasks to all sorts of modules, whether in sales, marketing, or whatever. In Zoho CRM, tasks allow you to keep track of something you have to do on a specific schedule. Add as many tasks to Zoho CRM as you like; they appear on the Activities tab. Create new tasks from the Campaigns tab.

Welcome to the Sales modules

Businesses know that they survive on sales, and Zoho CRM has plenty of modules here. From tracking sales leads to creating sales forecasts, it's all here (to access one of these modules, just click its tab):

✔ **Accounts:** Keep track of your existing customers with this module. You can track sales history, contact information, and outstanding balances.

✔ **Contacts:** *Leads* are potential customers; *contacts* are current customers (the contact people at your customers' companies). You can track contact information as well as associate contacts with a specific account, and track campaigns that generated the contacts.

✔ **Forecasts:** Track sales history and expected future sales with this module. Sales reps and managers can use this module to see whether they're on track to meet a quota.

✔ **Leads:** Track contact information of sales leads and product interest. Leads can be generated by marketing campaigns, trade shows, and more. The Leads module helps you make sure no leads get away.

✔ **Potentials:** Compared with the Leads module, the Potentials module is much more general, letting you target whole groups and track them all the way to closing the deal. You can track sales probability and expected revenue as well.

✔ **Quotes:** Your business will give different quotes to different potential customers, and you need to track those quotes. With this module, keep records of quotes for easy reference.

Welcome to the Inventory and Ordering modules

In any business, you have to keep track of where the money is going. How much is coming in, and how much is going out? To whom? For what?

Managers can keep track of the money flow with the modules discussed in this section.

And almost as important as tracking money is tracking inventory: How much do you have of what you sell? Where are the bottlenecks in production? What do you need more of, and what do you have too much of? With these modules, you can manage your production easily.

Here are the modules in this section:

- ✔ **Invoices:** With this module, you track your outstanding billings. Keep tabs on what invoices have been paid, and which have not. You can record the full details on each invoice: dates, line-by-line items, and mode.

- ✔ **Price Books:** This is where you keep track of the prices of what you have to offer. This module tracks unit prices as well as list prices. The *unit price* is a fixed price, and the *list price* may change, depending on the customer and the volume of the sale.

- ✔ **Products:** Use this module to organize the products you have for sale. Each record in the module corresponds to a different product. This module records prices and product specification. Use this module to keep your sales reps up to date at all times.

- ✔ **Purchase Orders:** This module is for purchases your company makes, ensuring you don't duplicate orders, and recording the full terms of each purchase order. Track invoices and shipments against your own records.

- ✔ **Sales Orders:** Here's where you track the purchases your customers are making. Use this module to record the full details of any purchase order, specifying price, number, delivery dates, and more.

- ✔ **Services:** This module keeps your salesforce up to date on the services your company offers. You can record all the details of the services you have to sell, and the module makes it easy to create invoices for those services as well as coordinate your sales reps.

- ✔ **Vendors:** Use this module to track your suppliers and what you purchase from them. It's like an address book with space for data on what you purchase from each vendor and descriptions.

 To customize quotes, invoices, purchase orders, and sales orders that you send to your customers, take a look at the templates that come with Zoho CRM. Click the Setup link in any Zoho CRM page, and then look in the templates section.

Welcome to the Customer Support modules

As important as sales and marketing are, you have to keep your current customers happy so that they'll become future customers as well. This section contains modules that let you deal with customer support, tracking customer issues and your resolutions.

Here's what's in this module:

- ✔ **Cases:** Keep track of customer issues. This module lets you assign individual case numbers and record the issue and all your responses to it, even as it's bumped up the chain of command.
- ✔ **Solutions:** This module contains a database of solutions to common problems. There's no need to solve each customer issue more than once if a solution already exists. This database is the one that your customer support staff can use to get what they need before creating a case for a specific customer issue.

Welcome to the Data Analysis modules

Data crunching is a good way to keep track of where your business is headed, and the Data Analysis modules give you ways of comparing data and spotting patterns. You can look at your data in tabular form with reports, or in chart form with the Zoho dashboards.

Here are the modules in this section:

- ✔ **Dashboards:** The Dashboards module allows you to create graphs of your data. For example, you can compare the performance of various sales reps, or chart how your sales have fared quarter to quarter.

  This module uses Flash to create its charts, so I recommend having the latest version of Flash installed on your machine.
- ✔ **Reports:** This module lets you track data to spot trends early on. More than 40 reports are built in to Zoho CRM, and you can also create your own.

Putting a Zoho CRM Module to Work

Zoho modules have many similarities. Although the data they work with differs from module to module, how you work with that data is usually very much the same.

Modules are all record based: You can create, edit, and delete records. You can search through and organize your records in a module. You can graph them, create reports, and more.

Start by looking at one of the most popular modules: the Marketing Campaign module.

Dissecting a module

The Campaigns module is typical of Zoho CRM modules. To access a module, click the tab corresponding to that module. You can see the Campaigns tab in Figure 12-11.

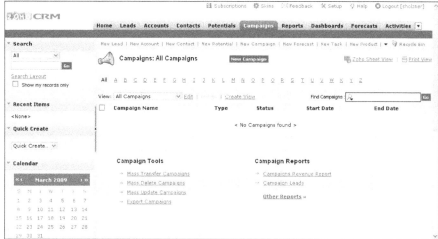

Figure 12-11: The Zoho CRM Campaigns module.

At the top of the tab is the New Campaign button, with which you create a new campaign. Each new campaign will represent a new *record* in the module.

That's the usual way things work in a module: Each item in a module is a record. For example, a new invoice in the Invoices module is a new record in that module, and a new vendor in the Vendors module is a new record in that module. Each module usually has a button at the top center to let you create a new record, which is what the New Campaign button lets you do here.

Directly beneath the New Campaign button is a set of alphabetic links (letters A–Z), which you use to easily find records (in the Campaigns module, these correspond to marketing campaigns) based on their names.

Below the alphabetic links is the View bar, which Zoho CRM modules also usually offer. This bar lets you filter the records in the module by specifically searching for matches as well as letting you select all records marked as active.

Underneath the View bar is the section that displays your campaigns. Each campaign (that is, each record) gets a line here. This section lists each campaign's name, type, status, start date, and end date.

Beneath the section that lists your campaigns, you find links to tools and reports, which is typical for a Zoho CRM module.

Creating a new record in a module

To create a new record in a Zoho CRM module, click the New button at the top of the module's tab. Because I'm in the Campaigns module, the New button is the New Campaign button. To create a new record in this module, follow these steps:

1. **Click the New Campaign button.**

   This opens the Create Campaign page you see in Figure 12-12.

   The window you see in Figure 12-12 is typical of Zoho CRM modules. To create a new record, you usually fill out a new form and then click Save.

2. **(Optional) Select the person who "owns" the new campaign.**

   Zoho CRM lists the users that you set up in Zoho CRM. (See the section "Getting People Involved: Managing Users," earlier in this chapter.)

3. **(Optional) Select the type of the campaign from the Type drop-down list box.**

   Some choices include Conference, Webinar, Trade Show, and others.

4. **Enter the campaign name.**

   This is the only required item to create a new campaign.

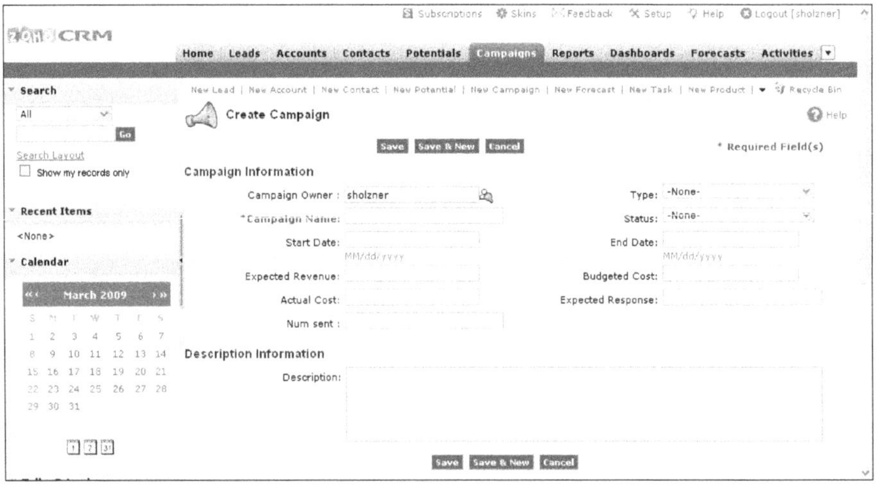

Figure 12-12: Creating a new campaign.

5. **(Optional) Select the campaign's status, choosing from Planning, Active, Inactive, or Complete.**

6. **(Optional) Enter the campaign's start date and end date in mm/dd/ yyyy format.**

   When you click the start date and end date boxes, a calendar appears, allowing you to click dates to enter them.

7. **Fill these remaining optional fields:**

   • The revenue the campaign is expected to generate

   • The budgeted cost and then the actual cost of the campaign (when that cost is known)

   • An expected response (such as an amount of income) for the campaign

   • Whether to track the number sent (a mass mailing, for example) in the Num Sent field

   • A description for the campaign

8. **Click Save to create the new campaign, or click the Save & New button to save the current campaign and create a new one.**

   Zoho CRM displays a summary of the new record, as you can see in Figure 12-13.

To edit a record that's open, click the Edit button. To close a record, click the Close button.

After you create a new record, that record is displayed on the module's tab. You can see a new campaign — Townhouse Rentals, in this example — in Figure 12-14.

Editing and deleting a record

To edit a record, follow these steps:

1. **Click the containing module's tab to open that module.**

2. **Click the name of the record you want to edit.**

   The record will be displayed in a details page (in this example, Campaign Details on the Campaigns tab).

Figure 12-13: The summary of the new record.

3. Make the edits you want.

4. Click Save.

To delete a record, follow Steps 1 and 2 of the preceding step list. Then click the Delete button.

Figure 12-14: A new record in the Campaigns module.

Creating Custom Views

You can organize your records in many ways on the tab of a Zoho CRM module:

- ✔ **Sort:** Click a letter in the A–Z list of hyperlinks to find records whose names begin with the record you clicked.

- ✔ **Filter:** Filter by active records using the View drop-down list box.

- ✔ **Search:** Enter a search term in the Search field (left pane) and search for matching records.

If none of these methods work, you can create your own custom view, which lets you filter records based on the value of each field in the records. For example, say you want to find all campaigns with an expected revenue above a certain amount, or all campaigns belonging to a certain user. You can do that by creating a custom view.

To create a custom view for the records in a Zoho CRM module, follow these steps:

1. **In Zoho CRM, click the tab corresponding to the module for which you want to create a custom view.**

2. **Click the Create View link.**

   This opens the page you see in Figure 12-15.

3. **Enter a name for the view.**

4. **Select the field of the record you want to supply a criteria for in the first drop-down list box you see in Figure 12-15.**

   For the Campaign module, the fields to filter on include Campaign Owner, Campaign Name, Start Date, End Date, Expected Cost, and more.

5. **Select a condition from the second drop-down list box.**

   The possible criteria are: is; isn't; contains; doesn't contain; starts with; ends with; is empty; and is not empty.

6. **Click the third box to display possible values for the field you're filtering on.**

   For example, if you select Campaign Owner as the field to filter on, clicking the third box displays a list of all possible campaign owners. Click the one you want to sort on.

7. **To add additional criteria, click the Add Criteria button.**

   A new line with three boxes appears for the new criterion.

8. **Select the columns you want to appear in each line of the custom filter's display from the Available Columns list.**

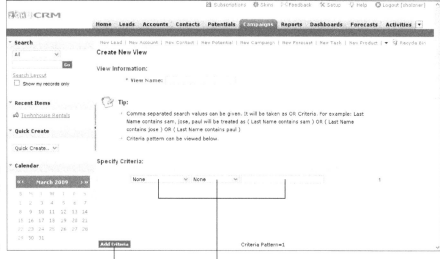

Figure 12-15:
Creating
a custom
view.

Add more criteria.   Choose view criteria here.

9. **Click the right-facing arrow to move your selected columns from the Available Columns list to the Selected Columns list.**

You can order the columns displayed by the custom view by selecting a column in the Selected Columns list and changing its position by clicking the up or down arrow to the right of the Selected Columns list.

10. **Select a radio button granting access to the custom filter in the Accessibility Details section. Choose from**

   • All Users Are Allowed to View This Custom View

   • Show This Custom View Only to Me

   • Allow the Following Users to View This Custom View. If you select this radio button, select User from the Select Source Type drop-down list box. Then select the users you want in the Available box and click the Add button to add them to the Selected box.

11. **Click Save.**

12. **To see which records the customer view displays, select the custom view by name in the View drop-down list box that appears in the module's tab.**

Creating custom views this way lets you filter the records in a module with complete precision, and you can filter on as many criteria as you like.

Part V
The Part of Tens

The 5th Wave
By Rich Tennant

CAUTION
LIVE SNAKES

So old Dave's presentations are boring? They're dull, huh? "Add some dynamic content," they said. I'll give you dynamic content...

In this part . . .

In this part, I give you two collections of the most important resources available for Zoho: the top ten best Zoho help resources and the top ten best online Zoho tutorials.

Chapter 13

Top Ten Zoho Help Resources

In This Chapter

▷ Zoho help resources and FAQs

▷ Zoho Forums

▷ Zoho application manuals

▷ Videos on Zoho applications

The Zoho help system is still a work in progress; you'll find far more in this book than you will in the Zoho help files. Thus, the help system is currently very spotty: a user manual for one application, FAQs for another, and nothing for another. For example, no official online help is available for Zoho Reports or Zoho Sheet.

When you're working in an application, sometimes you see a Help link at the top of the application — but in most cases, you don't. As a result, tracking down help resources is not the easiest thing to do, which is why I collected them for you in this chapter.

If nothing else, Zoho has a toll-free number (888-900-9646) that you can call day or night, and a person usually answers promptly. Try that route if you're really stuck.

The Zoho FAQ

```
www.zoho.com/zoho_faq.html
```

Zoho emphasizes frequently asked questions (FAQ) lists instead of help files. This is a good general resource on Zoho and what it has to offer. Individual FAQs are also available for specific applications, as I describe in this chapter.

Zoho Forums

http://forums.zoho.com

Zoho Forums is the place for interactive help. You can post questions here and often get a helpful answer.

Zoho Writer FAQ

http://writer.zoho.com/public/help/zohowriterfaq/fullpage

Zoho Writer is one of those applications that doesn't have a user manual, but it does have FAQs.

You'll find questions like these answered in the FAQ list:

- What is Zoho Writer?
- What can I do with Zoho Writer?
- What browsers does Zoho Writer support?
- I can't sign in to my Zoho Writer account even after entering details. What am I doing wrong?
- The browser shows an error on the page and I am unable to access documents in Zoho Writer. What's wrong?

Zoho Notebook Help

http://writer.zoho.com/public/mdsadiqms/Notebook-Help

Although it's brief, a help document for Zoho Notebook is available. This help file lists key features of Zoho Notebook and goes over them. For example, here's the key features list from the Notebook help file:

- Creating, aggregating, and sharing multiple types of content
- Drawing tools to draw and add shapes to compliment content
- Integration with other Zoho Applications
- Recording video and audio within Notebook
- Versioning control and commenting

✔ Collaborative/simultaneous editing and content sharing

✔ Firefox plug-ins for instant Web clipping

✔ Skype integration for instant chat and IP telephony

Video on Zoho Sheet

```
www.viddler.com/explore/raju/videos/22
```

Although Zoho Sheet doesn't have any official Zoho help documentation yet, here is where you can find a video covering it.

Zoho Show FAQ

```
http://show.zoho.com/help/faq/faq.html
```

Zoho Show is another application for which there's no formal help file. However, you can find FAQs at the preceding address.

Zoho Projects Help

```
http://zohoprojects.wiki.zoho.com
```

Zoho Project offers a help file online. This is a really useful resource that lets you dig deep into Projects. What you see first is a table of contents — click the item you're interested in.

Zoho Invoice User Manual

```
http://invoice.wiki.zoho.com
```

Zoho Invoice doesn't have FAQs or help files, but it does have a user manual, available online.

The manual covers Invoice's key features. Here is a much-condensed list of topics:

✔ Create and send branded invoices, quotes, or estimates.

✔ Automate repeated invoicing with recurring invoices.

✔ Customize invoice layout and look and feel with templates.

✔ Print and save invoices as PDF.

✔ Track invoices and send overdue reminders.

✔ Customer payment options; expand overseas business with support for multiple currencies.

✔ Visualize the latest business standings with powerful reports.

Zoho CRM Help

http://zohocrm.wiki.zoho.com

Perhaps because Zoho CRM has paid versions, it has a great online help system, including FAQs, a user manual, and tutorials.

Zoho CRM Blog

http://lounge.zohocrm.com

Zoho CRM has a blog where you can keep track of the latest developments with CRM. (See Figure 13-1.) This blog has all kinds of posts related to what's going on with CRM, such as new functionality being added to the Campaigns module or support for a new currency.

Figure 13-1: The Zoho CRM Lounge.

Chapter 14

Top Ten Online Zoho Tutorials

In This Chapter

▷ All application video tutorials

▷ Zoho Projects tutorial

▷ Zoho Notebook tutorial

▷ Zoho Planner tutorial

▷ Zoho Sheet tutorial

▷ Zoho Writer tutorial

▷ Official Zoho CRM video tutorials

A number of Zoho tutorials are readily available online. Most are video tutorials; that is, you get to watch what you're interested in. Take a look. All of them can be very helpful.

Zoho App Videos

```
http://www.zoho.com/product_videos.html
```

Zoho offers a video introduction for all its applications. At this site, you can find official introduction videos for all Zoho applications. Just scroll down the page and make your choice from the palette of applications, as shown in Figure 14-1.

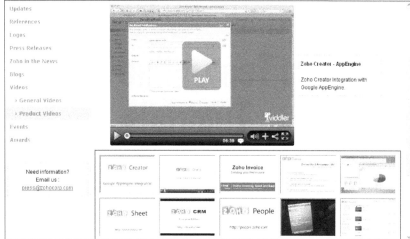

Figure 14-1:
The official Zoho application videos.

A Guided Tour of Zoho

www.metacafe.com/watch/2389816/using_zoho_apps_to_
create_an_integrated_web_office_suite

At this site, you can find a guided tour of Zoho. This hip video presents an overview not only of Zoho but also of the applications.

Zoho Projects Tutorial

www.mpagbyorksregion.co.uk/tomsmith/MoodleTutorials

This tutorial is divided into Projects tasks, and it covers many common things you want to do with Projects, from adding milestones to adding tasks.

Zoho Notebook Tutorial

http://technorati.com/videos/
youtube.com%2Fwatch%3Fv%3DXabm8hRyXrk

This video tutorial on Zoho Notebook is a copy of the announcement of Zoho Notebook from the Zoho people, and it covers all that Notebook does in overview.

Zoho Planner Tutorial

```
http://it.toolbox.com/blogs/matthewmoran/zoho-planner-
         and-email-integration-my-video-tutorial-20882
```

This video tutorial on Zoho Planner emphasizes integrating e-mail into Zoho Planner. You'll find a lot of great tips and tricks on the subject here.

Zoho Sheet Tutorial

```
www.youtube.com/watch?v=bEx4v_-7ZTc&feature=PlayList&p=
         BF056106BFE14504&playnext=1&playnext_from=
         PL&index=45
```

This excellent video tutorial of Zoho Sheet covers all the Sheet basics well. This tutorial is very slick with zooms, highlights, and screen shading. It gives you an excellent introduction to Sheet.

Creating Macros in Zoho Sheet

```
http://mefeedia.com/entry/zoho-sheet-
         macro-recording/11012611
```

This video tutorial is a useful one for creating macros in Sheet. See how to record a series of Sheet commands and play them back using a macro.

Zoho Writer Tutorial

```
www.youtube.com/watch?v=uf71nos7Qag&feature=PlayList&p=
         BF056106BFE14504&playnext=1&playnext_from=
         PL&index=38
```

Zoho Writer is a big topic, and this is a good video tutorial that serves as an introduction to the topic. It's a well-done video with all kinds of special effects. All the basics of entering and formatting text are covered handily.

Taking Zoho Writer Offline

`www.zoho.com/zohowriter-zoho/zohowriter-zoho.html`

If you want to learn all about taking Zoho Writer offline with Gears by Google, take a look at this video tutorial. It offers good coverage on taking Writer offline, including troubleshooting in case you run into problems.

Zoho CRM Tutorials

`http://zohocrm.wiki.zoho.com`

Zoho has 20 — count 'em, 20 — great video tutorials on Zoho CRM.

At this site, you can find videos on managing the B2C process; getting started; customizing the home page, tax settings, and tabs; changing currency; personalizing date format, language, company logo, and time zone; renaming tabs; and more.

Index

• A •

accounts
  CRM, 276–277
  Zoho, setting up, 8–10
Accounts module, CRM, 288
action shortcuts, Sheet, 172
Action toolbar, Sheet, 170
active cells, Sheet, 171–172
Active Contacts link, Invoice, 262
Active Contacts page, Invoice, 264
Active Customers page, Invoice, 258, 264
Add Appointment link, Planner, 128–129
Add Audio dialog box, Notebook, 96
Add Bcc link, Compose dialog box, 142
Add Blank Page link, Notebook, 89
Add Chart dialog box, Sheet, 181–182
Add Column option, Reports, 213
Add Comment button, Writer, 46
Add Comment dialog box, Writer, 46
Add Component dialog box, CRM, 280–282
Add Custom Message check box, Share
    dialog box, 110
Add File dialog box, Notebook, 100
Add Formula Column option, Reports, 213
Add Groups link, Share This Document
    dialog box, 54
Add HTML dialog box, Notebook, 97
Add Image dialog box, Notebook, 93
Add List Item link, Planner, 121
Add New Customer page, Invoice, 258–260
Add New Estimate page, Invoice, 268–270
Add New Invoice page, Invoice, 271–272
Add New Item page, Invoice, 265
Add New User box, Projects, 232
Add Note link, Planner, 130
Add Payment for This Invoice icon,
    Invoice, 272
Add Payment page, Invoice, 272–273
Add Project dialog box, Projects, 230–231
Add Row option, Reports, 213
Add RSS dialog box, Notebook, 98–99
Add Sheet link, Notebook, 90, 100
Add Show dialog box, Notebook, 101
Add Tags link, Planner, 136

Add Task link, Projects, 237
Add Text link, Notebook, 91
Add Text Page link, Notebook, 90
Add URL dialog box, Notebook, 98
Add User button, CRM, 282
Add Video dialog box, Notebook, 94–95
Add Web link, Notebook, 90
Add Writer link, Notebook, 90, 100
address book contacts, Mail, 160–161
Admin Settings, CRM, 284
Administrator profile, CRM, 285
Advanced Options link, Projects, 241
Advanced Options section, Projects,
    234–235
aligning page elements, in Writer, 30–32
Alignment menu, Sheet, 175
Allow Others to Give Comments check box,
    Writer Public Share dialog box, 48
alphabetically ordered cells, Sheet,
    178–179
AMORDEGRC function, Sheet, 186
Anchor field, Writer Insert/Modify Link
    dialog box, 36
API key, CRM, 262
application videos, 303–304
applications, home page of, 12. *See also*
    specific applications by name
Apply On field, Invoice Tax Settings page,
    257
appointments, Planner, 125–129
Appointments dialog box, Planner, 126
Appointments section, Planner, 128–129
Archive option, Mail, 154
arrows, Notebook, 104
Ascending radio buttons, Sheet Sort dialog
    box, 180
ascending rows, Sheet, 179
Ask Receipt check box, Compose dialog
    box, 143
Attach from Zoho Docs dialog box, Mail,
    155
attachments
  e-mail, 154–157
  Planner, 131–133
audio files, adding to notebooks, 96

Authorize.Net, 266–267
Auto Number formats, Reports, 201
AVERAGE function, Sheet, 185–186

• *B* •

Basic plan, Invoice, 253
Bcc field, Compose dialog box, 142
billing information section, Invoice,
    259–260
Billing Status drop-down list, Projects, 245
blank notebook pages, 89
Blank Slide option, Create New Slide dialog
    box, 68
blind carbon copy (bcc), 142
Block Arrows category, Show shape
    palette, 76–77
blogs, publishing to, 48, 191
boilerplate text, 40–41
bolding, marking e-mail with, 153–154
border, of shapes in presentations, 79
bullets, using in presentations, 71–72

• *C* •

calendar
  CRM, 278
  Planner, 122–123, 126
  Zoho Projects, 242–244
callouts, 74–76, 104
Campaigns module, CRM, 287, 290–292, 294
Cascading Style Sheet (CSS), 33
Case Sensitive check box, Sort dialog box,
    180
Cases module, CRM, 290
Category pane, Show, 64
Cc box, Compose dialog box, 141
CEILING function, Sheet, 186
cells
  Reports database table, 209–210
  Sheet spreadsheet, 171–173, 176–178,
    183–184
  Writer table, 36–37
center alignment, Writer, 31
Change Datatype option, Reports, 213
Change link, Invoice, 255
charges, Project, 228
charts
  Reports, 219–220
  Sheet, 180–182

chat area
  Sheet, 189–190
  Show, 85–86
Checkout, Google, 266–267
Clear Flag option, Mail, 154
client users, Projects, 233
clients, Invoice, 258
ClipArt category, Show shape palette, 77
clips, Web page, 97–98
clock icon, Projects, 246
Closing This Month section, CRM, 278
cloud computing, 1, 7
Collaborators pane, Writer, 53–54
collapsing lists, Planner, 119
Collection tab
  Add Audio dialog box, 96
  Add File dialog box, 100
  Add Image dialog box, 93
color
  of borders in Show, 79
  filling shapes in Show presentations with,
    77–78
  font, in Writer, 32–33
  of Mail labels, 162
  of Notebook shapes, 102
COLUMN function, Sheet, 186
columns
  Reports database table, changing,
    212–213
  Reports lookup, 208, 211–212
  Sheet pivot table, 192–193
  Sheet spreadsheet, 174–175, 178–179
  Writer table, 37
comma-separated values (CSV) format,
    198, 261–262
comments
  Projects forum post, 248
  Sheet spreadsheet, 176–177
  Writer, 45–47, 52–53
company logo, adding to invoices, 254–255
company profile, setting up on invoices,
    253–254
Company Settings tab, Projects, 230
Completed section, Planner, 120
components, CRM, 279–282
Compose dialog box, Mail, 141–143,
    154–155, 160–161
composing e-mail, in Mail
  overview, 141–142
  priority level, setting, 143
  return receipts, 142–143

sent mail, viewing, 144–145
signatures, adding, 143–144
CONCATENATE function, Sheet, 186
confirmation e-mail, Zoho, 10
Contact Details section, Add New
  Customer page, 259
contacts, Invoice
  deleting, 264–265
  editing, 263–264
  importing, 262–263
  overview, 257–258
Contacts module, CRM, 288
Contains Header check box, Sort dialog
  box, 180
Content field, Mail Vacation Reply tab, 150
copying shapes in notebooks, 103
COSH function, Sheet, 185
COUNT function, Sheet, 185–186
Create a Zoho Account page, 8–9
Create Blank Database dialog box, Reports,
  205
Create Campaign page, CRM, 292–293
Create Database from Template dialog box,
  Reports, 202–203
Create Database (Import) dialog box,
  Reports, 199–201
Create Desktop Icon check box, Offline
  Settings dialog box, 165
Create New button, Show, 64
Create New Filter option, Reports, 215–216
Create New Page button, Planner, 133
Create New Presentation page, Show, 64
Create New Project button, Projects, 226
Create New Slide dialog box, Show, 68
Create New Table page, Reports, 205–207
Create New View page, CRM, 295–296
Create Pivot Report dialog box, Sheet, 193
Create View link, CRM, 295
Create Your Personal Group dialog box,
  Writer, 54–55
CRM. See Zoho CRM
CRM Requirements field, CRM, 277
CSS (Cascading Style Sheet), 33
CSV (comma-separated values) format,
  198, 261–262
currency
  Invoice, setting, 256
  Sheet, 177–178
Currency format, Reports, 201
Custom Fields section, Invoice, 253

Customer Details page, Invoice,
  260, 264–265
customer relationship management. See
  Zoho CRM
Customer support modules, CRM, 289–290
customers, Invoice
  adding manually, 258–260
  deactivating and reactivating, 264
  editing, 263–264
  importing, 260–262
  overview, 257–258
customizing
  CRM, 279–282
  notebooks, 106–108
  Projects, 228–230
  Show presentations, 70–81

• •

dashboard, Projects, 231–232
Dashboards module, CRM, 290
dashed borders, Show, 79
Data analysis modules, CRM, 290
Data Labels drop-down list, Add Chart
  dialog box, 182
Data Range field, Create Pivot Report
  dialog box, 193
data types, Reports, 208
database tables, Reports
  columns, changing, 212–213
  creating, 203–204, 206–209
  filtering data in, 214–217
  querying data with SQL, 217–219
  related, 210–212
  rows, changing, 213
  sorting data in, 214
  standard, 209–210
databases. See Zoho Reports
Date Format field, Currency and Time Zone
  page, 256
Date Format Settings category, Projects,
  230
date format, Sheet, 177–178
DAY function, Sheet, 186
deactivating Invoice customers, 264
Decrease List Level button, Show, 71
DEGREES function, Sheet, 186
Delete All Rows option, Reports, 213

Delete button
  Mail, 151
  Notebook, 90
  Writer, 23
Delete Column option, Reports, 213
Delete Row option, Reports, 213
deleting
  cell comments, Sheet, 177
  components, CRM, 280–282
  contacts, Invoice, 264–265
  content, Notebook, 108
  e-mail, Mail, 151
  milestones, Projects, 238–239
  module records, CRM, 293–294
  notes, Planner, 130
  shapes, Notebook, 103
  slides, Show, 69
  spreadsheets, Sheet, 173
  tasks, Projects, 236
  to-do list items, Planner, 122
  users, Projects, 240
Descending radio buttons, Sort dialog box,
    180
descending rows, Sheet, 179
Description (Optional) field, Create Your
    Personal Group dialog box, 54
Description column, Reports, 208
Design Pivot dialog box, Sheet, 193–194
Design view, Reports, 206–209
desktop sharing, Show, 86
DOC (Microsoft Word document) files, 58
Document properties button, Writer, 23
documents, embedding in Notebook,
    99–101. *See also* Zoho Writer
Documents tab, Projects, 249
DOCX (Microsoft Word document) files, 58
download dialog box, Writer, 59
Download Images and Attachments check
    box, Offline Settings dialog box, 165
downloading
  attachments, Mail, 156–157
  e-mail to computer, Mail, 159–160
  Writer templates, 41
drafts, Mail, 142
drawing shapes, Notebook, 102
Drawing toolbar, Notebook, 102, 105
due dates, Planner, 122–124
Duration field, Projects, 234

• E •

Edit dialog box, Planner, 122
Edit Group dialog box, Writer, 57
Edit Invitation Mail button, Share This
    Document dialog box, 50, 83
Edit Template link, Writer, 43
Edit User Details page, CRM, 284–285
editing
  appointments, Planner, 127–129
  cell comments, Sheet, 177
  collaborator groups, Writer, 57
  company profiles, Invoice, 254
  contacts, Invoice, 263–264
  customers, Invoice, 263–264
  database tables, Reports, 212–214
  formulas for cells, Sheet, 184
  items on to-do lists, Planner, 122
  milestones, Projects, 238–239
  notes, Planner, 130
  presentation titles, Show, 70
  records, CRM module, 293–294
  shapes, Notebook, 105
  shared Planner pages, 137
  Sheet keyboard shortcuts for, 172
  tasks, Projects, 236
  templates, Writer, 43
  user roles, Projects, 239–240
editing area, Show, 66
editing space, Writer, 26
Elite plan, Invoice, 253
e-mail. *See also* Zoho Mail
  about spreadsheet changes, Sheet, 190
  acknowledgement of payment, Invoice,
    273
  appointment reminders, Planner, 128
  invitations, Planner, 137
  invitations, Writer collaborator, 50–51, 56
  invitations to view databases, Reports,
    222
  invitations to view online slide
    presentations, Show, 85
  invitations to view spreadsheets, Sheet,
    188–189
  meeting participants, Projects, 242
  member tasks, Projects, 235–236
  notifications, Invoice, 267–268
  to Projects users, 240
  registration confirmation, Zoho, 10
  signatures, 143–144

spam, 153
welcome, Projects, 226–227
embed code, video, 94–95
Embed to Website Blog dialog box, Sheet,
191–192
embedding documents, in Notebook,
99–101
Enable Vacation Reply radio button, Mail,
150
End Date box, Create Campaign page, 293
End Date field, Projects, 234
Enter a Short Message field, Create Your
Personal Group dialog box, 55
Enter Data Right Away dialog box, Reports,
204–205
Enterprise Edition, CRM, 276
Enterprise plan prices, Projects, 228
estimate e-mail template, Invoice, 267
estimates, Invoice, 268–270
Events module, CRM, 288
Excel (XLS) format, 198
EXP function, Sheet, 186
Export button, Writer, 23, 59
Export Contacts link, Invoice, 263
Export to Template Library link, Writer, 44
exporting, in Writer, 44, 58–60
Express plan prices, Projects, 228

FAQ, Zoho, 299
FAQ option, Writer Help menu, 25
Feedback link, Writer, 25
Feeds link, Writer, 25
Fetch button, Mail, 146
field formats, Reports, 201
fields, Reports database, 197
File Type drop-down list, Create Database
(Import) dialog box, 200
File Upload dialog box, 131, 154,
200, 255, 263
fill color, Notebook shape, 102
filter, CRM module, 295–296
filtering data in database tables, Reports,
214–217
FIND function, Sheet, 186
finding Writer templates, 41
Firefox
adding Web page snapshots to
notebooks, 108–109
viewing Planner attachments, 132

fixed price templates, Invoice, 269, 271
flags, marking Mail e-mail with, 153–154
Flip Type button, Notebook, 105
flipping images, Show, 76–77
Flow charts category, Show shape palette,
76–77
flowcharts, Notebook, 104
Folder Name text box, New Folder dialog
box, 164
folders, Mail, 140, 152, 163–164
Follow Up option, Mail, 154
font, in Writer, 32–33
Forecasts module, CRM, 288
Format Column option, Reports, 213
Format toolbar, Writer, 23
formats
Reports field, 201
Sheet, 177–178
formatting, in Writer, 29–33
Formatting toolbar
Sheet, 170, 177–178
Show, 70–71
Formula bar, Sheet, 171, 184
Formula column, Reports, 208
formulas, Sheet, 182–184
forums, Projects, 246–248
forwarding e-mail, Mail, 148–149
Free Edition, CRM, 276
Freeze Column option, Reports, 213
From Beginning option, Show, 83
From Current Slide option, Show, 83
From date box, Mail, 150
From URL tab
Add Audio dialog box, 96
Add File dialog box, 100
full-screen slide shows, Show, 85
functions, Sheet, 182, 185–186
FV function, Sheet, 186

Gantt charts, Projects, 248–249
Gears, Google, 60–61, 164–165
Gears Security Warning dialog box, 61
GearsSetup.exe file, 61
General Information section, CRM, 283
General Settings tab, Projects, 228–229
Go Offline link, Writer, 25, 61
Google Adword Campaign Performance
Analysis template, Reports, 202
Google Checkout, 266–267

Google Gears, 60–61, 164–165
gradient, for shapes in Show presentations, 78–79
Group Name field, Create Your Personal Group dialog box, 54
Groups dialog box, Writer, 57
Groups List dialog box, Writer, 54, 56–58
Groups Summary dialog box, Writer, 55
guided tours, application, 304

• *H* •

Help link, Writer, 25
help resources, 299–302
Helper plugin, Notebook, 108–109
hex code, 33
Hide Column option, Reports, 212
hiding CRM tabs, 279–280
history, Writer document, 38–39
home pages
  application, 12
  Gears, 61
  Mail, 140
  Planner, 116–120, 128–130
  Projects, 228, 241, 247, 249–250
  Writer, 21
HTML, 59, 97, 198–199
HTML Editor button, Compose dialog box, 142
hyperlinks, inserting into Writer documents, 35–36

• *I* •

icons used in book, 3
images
  adding, Notebook, 93–94
  inserting into Writer documents, 34–35
  Show presentation, 80–81
Import button
  Show, 65
  Writer, 23, 58
Import Contacts page, Invoice, 263
Import Customers page, Invoice, 262
Import Document dialog box, Writer, 58
Important option, Mail, 154
importing
  contacts, Invoice, 262–263
  customers, Invoice, 260–262
  databases, Reports, 198–202

documents, Writer, 58–60
  presentations, Show, 65–66
Inactive Customers folder, Invoice, 264
Inbox folder, Mail, 146–147, 151–154
Increase List Level button, Show, 71
Info option, Mail, 154
Info tab, Show, 67
Insert button, Show, 71
Insert Comment dialog box, Sheet, 176
Insert Image button, Writer, 34
Insert Image dialog box, 34, 80–81
Insert Table button, Writer, 36–37
Insert toolbar, Writer, 24
inserting
  hyperlinks into Writer documents, 35–36
  images into Writer documents, 34–35
  shapes into Notebook, 104
  shapes into Show presentations, 72–74
insertion point, Writer, 26
Insert/Modify Link dialog box, Writer, 35–36
Install Gears button, Gears home page, 61
INT function, Sheet, 186
Internet Explorer, 132
inventory, creating with Invoice, 265–266
Inventory and Ordering modules, CRM, 288–289
invitations
  collaborator, Writer, 50–51, 56–57
  to online slide presentations, Show, 85
  sharing Planner pages, 137
  to view databases, Reports, 222
  to view spreadsheets, Sheet, 187–189
Invoice. *See* Zoho Invoice
Invoice Details page, Invoice, 272
invoice logo, Invoice, 254
Invoice Notification page, Invoice, 268
Invoices module, CRM, 289
Invoices tab, Invoice, 271–272
Issue Manager template, Reports, 202
Items tab, Invoice, 265–266

• *J* •

justification, Writer, 30–31

• *K* •

keyboard shortcuts, 25, 29–30, 172–173

• L •

Label field, Add New Customer page, 260
labels, organizing Mail with, 161–163
Language category, Projects, 229
Latest Project Activity section, Projects, 232
LaTeX files, 58
layers, Writer, 30
Leads module, CRM, 288
left alignment, Writer, 31
List options, Sort dialog box, 180
list price, CRM Price Books module, 289
log out, Writer, 25
logging time, in Projects, 245–246
login page, Projects, 227
logo, company, adding to invoices, 254–255
Logo category, Projects, 230
lookup columns, Reports, 208, 211–212

• M •

macros, Sheet, 305
Mail. *See* Zoho Mail
Make Active button, Invoice, 264
Make Inactive button, Invoice, 264
Make Remote & Continue button, Play This Presentation Remotely dialog box, 84
Mandatory column, Reports, 208
Mark As button, Mail, 154
Marketing modules, CRM, 287–288
Master View option, Show, 67
math operators, Sheet, 183
MAX function, Sheet, 186
Maximize Editor button, Writer, 26
MEDIAN function, Sheet, 186
meetings, Projects, 241–242
member roles, Projects, 232
Members Mail IDs field, Create Your Personal Group dialog box, 54
Microsoft Excel (XLS) format, 198
Microsoft Word document (DOC or DOCX) files, 58
Milestone Report link, Projects, 249
milestones, Projects, 237–239
Minimize Editor button, Writer, 26
Module drop-down list, Add Component dialog box, 281
modules, CRM
    creating records in, 292–293
    Customer support, 289–290

Data analysis, 290
    deleting records from, 293–294
    editing records, 293–294
    Inventory and Ordering, 288–289
    Marketing, 287–288
    overview, 291
    Sales, 288
More button, Show, 84
More Options button, Compose dialog box, 143
More Options drop-down menu, Mail, 159–160
My Account link, Writer, 25
My Docs pane, Writer, 24
My Sheets section, Sheet, 171

• N •

Name Your New Page text box, Planner, 133
navigation, Show presentation, 85
navigation bar, in Zoho applications, 12
navigational keyboard shortcuts, 30, 172
New button, Writer, 23, 26
New Campaign button, CRM Campaigns module, 291–292
New Document button, Projects, 250
New Document item, Writer, 28
New Folder dialog box, Mail, 152, 163–164
New Forum Post button, Projects, 247
New Invoice button, Invoice, 271
New Label dialog box, Mail, 162
New Meeting link, Projects, 241
New Milestone link, Projects, 238
New Profile page, CRM, 285–286
New Project link, Projects, 230
[New Query Table]* tab, Reports, 218
New Role page, CRM, 284
New Slide button, Show, 68
New Spreadsheet button, Projects, 250
New Task button, Projects, 233–234
New Task List link, Projects, 237
Normal View option, Show, 67
Notebook. *See* Zoho Notebook
notes, in Planner, 129–130
Notes box, Add New Customer page, 260
notes field, Show, 67, 85
Notify Me check box, Share This Document dialog box, 82, 188
Notify This Document To list, Upload New File dialog box, 249

NOW function, Sheet, 186
Number of Mails to Download Initially, to Setup Offline Mode drop-down box, Offline Settings dialog box, 165

• O •

objects, Show, 68
ODF or ODT (OpenOffice.org) files, 58
Offline Settings dialog box, Mail, 165
Online Payment Settings page, Invoice, 266–267
Open Tasks section, CRM, 278
OpenOffice.org (ODF or ODT) files, 58
Options page, Add Chart dialog box, 181–182
Organize Tabs page, CRM, 279–280
Orientation options, Sort dialog box, 180
Outlook Express CSV format, 262
Overdue Invoices link, Invoice, 273
Owner box, Projects, 234

• P •

page elements, aligning in Writer, 30–32
Page Setup toolbar, Writer, 24
Page Sharing link, Planner, 136
pages
  adding, Notebook, 89–90
  creating in Planner, 133–134
  width of in Writer, 31–32
parent folders, Mail, 164
password, Zoho account, 8–9
Password category, Projects, 229
pasting shapes, in Notebook, 103
payment gateway, selecting with Invoice, 266–267
payment terms, Invoice, 258
payment-received notice, Invoice, 268
PayPal, 266–267
PDF (Portable Document Format) files, 58, 270, 272
pencil icon
  Invoice, 264
  Planner, 122, 124, 127, 238–240
  Projects, 236
% Completed drop-down list box, Projects, 235
percentage format, Sheet, 177–178
permissions, 51, 82, 286

phone number, Zoho, 299
Photo category, Projects, 229
pinning content, in Notebook, 106
Pivot button, Sheet, 193
Pivot view, Reports, 220
Planner. *See* Zoho Planner
Play This Presentation Remotely dialog box, Show, 84
player, Notebook Add Audio, 96
plugins, Firefox Notebook, 108–109
PMT function, Sheet, 186
Popout icon, Mail, 146
Populate with Sample Data check box, Create Database from Template dialog box, 203
Portable Document Format (PDF) files, 58, 270, 272
posts, Projects forum, 247–248
Potentials module, CRM, 288
Powered by Logo category, Projects, 230
Premium plan
  Invoice, 253
  Projects, 228
presentations, 101. *See also* Zoho Show
Price Books module, CRM, 289
prices, Projects, 228
pricing plans, Invoice, 252–253
primary sort, Sheet, 180
Print button, Writer, 23, 47
printing
  documents, Writer, 47–49
  e-mail, Mail, 159–160
Priority drop-down list, Projects, 234
priority level, Mail e-mail, 143
Privacy Policy, Zoho, 9
Private Sharing section, Planner, 136–137
product templates, Invoice, 269, 271
Products module, CRM, 289
Professional Edition, CRM, 276
profile, company, setting up on invoices, 253–254
Profile category, Projects, 229–230
Profile field, Create User page, 283
profiles, CRM, 282, 285–287
Project Manager template, Reports, 202
Project Members list, Projects, 241
project portal, Projects, 226
Projects. *See* Zoho Projects
Properties dialog box, Show, 77–79
Public Info item, Writer, 47

Public Share dialog box, Writer, 48
Publish to Blog option, Writer, 48
publishing, Web
  Sheet spreadsheets, 191–192
  Writer documents, 47–49
Purchase Orders module, CRM, 289
PV function, Sheet, 186

• Q •

querying database tables, in Reports,
  217–219
Quick Create, CRM, 278
Quick Setup page, Invoice, 252
Quotes module, CRM, 288

• R •

RAND function, Sheet, 186
ranges, Sheet cell, 173
reactivating Invoice customers, 264
Read Only Members field, Share This
  Document dialog box, 50, 82, 188
Read option, Mail, 154
reading Mail e-mail, 146–147, 164–165
Read-Only button, Share dialog box, 110
read-only mode, Show, 65
Read/Write button, Share dialog box,
  110–111
Read/Write Members field, Share This
  Document dialog box, 50, 82, 188
receiving e-mail, Mail, 146–147
Recent Documents section, Projects, 231
Recent Forum Comments section, Projects,
  232
Recent Forum Posts section, Projects, 232
Recent Items, CRM, 278
Record tab
  Add Audio dialog box, 96
  Add Video dialog box, 95
records
  CRM module, 291–294
  Reports, 197
recurring appointments, Planner, 127–128
red font, in Writer, 33
red X icon
  Invoice, 265
  Planner, 133
  Projects, 236, 239–240
reference number, Invoice estimate, 269

registration confirmation e-mail, Zoho, 10
Related Milestone drop-down list box,
  Projects, 237
relational databases, Reports, 208, 210–212
Remind All list, Projects, 241
Remind Me drop-down list, Planner,
  124, 126
reminders, setting in Planner, 123–124
Remote button, Show, 84
Remote URL dialog box, Show, 84–85
Rename Column option, Reports, 213
renaming
  CRM tabs, 280
  notebooks, 88–89
reordering to-do lists, Planner, 121
Repeat drop-down list, Projects, 241
REPLACE function, Sheet, 186
replying to e-mail, Mail, 147–151
Report Spam button, Mail, 153
Reports. *See* Zoho Reports
reports, Projects, 248–249
Reports module, CRM, 290
return receipts, Mail, 142–143
Review toolbar, Writer, 24, 39
Rich Text Format (RTF) files, 59
roles
  CRM, 282, 284–285
  Projects, 239–240
rotating shapes, Show, 74
rows
  database table, Reports, 213
  spreadsheet, Sheet, 175–176, 179
  table, Writer, 37
RSS feeds, adding in Notebook, 98–99
RTF (Rich Text Format) files, 59

• S •

Sales modules, CRM, 288
Sales Orders module, CRM, 289
Save As button, Writer, 28
Save As dialog box, 27, 209, 218
Save as Template dialog box, Writer, 44
Save button
  Notebook, 89
  Sheet, 173
  Writer, 23, 27
Save Draft button, Compose dialog box,
  142
Save Order link, Planner, 121

Save Template link, Writer, 43
saving
  e-mail in Mail, 159–160
  notebooks in Notebook, 88–90
Schedule Meeting button, Projects, 242
SEARCH function, Sheet, 186
searching
  CRM modules, 278, 295
  e-mail, Mail, 157–159
  for Planner pages with tags, 136
  for Templates, Writer, 41
  in Writer, 23
Select a Parent Folder field, New Folder
  dialog box, 164
Select Custom View section, Add
  Component dialog box, 281
Select Folder drop-down list, Upload New
  File dialog box, 249
Select Invitation Language field, Create
  Your Personal Group dialog box, 55
Select Slide Number option, Show, 83
SELECT statement, Reports, 217
Select tool button, Notebook, 92, 103,
  106–107
Selected Tabs list, CRM, 280
Selected Text field, Insert/Modify Link
  dialog box, 36
selection keyboard shortcuts, 30, 173
Send Mail Notification check box, Projects,
  234
Send Message link, Projects, 240
Send Vacation Reply To radio button, Mail,
  150
Sending Interval item, Mail, 150
Sent folder, Mail, 144–145
service templates, Invoice, 269, 271
Services module, CRM, 289
Settings link
  Mail, 144, 150–151
  Writer, 25
Settings page, Projects, 228–229
Setup page, CRM, 280
shapes
  in Notebook, 101–105
  in Show presentations, 72–79
Shapes tab, Show, 67, 72–73
sharing
  databases, Reports, 222
  documents, on Projects, 249–250
  in Notebook, 110–111
  Planner pages, 136–138

presentations, Show, 82–83, 86
  Sheet spreadsheets, 186–192
  Writer documents, 24, 49–58
Sheet. *See* Zoho Sheet
shipping information section, Invoice,
  259–260
shortcuts, keyboard, 25, 29–30, 172–173
Show. *See* Zoho Show
Show Legend check box, Add Chart dialog
  box, 182
Show Notes button, Show, 85
Sign Out link, Writer, 25
signatures, adding to Mail e-mail, 143–144
signing in
  to CRM, 276–277
  to Zoho, 10–12
sizing handles
  shape, Show, 72–73
  table, Writer, 37
  text box, Show, 71
Skins category, Projects, 229
Slide Show Time item, Show, 84
Slide View drop-down menu, Show, 67–68
slides, adding to Show presentations,
  68–69
Slideshow option, Show, 68, 83
snapshots, Web page, in Notebook,
  108–109
solid borders, Show, 79
Solutions module, CRM, 290
Sort submenu, Reports, 212
Sorter View option, Show, 67
sorting
  CRM module, 295
  data in database tables, Reports, 214
  Mail e-mail, 145
  Sheet spreadsheet data, 178–180
  slides, Show, 69
Source Data page, Add Chart dialog box,
  181
spam, 153–154
Specific Sheets radio button, Share This
  Document dialog box, 187
speech bubbles, Show, 74–75
Spell Check button, Compose dialog box,
  142
spreadsheets. *See* Zoho Sheet
SQL, querying database tables with in
  Reports, 217–219
stacking content, in Notebook, 107–108

Standard plan
  Invoice, 253
  Projects, 228
Standard profile, CRM, 285
Star Office (SXW) files, 59
star shapes, 75–76
Start Date box, CRM, 293
Status field, CRM, 293
STDEV function, Sheet, 186
Stop Remote button, Show, 86
style sheets, 33
Sub Type area, Add Chart dialog box, 181
sub-bullets, Show, 71
Subject field
  Compose dialog box, 142
  Vacation Reply tab, Mail, 150
Sum button, Sheet, 182–183
SUM function, Sheet, 185–186
Summary view, Reports, 221
Switch To link, Writer, 25
SXW (Star Office) files, 59
Symbols category, Show shape palette, 77
synchronizing offline documents, with
    Writer online, 62
system logo, Invoice, 254

• *T* •

table-creation options, Reports, 206
tables, Writer, 36–38. *See also* database
    tables
tab-separated values (TSV) format,
    261–262
Tabular view, Reports, 219
Tag Folders pane, Writer, 24, 40
tags
  organizing Writer documents with, 39–40
  Planner item, 134–136
  Projects, 249
Tags field, Show, 64
Tags link, Planner, 135
Target field, Insert/Modify Link dialog
    box, 36
Task - Graph View link, Projects, 249
Task - List View link, Projects, 249
task lists, Projects, 233, 236–237
tasks
  CRM, 278
  Projects, 233–236
Tasks & Milestones tab, Projects,
    233–238, 246

Tasks module, CRM, 288
tax information, specifying, Invoice, 257
Tax Settings page, Invoice, 257
telephone number, Zoho, 299
Template Library, Writer, 25, 41, 44
templates
  creating databases from, Reports,
      202–204
  CRM, 289
  Invoice, 267–269, 271
  Writer, 28, 40–44
Templates pane, Writer, 24
Terms of Service, Zoho, 9
text
  appearance of, in Writer, 32–33
  in Notebook, 91–92
  in Show presentations, 70–71, 74
Text (TXT) files, 59
text boxes
  Compose dialog box, 142
  Notebook, 91
  Show, 70–71, 74
text mode, Notebook, 92
text pages, Notebook, 90
Text tool button, Notebook, 92
themes, Show presentation, 64, 79–80
Themes tab, Show, 67, 79–80
time zone, setting
  in Invoice, 256
  in Planner, 125–126
timer, Projects, 246
Timesheet, Projects, 245–246
timing, Show slide presentation, 84
Title (tooltip) field, Insert/Modify Link
    dialog box, 36
title bar, Notebook, 91
Title Slide option, Create New Slide dialog
    box, 68
Title with Points option, Create New Slide
    dialog box, 68, 71
Title with Text option, Create New Slide
    dialog box, 68
titles, Show presentation, 70
To date box, Mail, 150
To field, Compose dialog box, 141
Todays Leads section, CRM, 278
to-do lists, Planner
  adding items, 121–122
  checking items off, 120
  creating, 116–119
  deleting items, 122

to-do lists, Planner *(continued)*
  due dates, setting for items, 122–123
  editing items, 122
  overview, 119
  reordering, 121
To-Dos link, Planner, 117
To-Dos Overview link, Planner, 127
toll-free number, Zoho, 299
toolbars. *See also* specific toolbars by
    name
  Compose dialog box, 142
  Notebook text box, 91
  Writer, 23–24
Trash folder, Mail, 151
Trash pane, Writer, 24
Trash section, Sheet, 173
TSV (tab-separated values) format,
    261–262
tutorials, 303–306
Two Text Blocks option, Create New Slide
    dialog box, 68
TXT (Text) files, 59
Type drop-down list box, CRM, 292
Type Your Notes for This Slide Here text
    box, Show, 67

• *U* •

unfixing content, in Notebook, 106
unit price, CRM Price Books module, 289
Unread option, Mail, 154
Upcoming Milestones tab, Projects,
    238–239
updates, Zoho, 7
Upgrade link, Projects, 227
Upload dialog box, Notebook, 93
Upload File dialog box, Invoice, 262
Upload New File dialog box, Projects,
    249–250
Upload tab
  Add Audio dialog box, 96
  Add File dialog box, 100
  Add Image dialog box, 93
URL field, Insert/Modify Link dialog box, 36
URLs, adding in Notebook, 97–98
Use This Template link, Writer, 42
User Details page, CRM, 284
user management
  CRM, 282–287
  Projects, 232–233, 239–240

User Name/E-Mail Separated by Comma
    field, Share dialog box, 110
username, Zoho, 8
Users page, CRM, 282, 284
Users tab, Projects, 232–233, 239–240

• *V* •

vacation reply, Mail, 149–151
Value field, Invoice Add New Customer
    page, 260
VALUE function, Sheet, 186
VAT IDs, Invoice, 253
vCard format, 262
Vendors module, CRM, 289
Version Details tab, Show, 67
video, adding in Notebook, 94–95
videos, application, 303–304
View bar, CRM Campaigns module, 291
View toolbar, Writer, 24
viewing
  data in databases, Reports, 219–221
  sent e-mail, Mail, 144–145
views, CRM custom, 295–296

• *W* •

Web page snapshots, in Notebook, 108–109
Web pages, in Notebook, 90
Week Ahead section, Projects,
    231, 236, 238, 242
WEEKDAY function, Sheet, 186
Welcome page
  Invoice, 252
  Writer, 22
Whole Document radio button, Share This
    Document dialog box, 187
Word document (DOC or DOCX) files, 58
Word Verification section, Create a Zoho
    Account page, 9
Writer. *See* Zoho Writer

• *X* •

XLS (Microsoft Excel) format, 198

• *Y* •

YouTube, 94

• Z •

Zoho. *See also* specific applications by
     name
  account, setting up, 8–10
  overview, 1–4, 7–8
  signing in for first time, 10–12
Zoho Accounts page, 11
Zoho API option, Writer Help menu, 25
Zoho Blogs option, Writer Help menu, 25
Zoho CRM
  accounts, creating, 276–277
  blog, 302
  choosing edition of, 276
  creating records in modules, 292–293
  Customer support modules, 289–290
  customizing, 279–282
  Data analysis modules, 290
  deleting records from modules, 293–294
  dissecting modules, 291
  editing records, 293–294
  help system, 302
  importing customers to Invoice, 262
  interface, 278
  Inventory and Ordering modules, 288–289
  Marketing modules, 287–288
  overview, 19–20, 275
  Sales modules, 288
  tutorials, 306
  user management, 282–287
  views, creating custom, 295–296
Zoho CRM ID field, CRM, 283
Zoho CRM Lounge blog, 302
Zoho FAQ, 299
Zoho Forums, 300
Zoho Invoice
  company logo, adding, 254–255
  company profile, setting up, 253–254
  contacts, 257–258, 262–265
  creating invoices, 271–272
  currency, setting, 256
  customers, 257–264
  e-mail notifications, 267–268
  estimates, creating and sending, 268–270
  inventory, creating, 265–266
  marking invoices as paid, 272–273
  overview, 18–19, 251
  payment gateway, selecting, 266–267
  sending invoices, 271–272
  starting, 252–253

  tax information, specifying, 257
  time zone, setting, 256
  user manual, 301–302
Zoho Mail
  address book contacts, 160–161
  attachments, 154–157
  composing e-mail, 141–145
  forwarding e-mail, 148–149
  Inbox, 151–154
  organizing e-mail, 161–164
  overview, 15–16
  printing e-mail, 159–160
  reading e-mail, 146–147, 164–165
  receiving e-mail, 146–147
  replying to e-mail, 147–151
  saving e-mail, 159–160
  searching e-mail, 157–159
  starting, 139–140
Zoho Notebook
  audio files, adding, 96
  customizing notebooks, 106–108
  embedding documents, 99–101
  help document, 300–301
  HTML, adding, 97
  images, adding, 93–94
  overview, 14, 87
  pages, adding, 89–90
  renaming notebooks, 88–89
  RSS feeds, adding, 98–99
  saving notebooks, 88–90
  shapes, adding, 101–105
  sharing notebooks, 110–111
  text, adding to pages, 91–92
  tutorials, 304
  URLs, adding, 97–98
  video, adding, 94–95
  Web page snapshots, adding, 108–109
Zoho Planner
  appointments, 125–129
  attachments, 131–133
  creating pages, 133–134
  due dates, setting for items, 122–123
  notes, recording details with, 129–130
  overview, 15, 115
  reminders, setting, 123–124
  sharing pages, 136–138
  starting, 116
  tags, 134–136
  to-do lists, amending, 119–122
  to-do lists, creating, 116–119
  tutorials, 305

Zoho Projects
  calendar, 242–244
  customizing, 228–230
  dashboard, 231–232
  documents, 249–250
  forums, 246–248
  help file, 301
  logging time, 245–246
  meetings, setting up, 241–242
  milestones, creating, 237–239
  overview, 18, 225, 230–231
  reports, generating, 248–249
  starting, 226–228
  task lists, creating, 236–237
  tasks, adding, 233–236
  tutorials, 304
  user management, 239–240
  users, adding, 232–233
Zoho Reports. *See also* database tables,
    Reports
  creating databases, 197–198, 202–206
  importing databases, 198–202
  overview, 16–17
  sharing databases, 222
  viewing data, 219–221
Zoho Sheet
  adding documents to Notebook, 90
  charts, 180–182
  columns, adding, 174–175
  comments, adding, 176–177
  embedding documents in Notebook, 100
  entering data, 171–174
  formats, 177–178
  formulas, 182–184
  functions, 182, 185–186
  macros, creating, 305
  overview, 16, 17, 169–170
  pivot tables, 192–195
  rows, adding, 175–176
  sharing spreadsheets, 186–192
  sorting data, 178–180
  starting, 170–171
  Sum button, 182–183
  tutorials, 305
  video, 301
Zoho Show
  bullets, 71–72
  creating presentations, 63–65

  embedding documents in Notebook,
    100–101
  FAQs, 301
  images, adding, 80–81
  importing presentations, 65–66
  interface, 66–67
  overview, 13–14
  presenting presentations, 83–86
  shapes, 72–79
  sharing presentations, 82–83
  slides, adding, 68–69
  text, adding, 70–71
  themes, changing, 79–80
  views, 67–68
Zoho Sign In page, 11
Zoho Writer
  comments, 45–47
  creating documents, 26–29
  document pages in Notebook, 90
  embedding documents in Notebook, 100
  exporting documents, 58–60
  FAQs, 300
  formatting, 29–33
  history of documents, 38–39
  home page, 21
  importing documents, 58–60
  inserting elements in documents, 34–36
  interface, 22–26
  naming documents, 26–29
  organizing documents with tags, 39–40
  overview, 12–13
  printing documents, 47–49
  publishing to Web, 47–49
  saving documents, 26–29
  sharing documents, 49–58
  starting, 21–22
  tables, 36–38
  taking offline, 306
  templates, 40–44
  tutorials, 305–306
  working offline, 60–62
Zoho Writer Forums option, Writer Help
    menu, 25

Lightning Source UK Ltd.
Milton Keynes UK
UKHW031321030320
359646UK00004B/17